More praise for

HOW TO WRITE AN AUTOBIOGRAPHICAL NOVEL

"Alexander Chee is the very best kind of essayist, a boon companion in good times and bad, whose confiding voice you'd follow anywhere, just for the wonderful feeling of being understood like never before."

—Charles D'Ambrosio

"Alexander Chee's first collection of nonfiction is a lovely reminder that there is indeed an art to the personal essay, and he is a master artist."

—Maris Kreizman, *Esquire*

"As profound as they are beautiful, Chee's essays impart wisdom from a life fully lived, and speak to what it means to be a writer and reader in contemporary times."

—Jarry Lee, *BuzzFeed*

"In his first collection of essays, novelist Alexander Chee immortalizes himself through his art and literature . . . Enlightening, revealing the true impact of the arts."

—*Bitch*

"*How to Write an Autobiographical Novel* is a rare hybrid of a book: an act of poetry, a gift of entertainment, and a primer for life. Alexander Chee is one of our most important writers, and we should listen to every damn thing he has to say."

—Jami Attenberg

BOOKS BY ALEXANDER CHEE

Edinburgh

The Queen of the Night

How to Write an Autobiographical Novel

HOW TO WRITE AN AUTOBIOGRAPHICAL NOVEL

ESSAYS BY ALEXANDER CHEE

A Mariner Original MARINER BOOKS

Houghton Mifflin Harcourt Boston New York

For information about permission to reproduce selections from this book, write to trade.permissions@hmhco.com or to Permissions, Houghton Mifflin Harcourt Publishing Company, 3 Park Avenue, 19th Floor, New York, New York 10016.

hmhco.com

Library of Congress Cataloging-in-Publication Data is available.
ISBN 978-1-328-76452-2

Book design by Greta D. Sibley

Printed in the United States of America
DOC 10 9 8 7 6 5 4 3
4500716903

To my mother and father, who taught me how to fight

CONTENTS

THE CURSE

I SPENT THE SUMMER I turned fifteen on an exchange program in Tuxtla Gutiérrez, the capital of the state of Chiapas, in Mexico, some three hundred miles north of the Guatemalan border. My host family was named Gutiérrez, and I never asked them if the town took its name from their forebears, but if it did, they wore their fame lightly, though they were a powerful and prosperous family. The father, Fernando, had been a stevedore, of the kind who worked for him now, and the mother, Cela (pronounced *Che*-la), was a dance teacher. They lived like people who felt lucky to be alive, and I loved them right away.

Their son, Miguel Ángel, had lived the previous year with me and my family in Cape Elizabeth, Maine. He had told his parents stories of me, and so they greeted me like a child they'd always known but never met. They had a handsome modern house of gleaming wood, glass, and stucco, surrounded by high walls topped with barbed wire and trees with enormous crowns, their leaves arrayed in stars, that I would learn were mangoes.

The first night, the family told me over a cheerful and friendly dinner that they were not going to speak to me in English for the rest of the summer, no matter how confusing it was. And that this was to teach me to speak Spanish. I laughed as I agreed, in Spanish, to their terms, intimidated but sure of my purpose and already wanting to please them.

That night, as I lay awake trying to sleep, I heard the knock of ripe mangoes falling from the trees that circled the house and ran up and down the street. The noise ranged, depending on the ripeness, from the plop of a tennis ball to a pulpy sort of splash to the occasional smash when one of them would crash through a car windshield.

We need to cut that tree down, my host mother said the next morning. She would say it whenever this happened, but they never did. It was as if they accepted the broken windshields as the price of the mangoes, which we ate as fast as we could. They had their gardener collect the fruit instead, and replaced the windshields as if they were changing a tablecloth. And that would be among the first of my object lessons in the ways of the very rich.

Years later, and only when I learned of the deep poverty in Chiapas—the reason they had those walls topped with barbed wire—did I think to question whether it was really just mangoes breaking their windshields—if mango season lasted as long as a summer.

❖

I WAS ONE OF TWELVE STUDENTS in Chiapas from my high school that summer, on what now seems like an odd program: we lived there with the Mexican students who lived with us during the year, but unlike them, we did not attend any classes. The summer itself was supposed to be a class. If my host family had not made me promise never to speak English, I don't know what I would have learned. Our teacher came with us, as a chaperone, but he did not teach us. Whatever else he did there, he also accompanied us on intermittent group field trips to explore the mostly well-trodden ruins and to shop in places like the nearby San Cristóbal de las Casas, formerly the capital of Mexico, a quiet, sun-struck city, cheated out of the prosperity of being the capital. These trips were set apart for me by stretches of nameless, numberless days spent wandering the empty, luxurious house while the Gutiérrezes were either at school or at work. I was fascinated by my host father's many toupees, which were kept on mannequin heads in his bedroom dressing room, and the life they suggested, entirely alien, of hair that was public and hair that was private.

It was just one detail of many that I eagerly collected that summer, and if it seems I was snooping, I was. I was lost in the books I had brought with me, the *Dune* novels by Frank Herbert —the story of a young boy without playmates, suspected of being a messianic figure, and undergoing training in the ways of the Bene Gesserit, a secretive society of women with extraordinary powers, born in part through their obsessive observation of detail. The boy was the latest iteration of a series of heroes like this for me—Encyclopedia Brown, Sherlock Holmes, Batman—who went from being ordinary people to heroes through their ability to perceive the things others missed. I wanted to see if I too could obtain these powers through observation.

And when I wasn't reading those novels, I wrote my own stories, stories no one has seen to this day, about mutants with psychic powers who were running from a government that, of course, hoped to control them. *X-Men* fan fiction, essentially, before I knew what it was.

It was my greatest dream to live out this kind of story, of power gained through either inborn abilities or persistence, and though I couldn't have said this at the time, this dream coming true would have meant all of my struggles were worth it.

The closest thing I had to a routine that summer was my time spent sitting with the cook, Panchita, in front of the kitchen television, chomping on the fried tortillas she served me, spread with some sort of light, fresh tomato sauce and sprinkled with white cheese. Together we watched *El Maleficio,* a *telenovela* about a wealthy family of witches living in Oaxaca and the various troubles they got into. I liked the look of that soap opera, those men and women who seemed straight out of *Dallas* or *Falcon Crest* all shouting at each other, casting spells, promising revenge, and lit by the cheesy special effects that made their already spectral appearance even more incredible. I couldn't understand most of what was being said at first, having had just two years of high school Spanish before this. But about a month into my stay, while watching the show, I had the realization that I understood everything the witches were saying. The ads came on and I understood those also. The news came on and I understood that as well. It was as if the show had cast a spell on me.

I had crossed over into fluency. I said something to that effect to Panchita, and she smiled and laughed, congratulating me. She herself spoke only a little more Spanish than me, she joked, and made me the treat of an extra tortilla that day.

❖

MY HOST BROTHER, Miguel Ángel, snorted almost nightly at the unfairness of my program when he came home from summer school to find me tanned and reading. He was a tall, lanky seventeen-year-old with a sort of dreamy teen-idol beauty gone slightly, if adorably, awry. He had large front teeth that were endearingly crooked, and he wore the tightest, thinnest jeans of anyone I knew, his hair cut in a Leif Garrett shag. At some point after arriving home from school, Miguel would begin getting ready for the evening, showering and dressing carefully for the disco. I found these preparations alien and thrilling—the application of cologne being nearly mystical to watch.

And I watched it all.

I felt sometimes like a camera, shocked when people noticed me. I was a little in love with him and his friends, young men of sixteen or seventeen, a year or two older than me, all beauties, and I wanted to know everything I could, as if, per the *Dune* novels, all of this detail might confer some greater mastery over the objects of my desire. There was a code to it all, it seemed, something underneath the smooth rhythm of the day and night, and that was what I wanted to crack.

Miguel and I would meet up with his friends at the overlook of the town's dump, a hillside where we parked and drank, tailgating with brandy and Coca-Cola, mixed into a sticky-sweet and satisfying drink for the hot summer nights, before they all went out to the discos. Drinking with these young men left me a little drowsy from the liquor, and a sensual sort of atmosphere took hold of my imagination, a sense that something was almost about to happen.

These boys were all waiting for the girls, who took longer to get ready, and we drank as they dressed and made themselves up. I watched for the moment the girls would arrive, the way the group of boys at the overlook would change when they did. I already knew at this point that I was gay, and so I was forever looking for other signs of it in the landscape. What I was looking for was what seemed to vanish then. The girls arrived in their own cars, the headlights sweeping the scene where we stood, illuminated by them. Out they'd step, confident, glamorous in their makeup, their legs shining, lips flashing wet with lip gloss, their new manicures and pedicures giving off sparks in the night. The boys would growl hellos, smiling like cartoon wolves.

Two of Miguel's friends in particular held most of my attention. They seemed to be deeply in love with each other, in a kind of easy masculine protectorate that we all respected without quite acknowledging it. They weren't what I thought of as macho per se, but they seemed manlier than I could ever be, and they kept very close to each other, always. Before the girls' arrival, they would sit together, arms around each other, handsome and easy, and from where I sat I could feel everywhere their skin touched, as if the heat of it could be felt with my eyes. Sometimes, at the end of the night, one would lay his head on the other's shoulder, and I would ache for the rest of the night from that sight. But on seeing the girls' cars, they lifted off each other, as if what was there was not there.

Everyone was friendly with me, but to my knowledge, no one was flirting with me. I was too young. I was not stylish. I did not have a gold chain. I did not have anything special about me, to my mind, except my eyes, which I was proud of, and which people often said were beautiful. And which I was using, sure that my dream of power was something they could make come true. I was probably a starer, to be honest. I was from Maine, with my ordinary side-parted brown hair cut in an ordinary way, jeans of an ordinary cut, ordinary polo shirts.

Most of my notebooks have a doodle in them of a staring eye. Sometimes as I drew it, I was staring at myself. Sometimes I had the sense, as I finished the drawing, that I was staring back at me. I still draw these. The eye a perfect talisman for a boy who believed his watching both hid him and gave him power.

❖

SOMETHING WAS HAPPENING, though it had, in a sense, already happened. I felt at home in Mexico in a way I never had before.

My new fluency in Spanish was part of it. I was the first of the twelve students in my high school group to accomplish this —undeniably the main purpose of being in Chiapas. I was also the only Asian, nonwhite student in the group. On field trips the other kids started asking me what "they" were saying, or they'd ask me to speak for them. The only exchanges the students had mastered were basic— ¿Cuánto cuesta? How much does this cost? —and so I felt a tiny contempt whenever I conceded and helped them.

As we were otherwise left on our own when the trips were not happening, I kept to myself as much as I could and never knew how the other Americans spent their time without me. Nick Stark was the only one of these students I sought out. He was, like all of them, hopelessly bad at pronunciation and with no memory for vocabulary, but I was friends with him mostly because I found him very handsome. He had become my best friend out of all the American students, by default. We often swam together in the afternoons, after my television show hour, at the Tuxtla country club's outdoor pool, where our host families were both members, and in doing so, the sun had turned us completely brown, except for the space barely covered by our swimsuits. I went along with it because Nick never mocked me, and I enjoyed looking at him. When he took off his Speedo or put it on, his tan line flashed white in the changing room, so bright it was like a camera flash.

Nick had dark hair and eyes like me, and looked, with his mouth closed, like many of the Mexican members of the club, most of them from European backgrounds, and so when we swam there, by and large we attracted little attention unless we spoke. But when Nick opened his mouth, he showed his giant white, straight American teeth, the product of perfectly attended orthodontist visits. Mine were also large and white, but a little crooked, like my mother's teeth, and like theirs—not enough to get fixed but enough to assist me, along with my better accent, in passing. I had already noticed that the Mexicans here in Tuxtla were less obsessed with braces than we were back in America, even the rich ones I had met. Orthodontics, in the 1970s, was a very American obsession. And I had noticed what Nick would now point out to me: that I also looked Mexican. Or, really, it was a little more than that.

"You're going native," he said to me one day as we changed after swimming. The smell of chlorine and rust hung in the cold green lockers of the country club, and I closed mine carefully, which dimmed the odor only slightly. I was pleased by him saying this and wanted more information, but also the pleasure of watching him change clothes distracted me. By now I was aware that I was attracted to him, and I had learned to modulate my attention to him so that it seemed like I was no more interested in his beauty than anything else around us. But that day, his penis swung up and down as he spoke, as if his vocal cords were strung to it, and was a rosy pink in the center of that blinding white border of skin between his beautifully brown top and bottom halves. He looked like a very sexy Neapolitan ice cream treat.

He was waiting for me to turn and face him, holding out his navy swimsuit, waiting to step inside of it.

"How exactly do you mean 'native'?" I asked him.

Nick struggled with this for a moment. I think he had hoped I'd know what he meant. "Uh, well, you know. You could, like, pretend to be Mexican. Your Spanish is really good. You sound Mexican."

"Yeah?" I sat down on the bench by the locker. Nick stood as if waiting to be released from this conversation in order to put on his suit.

In retrospect, he may have been flirting with me also.

"Yeah," he said. "I'm sure you could convince anyone here. You could totally play Mexican." His penis swung again, and now that I was seated, it was at my eye level. I looked up at his face so he wouldn't notice me noticing it, but I could see it in and out of the edge of my vision, tantalizing. I asked more questions. "Are you bored yet? Isn't it weird that we have no classes? Pablo's a madman to have set the summer up this way." Pablo was our Spanish teacher, Mr. Castellanos, whom we always referred to as Pablo. We never called him Mr. Castellanos.

"No," he said. "I'm having a blast." This produced at least a few more swings. He finally put on his suit and smiled at me as he settled the drawstring inside, as if he'd accomplished something quite difficult. Then I stood and we went out to the pool.

At dinner that night, I told my host family at last the news about my fluency, and they bragged to one another about how I was the best of the American students, and how proud of me they were. Each of the other Americans was brought up and dismissed as lesser than me. "Lo más bueno," my host father said, pointing to me. Cela beamed as they congratulated themselves on their plan of not speaking to me in English, and confirmed that I sounded just like a Mexicano. As they said this, I saw a change come over their eyes, as if I had been revealed as one of their own.

❖

THE GUTIÉRREZ FAMILY were bewilderingly rich to me. Miguel's youngest sister, for example, was away at a finishing school in Switzerland. His older sister had also been to one, the same one. I'd never met a family with this tradition. I understood that Mr. Gutiérrez ran an import-export business, but when I tried to imagine what that was, I could only picture bales of cash being unloaded off of enormous ships.

They were the first family I ever knew to employ a houseboy. His name was Uriel, and he tended the garden in the courtyard, washed the three cars every other day, and picked the mangoes up off the ground, in addition to whatever he did out of my sight. Uriel worked shirtless in the heat, spraying the cars down, himself glazed by the water and the sweat, and in a way, of all the boys I was in love with that summer, he was chief among them.

I had watched him for weeks from my window, too shy to approach him, too unsure of my Spanish, but now that I was fluent—such that I was—I went down at last and reintroduced myself. He had met me on my arrival but we hadn't really spoken since, just the occasional smile and nod. He was shy too, and when he smiled it was as if we were in a movie and the soundtrack changed. He was deeply tanned from working in the sun all day. I knew his name was an angel's name—an archangel, really. Which only made him glow more in my eyes.

I was young enough, naïve enough, to imagine we could be friends, and I did eventually write a short story about a boy like me on a trip like this, the two of us in love. But this was a fantasy. I was learning there was a gulf between us that could not be as carelessly crossed by my learning Spanish. For all I was trying to vanish into the surroundings, I was still the American visitor, and he knew it well, whatever he also felt. He kept our interactions polite and ordinary. If he was aware of my crush on him, he did

not let on. I did not yet understand how the class difference between us was, at the time, a greater barrier than the language. He
had to be polite to me, no matter what he felt.

I wished I had asked more questions. On the nights at the
disco, or at home later, in my room, I often found myself thinking
of Uriel. Did he sleep in the house also, and if not, where? Where
did he go home to, and what was his life like? And, of course,
what was he thinking about? Which was only a way of hoping he
thought about me.

◈

THE FIELD TRIP I remember best was the one to Palenque. At
the time, it was an archeological site, according to our guide, still
very remote, full of scorpions, and surrounded by what the guide
said were cannibal tribes. For several hours our bus took countless
hairpin turns through the mountains, and I remember the electric
fear of feeling close to death as I looked out the bus window and
down a cliff. All along the roads were crosses and candles marking where people had died in accidents.

Palenque was a Mayan ruin in the center of the Mexican rainforest. This location, we learned, was thought to be strategic. The
stones were the color of the white summer sky. We exited the bus,
and I was in awe of the dense rainforest jungle as the guide led
us into the single excavated temple cellar. There the other American students took pictures, the light bouncing off the plexiglass
erected between us and the discoveries, an aurora of camera flash.
"We know so little about the Maya," I remember the guide kept
saying, a litany of a kind. Palenque then was a sliver of what it is
now, which is a sliver of what it once was — it is estimated that
what we see of the ruin is just 10 percent of what is still there,

buried in the jungle. It was, for me, both thrillingly new and ancient at the same time. I was young and impatient upon learning that the world had not, in fact, been completely charted yet. Why did we not yet know more about the Maya when they had been around for so long?

The entire summer's program seemed like an education conducted through gestalt experiences: take kids to a place where they don't understand anything, and then take them on tours with other people who understand only a little more than they do. I was growing bored of these field trips, and I was still the only group member with any fluency. Being around the Americans, as I now thought of them, wore on me on that trip. Spanish, to me, was quieter, with a different tone and volume level, and their English rang in my head, discordant and forceful.

On the trip back to Tuxtla, Nick was gluey with sleep, his head tipped over, lips apart. I sat next to him, awake with the thrill of being close to him, and the knowledge I had of his body from all of those hours of swimming. I wanted nothing more than to slip a kiss on his mouth right then, but it was only pure lust, not affection, and the imagined scene of it turned in my mind like a worry stone as we passed again along the road's dangerous curves.

It was a summer of wanting impossible things.

◈

THE STUDENT I WAS THEN was puzzled by the lack of classes, but in truth the program was so effective it almost recommended itself as a method. I learned Spanish well enough to become fluent. The stories I was writing, which I did to entertain myself when I ran out of things to read, were their own kind of milestone, visible to me only much later: they were the first time I wrote for myself, for my own pleasure. There was something I wanted to feel, and I felt it only when I was writing. I think of this as one of the most important parts of my writer's education —that when left alone with nothing else to read, I began to tell myself the stories I wanted to read.

And there was the story I was living. Whatever I thought I was doing through my experiments in observation, I can see I was a boy losing himself as a way to find himself in the shapes of others. The classmates on this trip were kids I had grown up with since moving to town in the first grade. I longed to be rid of them, but also to be rid of me, or of the problem of me. This was not possible, but I tried.

Here, then, is that summer's last lesson.

❖

THE PREPARATIONS FOR THE CELEBRATION at summer's end were strenuous. A three-day party, the twenty-fifth wedding anniversary of my host family's closest friends. I'll call them the Márquez family. Guests were flying in from all over the world for the big event, and Cela, my host mother, would jump into spontaneous dances in front of me as she described it. She taught salsa and merengue, and now and then over the summer I would be drawn into dancing with her; I remember the delight in her eyes at the prospect of dancing. She had elegant legs, and her hips' quick movement surprised me, which made her laugh. "Merengue, salsa, merengue, salsa," she would chant, like a little girl asking to bake a cake, her hips shaking as she circled the dining room table, her heels ringing on the tile floor. Miguel always blushed, and at some point her husband would raise his hands and reach for his wife's waist.

She gave me a few lessons, insisting I would have to dance at the party.

The day of the party, we arrived at the Márquez house to find a white Jaguar parked in the driveway, a red bow on top. It was so clearly the señor's present to the señora that it needed no explanation: Mr. Márquez owned a luxury car dealership in town. I arrived with Miguel, and we were greeted by his friend Javier, the son of the celebrating couple. Javier wore a dry expression on his face, one I now know is common to those children who parent their parents. His mother chose that moment to come outside, and her diamond ring, the biggest I'd ever seen, flashed as she covered her mouth and screamed in joy. It was the sort of ring you could use to signal for help if you were ever lost on a desert island.

¿Qué onda? Miguel and Javier said to each other, and I said it too, the greeting the boys all used with one another, and as I did so, Miguel gave me a sidelong glance and a smile. You're ready, he said. You're ready. Javier's eyes glinted as Miguel set out the terms: I was to try to fool their friends, who had come in from Oaxaca, into thinking I was Mexican. And if I succeeded, I would win a case of beer.

Javier laughed. Yes, he said, you could be mestizo.

I knew what this word meant as soon as I heard it. Mixed. I think of it as a Mexican word, a word for the Americas — the secret self of the whole continent, north and south. And to me, it felt like the word for what I was. In the United States, if I said I was mixed, it meant too many things I didn't feel. Mixed feelings were confusing feelings, and I didn't feel confused except as to why it was so hard for everyone to understand that I existed. Living this way felt like discovering your shoe was nailed to the floor, but only one of them, so that you paced, always, a circle of possibility, defined by the limited imaginations of others.

I stared at Javier with love. His round head, his bowl-cut black hair, his sly little smile. He led us through the house to the friends in question.

They were a brother and sister, blond-haired, green-eyed, pure Spanish Mexican, as Miguel explained. They looked more American than I did. I don't remember their names, but we shook hands, were introduced, and began speaking.

I invented a past in Tijuana. Close to America but not quite. I don't remember the conversations that followed over the next three days. I remember only the way my accent stood up to scrutiny. They suspected nothing. When Miguel finally revealed the truth, their laughter and genuine astonishment were my real prize. Miguel and I took the case of beer and drank it with the boys, all of them there at the party also, and that was that. I may have had one beer.

For those days, "Alejandro from Tijuana" was real and happy. He was like me but more at ease in the world. Lighter. He didn't spend his days waiting to be caught out for not being whoever someone else thought he was, though that was sincerely the condition of the bet; it had nothing like the stakes of the life I lived back in the States. In Maine, my background — half white, half Korean — was constantly made to seem alien, or exotic, or somehow inhuman. In Mexico, I was only mestizo, ordinary at first glance. When people looked at me, they saw me, and they didn't stare at me as if at an object, the way my fellow American classmates did, all of whom were white and from the same small town in Maine.

After I won my bet with Miguel, the summer seemed to go away, the trip ending in a week's stay with my family in Mexico City, where, after a summer spent eating everything from fresh fruit to street tacos in Tuxtla, I finally got sick. I could only lie in bed, wishing that we'd skipped Mexico City, that we'd left the country before this had happened. This last evidence of my American constitution was a final reminder, not just that I was leaving, but that I was not from there. I really was only an impostor. I would never have this life. No life but the one I had. America now the exile of me.

THE QUERENT

IN 1980, the parapsychologist Dr. Alex Tanous tested my seventh-grade class for psychic abilities, an event so clear in my mind, and so important to me, that I have questioned whether this actually happened, or whether I simply invented him. Tanous was very real, though, as real as the town I grew up in, a conservative Maine town of extraordinary beauty with a population of about eleven thousand. I once heard Cape Elizabeth called a semirural suburb, which seemed a good way to describe it while still also misunderstanding it. This mix of public and private beaches, two lighthouses, farms, a golf course, a tiny museum of shipwrecks, and empty, decommissioned naval-base buildings together made the town feel at once prosperous and haunted.

Our public schools were good, and we excelled at swimming and theater, competing regularly in the state championships for each. And, at least during this period, we also excelled in psychic research. When I asked my former classmates if they remembered these tests, not only did they recall them, they described other tests I'd never heard about, earlier ones, different from mine.

Tanous had just published a book of his research titled *Is Your Child Psychic?* And it seems he had been using my middle school to test out his theories for some time. I still don't know whose idea it was. This was a period, I would learn later, when psychic abilities enjoyed a certain level of respectability with Republicans, due to the CIA's involvement in trying to develop them as a military tool, but this still doesn't explain it. My memory of the day begins only with the announcement that the doctor was coming, and the level of seriousness with which the visit was proposed to the class. "Dr. Tanous believes that all children are psychic naturally," my teacher said. "That it is just a matter of training your abilities. Tests and games that anyone can do."

For me, it was like a dream come true. My own private belief —and my long-held dream, in fact—was that I *was* psychic. The idea that we all were, and that some of us were just more aware of it than others, was news I greeted gladly: I was already good at studying. All morning long, as we waited for Dr. Tanous, I dreamed of being discovered as a prodigy and led from the classroom as a valued psychic asset, to join a team of psychics who would train me to use my powers, like in my *X-Men* comics. Together we would fight crime, of course. Or maybe, because my psychic powers were so overwhelmingly strong, I would be taken away, studied, for the protection of the town, as in my favorite Stephen King novel, *Firestarter*.

I was ready to be discovered, in other words, and for my story to begin.

Most of my fantasies then were of having to leave. Or they were fantasies of secret power. I felt trapped in this town, tired of my all-white classmates, who couldn't pronounce "Guam," where we'd moved from six years before. I still hoped someday we would move back.

Tanous, when he arrived, was a handsome man—friendly, charismatic, yet strangely, utterly ordinary in his carriage. He wore a blazer and tie, the knot a little too big, and looked like any of our teachers. But he was not.

◆

THE TEST I REMEMBER BEST was a guided meditation in which we were asked to close our eyes and imagine sinking through water, deeper and deeper, and then rising out of the water into the sunlight, before sending our consciousness under a magazine he had flipped open and laid out flat without our being able to see what was on the facing pages.

He asked each of us what we saw—I saw people in a canoe, on a river, with massive white columns rising behind them—and then he flipped the page over. A cigarette ad. The white columns I had seen were cigarettes, massive and rising above a canoe on a river.

The class turned and looked at me, suspicious. I was the only one who'd gotten it right. And my vision hadn't just been a close call; it was pretty precise. Dr. Tanous was pleased, and smiling. He turned to another magazine and asked that we all do it again.

My memory of the day is that I did well: I passed two of the three magazine tests, well enough to believe that I should have been rewarded with immediate admission into a government-funded psychic warfare program. Or anything more interesting than the seventh grade. Instead, Tanous left. But before he did, he taught us a game with cards to improve our psychic abilities. He asked us to think of a playing card and then run our fingers along the side of the deck, pulling the deck apart when it felt hot. Was that the card we had envisioned? It often was. I did this for years, until I lost interest in the game.

◈

THE BEGINNING OF THE STORY I had hoped for did not happen. Another beginning did.

I was, after all, a child. And like many children, I had wanted to be more powerful than the world around me. I had read novels of wizards and sorceresses, dragon-riding heroes and lost kings, hidden from their enemies, raised as commoners to protect them, and I had imagined becoming one of them. I had consumed first the mythology section of the town and school libraries, and soon found myself checking out *The Golden Bough* by Sir James George Frazer, a famous anthropological work on magic. I'd hoped it was a spell book. What I found seemed like instructions on how druids whistled up a wind, and any skill I have now at whistling began then.

After Dr. Tanous's visit, I began taking out books on parapsychology as well. I developed a plan to go to the University of Edinburgh in Scotland, where I would study parapsychology. The idea of studying grandmothers who felt they had "the sight" was the best thing I could think of for my life. And, of course, I would study me.

And then my world flew apart in just about every direction. My father was severely injured in a car accident, the safety-glass windshield blowing in instead of out during a head-on collision. The accident left him paralyzed on one side of his body, with internal injuries. The man driving the car he was in was injured less severely, but he died.

I was trying, I can see now, to hold on. I was prepared to declare allegiance to any other reality. I was thirteen at the time of the accident, sixteen when my father died of complications related to his injuries. When I ask myself why, of all the forms of the occult I'd found, the one that appealed to me most then was the Tarot, I know why. After my father's accident, I wanted to know how to tell the future. I never wanted to be surprised by misfortune again. I wanted one of those mirrors that could be used to see around corners, and for my whole life that's what I believed the Tarot could be. Given the results of my parapsychology tests, the next step seemed as simple as getting a Tarot deck —Tanous's card game, but with more features. And so I did.

❖

MY FAMILY had given me what I think of as a whimsical approach to fortunes at best, which is to say they were not something to be taken seriously, or they were taken seriously in ways that seemed comic. I remember my father, for example, reading palms while dressed as a gypsy for a Rotary Club fundraiser: he stuck his head out of a tent—wrapped in a ridiculous bandanna, an earring dangling off his ear—and winked at me. Or his sister, my aunt, who wept in fury when her North Korean inventor husband quit his highly paid chemical engineering job to try, unsuccessfully, to perfect a fortune-cookie-making machine. On their visits, my uncle brought us trash bags full of trial cookies, some with three fortunes inside, some with none. At first my friends loved eating them, but we wearied of them as they grew stale, and eventually used the trash bags they came in to throw them away.

Funny costumes aside, my father really did read palms, though he never read mine. I wonder if he ever read his own. He didn't live long enough to teach me what he knew or for me to even ask him. When I took to fortune-telling myself, in any case, I was serious. Too serious, in the way that makes you foolish.

I did not go to the University of Edinburgh in the end, but to Wesleyan University, a few hours south of Maine in the Connecticut River valley. I could not major in parapsychology there, but it didn't feel necessary. Wesleyan was full of people who read Tarot cards, for example, because it was full of people who believed everything. You could, in one week, attend Mass and a Seder, stay up all night consulting a Ouija board, get a Tarot reading, go to a Wiccan moon ritual, wake up and take Communion, and if anyone looked askance, shrug it off. Contradictions were defended proudly, and I joined in. I had left for college bristling still with grief after the death of my father—the numbness and shock had worn off and I could feel everything at once. The first thing I did with the trust fund that had been set up for me by the state—my father had left no will—was go to an Alfa Romeo dealership, pay for a new sedan with a check, and drive the car to college, where I called it my Italian lighter. I affected a lighthearted disregard for money, as if I was a character in *Brideshead Revisited*, even as I took a job, almost immediately, privately contrite, making sandwiches at 7 a.m. twice a week at a deli near my campus apartment. If some Wesleyan student ever looked at my car and told me I was privileged, in the class harrowing that passed for hazing there, I would shrug and say, "You're right. I'm privileged. I'm so privileged that my father is dead." And then whoever it was would run away.

Which is what I sought with this behavior.

My first Tarot deck was the Crowley deck, the brainchild of the famous early-twentieth-century occultist Aleister Crowley and Lady Frieda Harris. Crowley was a bisexual, opium-using crush-magnet, feral, fey, and floppy-haired, and Harris was his lover. At the time, men like Crowley were always getting me in trouble, and he was no different. In retrospect, it was the perfect deck for me, a great deal like buying an expensive sports car and using it to light your cigarettes. Crowley and Harris had attempted to take centuries of esoteric occult teachings and render them into a single deck of cards, whose regular use would, for the adept, also work as a kind of mnemonic exercise. While reading the cards you would also learn the relationships between ancient gods and goddesses, astrological signs, planets, alchemical sigils. Each card seemed to be one of seventy-eight windows into the secret life of the world, hidden somewhere beyond the air, under the skin of existence.

Much of what I love about literature is also what I love about the Tarot—archetypes at play, hidden forces, secrets brought to light. When I bought the deck, it was for the same reason I bought the car: I felt too much like a character in a novel, buffeted by cruel turns of fate. I wanted to feel powerful in the face of my fate. I wanted to look over the top of my life and see what was coming. I wanted to be the main character of this story, and its author. And if I were writing a novel about someone like me, this is exactly what would lead him astray.

The deck was, per Crowley's and Harris's wishes, published only after their deaths, a little in the way of E. M. Forster's famous decision to publish his novel *Maurice* posthumously, allowing only his friends to read it while he was alive. Forster was hiding his sexuality; I haven't been able to find out what Crowley and Harris were hiding.

❖

I'D BEEN TOLD that Tarot cards had to be given to you, but I wasn't prepared to wait. And so it was in my sophomore year that I appeared one day at the Magic Shop, a little purple cottage not far from the deli, intent on getting my Crowley deck. The dream catchers banged on the door as I went in, followed by the friend whom I'd brought along to buy my deck for me. I wanted my gift when I wanted it, which was right at that very moment. I felt exultant when my friend handed me the cards—just the sort of power I'd hoped for. But I also felt like I'd trespassed. Both feelings pushed at me as I took the deck home and spread the cards out, eager to master them—both have stayed with me ever since.

I never once thought to look into the history of the Tarot. I never asked, Where did this come from? From the beginning, the cards felt as if they'd always existed. But this is not true.

The conventional history given on most mainstream Tarot study websites says that Tarot began as Triunfo, a card game popular among the nobility in fifteenth-century Italy. It involved neither fortunes nor heresies, though it was informed by esoteric occult knowledge. It did not become what it is to us now until around the early twentieth century, through the efforts of the Society of the Golden Dawn, the group of spiritualists that Crowley and Harris belonged to, who were attempting to codify that esoteric knowledge. They saw their deck as a tool for educating students in everything from Egyptian mythology to astrology to kabbalah.

Tarot is thus said to be an ancient system, but it is more a way of knowing ancient systems than an ancient system itself. There are now many styles of decks, and our modern version of the Tarot is only about one hundred years old.

❖

IN THOSE FIRST DAYS reading the cards, I worked to learn the basics—in particular, the ten-card reading, the Celtic Cross, perhaps the most common layout. It begins by showing the querent

—the person who's having the reading done—at the edge of their fate, with cards representing the querent, the situation, what crosses them, what crowns them, what their foundation is, their recent past, their near future, their obstacles, allies, hopes, and final outcome. To draw the cross, you shuffle the deck, cutting it and either pulling cards from the top or spreading them in a fan, letting the querent choose their cards, and laying them down in the spread as they are handed to you.

My deck came with a guidebook of sorts, which recommended that I quietly hold the cards in my hand and ask the querent for guidance before drawing them. I remember tentatively closing my eyes and doing so. It was an uncomfortable thing to do at first, but that probably says more about who I was at the time than it does about the gesture. Now I find it consoling.

In the occult, good manners matter, as they do in life, and perhaps even more so.

A Tarot deck is composed of two kinds of cards, the Major and Minor Arcana. There are 22 Majors, numbered from 0 (The Fool) to 21 (The World), and they take you step by step along what's called The Fool's Journey, a journey to wholeness with 22 steps. The Fool passes from Innocence, in the first card, to the mastery represented by The World, which is the last. These cards typically have more weight in a reading than the Minor Arcana cards. The Major Arcana can be thought of as the gods; the Minor, as the mortals.

The Minors is divided into 4 suits: Pentacles, Swords, Wands, and Cups being the standard types. Pentacles are money, manifestation, bringing ideas into the world in a physical way, labor for which you're paid. Swords are the mind, the intellect, science, and plans. Wands are the fire of the spirit—creativity, passion for creation, inspiration. Cups are emotion, depths of the unconscious, and a way to measure sorrow and pleasure. Each of the suits is numbered 1 through 10, and each has a court of 4: a Page or Princess, a Knight or Prince, a Queen, and a King. There are 56 of these cards.

You turn the cards face-up as you lay them out, one by one, and consider the symbolism of each, as well as the fleeting impressions you get as you hold a card in your hand. Each card acts as a separate scene or chapter within a larger story, and as you go through the reading, you create a relationship between them. In that sense, it is, whatever truth it tells you, a terrific narrative exercise.

The cards all have standard meanings or associations — destruction, creativity, an affair, a lover, a fair-haired man, a dark-haired one, moving on, and so on. But there are also worlds within worlds, and patterns to learn: some suits are hostile to others, all of the cards mean different things in different positions, and the numbers have their own meanings too. And there are reversed-card meanings, provided you work with reversed cards (some readers do, some do not).

The friend who'd bought me the deck was my college roommate and best friend, Aaron, who, when we got home, asked me for a reading. I agreed. I placed my hand on the deck and closed my eyes, silently making that request for both truth and protection, described in the instructions for reading the cards. When I opened my eyes again, Aaron waited. I shuffled, fanned the cards out, and told him to use his nondominant hand to reach for the cards that felt hot.

This was my version of the instructions I remembered from the card game of my long-lost parapsychologist, Dr. Tanous.

We laid out the cards, and I did my best to interpret them. The Tetragrammaton appeared.

"Whoa!" Aaron said, without his customary tinge of irony.

The Tetragrammaton is a drawn symbol that replaces the name of God for those who believe it cannot be spoken or written in any language. Rendered in red and black, the card looked dramatic, even forceful. The Crowley deck is the only one to contain this card. The card has no meaning, according to the book accompanying the deck, and so it has no meaning within a reading. And yet it was in the deck, and here in the reading. And it did feel very much like it had meaning.

This, out of all of it, felt like a trick.

I don't remember the details of the reading otherwise. I just remember that at the end Aaron said, "Just for kicks, let's do another reading. See what we get."

"To see if we get the same cards?"

"Yeah," he said, and smiled.

I shuffled mightily and placed the deck down, spreading out the cards in a long aisle from which he drew again, before I laid them out.

Of the ten cards in the reading, seven were the same, and five of those were in the exact same places on the table, including the Tetragrammaton, which was starting to feel like the voice of God, if not His name, saying, "Go no farther down this path."

"Holy shit," Aaron said.

I agreed. We put the cards away.

And then, much later, I brought them back out. And did a reading for myself, for the first time.

❖

THE FEELING of something coming true, or of something speaking to you through the cards, is probably the hardest part of reading the Tarot. You read it because you want contact with something greater than yourself. You have questions, and you want the cards to answer them. The problem comes when they do.

Generally, the cards seem most relevant when describing hidden ambivalences or fears, things you normally hide from yourself and that emerge in synchronicity with the cards. Psychic powers are not required. They may even be in the way, or beside the point. Querents are not required to say anything to you about what they are after in a reading, and can spend an entire reading, for example, simply nodding as the reader describes what he or she sees. Frequently, it's better if the querent says nothing. If the querent leaves out personal information, the reader can read unimpeded by assumptions about the other person. Information from a querent creates an opinion in the reader, which clouds what might otherwise have been a better reading. This is because the reader is building meaning for the listener — making available a story in which the querent experiences his own truth. The real power in the Tarot is in the querent.

This is why, in my experience, you should never read for someone you're in love with, if you can help it. You may not be able to relate the story without your interpretation, based on what you know about them and what you hope will happen. And they deserve this distance, especially if you really love them.

When Aaron and I saw those seven cards repeated in his second reading, it was a shock to us both. I had shuffled the deck thoroughly, he had picked the cards by hand, the cards were new, so they weren't marked in ways that would have identified them — it didn't seem possible. Their reappearance — more than a coincidence, like a repeated message — was not just improbable, if you rely on statistics to guide you; it felt almost like a snarl. As if whatever it was that I'd naïvely asked for guidance from a second time had decided to mock our test even as it met it. When I put the cards away I was scared by how, when I'd asked them a question, something had answered. But when I finally took them out again, I was ready to speak again with whatever had answered me.

With time, I became accustomed to drawing recurring cards in readings, eventually thinking of them like weather that returned with the season. I stopped being afraid of the cards that terrify: Three of Swords, usually the card of a breakup or betrayal; Eight of Cups, which often tells you to move on; The Tower, the card of an explosive change of state—the powerful thrown down, the lowly made powerful; Nine of Swords, the card of mental anguish; Ten of Swords, total defeat. These descriptions are, of course, approximations. They lack the nuance you'd get in a reading, and much of Tarot is about nuance.

But I became impatient with the cards, reading too often, and then disappointed when whatever I thought was going to happen didn't happen. And so I put them away after a reading, as I always did, and years went by. There was perhaps too much nuance, and this tool I'd meant to guide me often left me confused. When I took the cards out again, I remember I was surprised to see them, but also uninterested in them. But I kept them.

And then one day I became a professional Tarot reader.

❖

IN 1999 I was working as a yoga teacher at a studio in SoHo, in lower Manhattan. At a staff meeting the owner asked if anyone read the Tarot and would be interested in reading for clients. I raised my hand. With this began one of the more interesting ways I've ever made money.

In New York State, I learned, fortune-telling is illegal, a class-

B misdemeanor. Per Article 165.35 of the New York Penal Code, it is legal only if you tell the questioner that the reading is for entertainment. The owner of the studio, an affable Colombian mystic who seemed indifferent to mortal laws, pointed this out to me once I volunteered. "Don't get us in trouble," he said. I was incredulous, but when I looked up the law, it was true. I tried then to think of what to say to clients. "This is just for fun" seemed not quite the right note. My eventual disclaimer was sarcastic: "Are you having fun yet? Because the State of New York requires me to tell you this is an entertainment."

Disclaimers about entertainment aside, reading for someone else is a tricky thing. To do so for money is even trickier. I had agreed to do it in a casual way because I needed extra cash, thinking it would be fun, but I immediately found myself in too close contact with the lives of others. Their pain, their ambition, their lust for power, achievement, money, or love—these can show up not so much in the querent's cards as in the questions they ask you about a reading, or their expressions as you answer. The mask of the querent drops in their pursuit of an answer much of the time, and you see them in ways they don't generally share with others. And if they pay, you can see in their face that this is not entertainment. They want real answers. They pay hoping, even believing, it will make the difference between guidance that is frivolous and guidance that is real. The best you can do, I think, is stay focused on the cards and not on the person. To let the Tarot cards be archetypes, impersonal metaphors, intimate experiences of an impersonal kind.

I learned to try to offer readings as a portrait of the possibilities of the present. And to receive them that way also.

IT WOULD BE UNETHICAL to describe in any detail the readings I have done. Luckily, I also can't remember them, either. Sometimes friends will ask if I recall a reading I gave them, especially if I predicted something that came true, and I can't. I don't know why. I don't even remember my own. I document readings with photos now. I can say that love and money are what most of my querents wanted to know about, and I think those topics are all that most of us want to know about. Will I be loved, will the love last, is my lover cheating? Will I have money, will it last, will I be cheated? Will I get the new job, the new promotion? Will my book sell? It's the shadow on every kiss and every dollar, that it might not be there tomorrow. If there's a demon lurking when you read your cards, it is inside the querent when they ask about love or money. And it is inside you too, as you read.

While training to be a yoga teacher, I learned about the *sid-dhis*—the gifts, roughly translated. They were an unexpected part of the literature, which said that the practice of yoga could purify your body such that you'd experience abilities like telepathy, clairvoyance, levitation. These same texts also warned that such gifts were obstacles to enlightenment, challenges—because to have them could make you feel like a god. Even being a yoga teacher could be an obstacle to enlightenment. Anything, in other words, that suggests to you that you'd have undue power over others, that you were somehow better than someone else—this is an obstacle.

It was in this light, then, that I came to view what I think of as the dark side of fortune-telling. I was not immune to wanting to know about love and money, and the more people told me how much my readings helped them, the more I heard from those I read for about how what I'd read had come true—book deals, new jobs, new loves—and the more I wanted to know for myself, and to be able to read for myself. This demon is so ordinary that it is no demon at all. It is the part of you that is so very human.

For all that I wanted to be extraordinary, I was no different from those I read for. I was sending my first novel out to publishers, and wanted to know if it would be sold. I was dating a man I felt seriously about for the first time in five years, and became obsessed with knowing how the relationship would turn out. Was I really going to sell the novel? Was the man really over his ex-boyfriend? Where was he the other night when he didn't want to come over? I might take the cards out to be reassured, but midnight, when you suspect your boyfriend of cheating, or of still being in love with his ex, is, shall we say, a bad time to draw the cards. I acted badly, I suspect, *because* of the cards, becoming more jealous or apprehensive than I might have if I'd only seen things as they were, if I'd only stayed within the bounds of what we experience of the world. I'd have false ideas by the time I spoke with the man again, ideas that had nothing to do with what was happening. My interest, I can see now, was in whether I could know the answers without asking questions regarding my own insecurities. Instead of conducting some basic relationship emotional hygiene — Is this working for you? Is this working for me? — I went to the cards and returned with a mind full of fictions. If I had good news from the cards, it made me lazy; bad news, and I couldn't sleep.

And this, of course, is why you should never read for yourself. You can't give yourself the impersonal reading you need. It's much like writing an essay or including autobiographical content in fiction — to succeed, it requires an ability to be coldly impersonal about yourself and your state, so as not to cloud what is there with what you want to see. I think few of us know enough about our lives to know our place in them — we can't see ourselves as we might a character in a novel, with the same level of detachment and appraisal. We can't, in other words, see ourselves as I wanted to that day when I entered the store and bought my cards. We think this means this, and that means that, and in the meantime the true meaning is somewhere else, and the omen lies on the ground, face-down, as good as mute. And the reader is sitting there looking at the cards in front of him, trying to read for himself as his life moves on in ways he can't see.

If I could, I'd go back in time and tell myself: This is how it turns out. You, sitting here, paralyzed by fear, alone in your apartment, reading cards.

◆

WHEN I DECIDED to write this essay, my editor suggested I get a Tarot reading. I was in Spain at the time, on vacation, and pondered the difficulties of locating one of the famous Galician witches, but Galicia was too far away, and few things are as intimidating in Spain as witches that Spaniards all swear by.

I wrote to my friend Rachel Pollack instead. Rachel is one of the world's foremost experts on the Tarot, the author of seventeen books on the subject, including authoritative texts for the Salvador Dalí and Haindl Tarot decks, and she is the creator of a deck of her own, The Shining Tribe. She's also a superb fiction writer. Her novel *Unquenchable Fire* is one I admire a great deal, a satire of magic and suburban America, like Jonathan Franzen's *Freedom* but with spells for green lawns. I met her as a colleague when I taught at Goddard College's low-residency MFA program for a year, where we spent weeklong residencies each semester with our students, doing the in-person part of the semester's work during the day and hunkering down in the Vermont woods together for cafeteria lunches. At those lunches, Rachel spoke elegantly to me about the Tarot as a tool for creative writing—using the Celtic Cross, for example, as a way to think about fictional characters. The questions of the reading—what is leaving the querent's life, what is about to enter, what is the root of the situation, what is the crown, how do people perceive them, what do they hope and fear?—these are all good things to ask yourself about any character you are writing about. But when she drew cards to help shape a graduation speech she gave, I understood just how differently, how powerfully, she used the Tarot. The speech used the cards as leaping-off points for different thoughts, which she then wove into a sense of the present moment, not the future. She gave the graduating class a collective Tarot reading, essentially. And they gave her a standing ovation.

What I understood, listening to her, is that the mirror I wanted, back when I wished to see around corners into the future, was never possible. The only mirror to be found in the cards was something that could show me the possibilities of the present, not the certainties of the future. The level of mastery Rachel had of Tarot was of another order entirely. She was an artist and I was a drunk. She could stand and speak through the cards' symbols in ways that reached past them, bringing out soulful depths and insights into the self and the world, while I had been addicted to the idea I might glimpse the lower truth, a literal one, about what happens next.

After returning from our second residency together, and finding myself in a particularly long episode of trying to second-guess another of the men at the edge of my life, and whether or not I should move to California, I got rid of my cards and made the decision to move without a reading. I told myself I couldn't have cards again until I could read in the same spirit as Rachel. If

I was going to get a reading for this essay, I wanted Rachel. So I wrote and asked her if she was game for an experiment, and she said yes.

◈

I PROPOSED TO RACHEL that she read my cards before I finish the essay. She asked if I wanted to draw my own cards or if she should draw them, and I decided I would draw them and send them to her.

I have a deck again, a gift from a friend, given to me honestly. She and I had gone with a group of friends to a restaurant where the backs of the menus were adorned with various Tarot cards. During dinner, I did a short reading based on the menu card each of us were handed. She was sufficiently impressed with what I managed to tell her that she bought me a deck.

The deck is the Blake Tarot, illustrated with William Blake's artwork and redefined by his philosophies. I shuffled and drew three cards, a very simple reading layout sometimes called The Three Fates, with cards for Past, Present, and Future.

First card: Ten of Science — also known, in a more common deck, as Ten of Swords. Second card: Error, or The Devil. Third card: Stars, or The Star.

It was a "good" reading for a querent to get, I noted as I looked them over, with the querent rising out of his utter defeat, an ascension. It was also, I noticed, like the conventional narrative of most personal essays: an author struggles with his bondage to something he came to as a result of a defeat in his past, and emerges with a better sense of his present place in the universe. I didn't let myself think of it as my future, not in any way I could rely on. I thought of it as something to aspire to.

I sent these results to Rachel. I told her what I asked, for a picture of my relationship to the Tarot, and she wrote back after a few days with this reading:

Reading for Alexander Chee: His evolving relationship to Tarot

    10 of Science (Defeat)

    15, Error

    17, Stars

Alex drew these cards as a group rather than with specific questions in mind. And yet, it's hard not to see them as a progression, with Defeat and Error representing a kind of dead end, or at least a limited direction, and Stars as a kind of spiritual and metaphysical breakthrough that opens up Alex's perspective to Tarot and maybe larger issues.

10 of Science

    These cards are from the William Blake Tarot, and Blake saw science as the outgrowth of a mechanistic worldview that he believed was not only wrong but led to misery and oppression. Thus the final numbered card of the suit shows a scene reminiscent of Laocoön and his sons being strangled by serpents for having offended the gods. In an overly dramatic way the card suggests Alex has tried to analyze the Tarot, or study it in a detached way, which can only lead to "Defeat."

15, Error

    In most decks this card is called The Devil, and in fact we see a Lucifer-like figure seemingly wrapping up souls in a kind of gluey web. This reinforces the limitations suggested in the first card. The error is somehow in the approach to Tarot, and the attempts perhaps to use it for information or analysis rather than a spiritual guide. The previous card suggests the error is primarily one of thinking, so Alex might ask himself just how he has looked at Tarot in his mind. Remember, however, that "Lucifer" means "Light-Bringer" and he is connected with the Morning Star, Venus, symbol of hope, and suggested in the next card. Card 15 is the light of love trapped in darkness, but with the energy of its own liberation held within it like a seed.

17, Stars

The central figure here emerges from darkness into light and a wider vision of the wondrous magical world. With an image as dramatic as the first two cards (this reading, and the Blake Tarot in general, are not trying to be subtle!) the card shows a great breakthrough for Alex in his understanding of the Tarot. The figures trapped in Error might be seen as released into the sky in Stars. Or, Alex's way of looking at people through the Tarot becomes transformed. The large open book on the table might be the Tarot, its mysteries now open to Alex's greater consciousness. The original name for card 17, The Star, probably referred to the Morning Star, Venus's light of love released from the Error of the previous approach.

Rachel's reading felt true to me, and as for the third card, that felt true to what I already hoped for.

◆

THERE ARE TWO KINDS OF PEOPLE, I think: those who want to know the future and those who do not. I've never met anyone ambivalent about this. I have been both kinds. For now, I think I know which one is better, but I'm prepared to change my mind again. It may be I am like that drunk who tells himself he can handle his alcohol now. But if I told you I could tell the future, you would laugh at me. And I would laugh at me too.

In 2006, I had a lesson in knowing the future. My father's oldest brother, my Uncle Bill, was visiting from Seoul and staying in New York's Koreatown at the small but decent hotel where he always stayed in New York. I went that night to come out to him and give him my first book. Before this, I had acted as if the entire world could know I was gay except for him, but this meant my career was hidden from him also. I wanted him to know I had succeeded, as a writer and as an openly gay man. I didn't want him to think I was a failure, and I wanted him to know me as I really was. And as I'd been doing Korean-language publicity in South Korea and America, there was now a remote chance that he might read an article about me. I didn't want this to be the way he learned about me.

The conversation went well, given that, historically, Koreans deny that gay people exist. But my uncle was a law professor who'd dedicated his career to international boundary, was a man of the world, the first one I knew who could wear tasseled loafers and look elegant, not silly. And so there we were, in his room, seated on the hotel's green club chairs, close to saying good night. It was after dinner, I'd given him the book, and we were now discussing the possibilities of my having a family as a gay man.

"Don't you want one of these?" he asked, pointing with energy at the photos of my siblings' kids that I'd passed along to him.

I explained to him that I could still have a family with another man, could still have a family if I was gay. As if to answer that, Uncle Bill told me this story:

Before he left for graduate school in the United States, he visited a fortune-teller in Korea. She told him that his younger brother would die young, and he would take his brother's children as his own, as he would father no children himself. He would either not marry or not stay married, the fortune-teller added.

Here Uncle Bill paused and looked at me. In his expression was someone braced against his life, betting his whole life against this fortune coming true. I saw him take the call with news of my father's car accident decades ago, saw him marrying late in life, in his forties, then divorcing.

After my father's foretold death twenty-seven years before this night, Uncle Bill, of my father's entire family, had stayed in touch with us the most, and though it was not frequent — cards at the holidays, a visit every three years — it had meant a great deal to us. What would it be like to look at the phone and think of calling us all those years, afraid even of this, taking his brother's children as his own, coming true?

As I hugged him good night, I wanted to stay, to somehow walk him back through the days of his life and remove the fortune's long shadow, to return him to who he was in the moment before he heard his future, or, to fulfill it all, at the very least to make true that he had become my second father. Of all the things that hadn't happened, this was maybe the most bitter to consider as I said goodbye. And yet I understood. Here, at least, was a choice to make. A way to feel free, even if that was all you felt.

ON THE SUBWAY HOME, I remembered the story of my own trip to a fortune-teller as an infant in Seoul. All she would say, apparently, was "This one, he has much to do." If she said anything else, no one remembers. I think sometimes of asking, but it seems to me now, after my uncle's story, that you only think you want to know the future, until you do. It would be like waiting for a bullet to pace its way to your side across the years, watching as it approached, knowing when it would hit, and not being able to move away.

Perhaps the only way to escape your fate is not to know it. Now, when I think of not knowing the future, I think of when, in a yoga class, my teacher had us begin our practice by doing sun salutations with our eyes closed, for as long as we could stand it. "What can you trust of what you can't see?" he would ask as we moved slowly and then faster, trying not to fall.

What can you trust of what you can't see?

THE WRITING LIFE

I

Dear Annie Dillard,

My name is Alexander Chee, and I'm a senior English major. I've taken Fiction 1 with Phyllis Rose and Advanced Fiction with Kit Reed, and last summer, I studied with Mary Robison and Toby Olson at the Bennington Writers Workshop. The stories here are from a creative writing thesis I'm currently writing with Professor Bill Stowe as my adviser. But the real reason I'm applying to this class is that whenever I tell people I go to Wesleyan, they ask me if I've studied with you, and I'd like to have something better to say than no.

Thanks for your time and consideration,
Alexander Chee

IN 1989, this was the letter I sent with my application to Annie Dillard's literary nonfiction class at Wesleyan University. I was a last-semester senior, an English major who had failed at being a studio art major and thus became an English major by default.

As I waited for what I was sure was going to be rejection, I went to the mall to shop for Christmas presents and walked through bookstores full of copies of the Annie Dillard boxed edition — *Pilgrim at Tinker Creek, An American Childhood, Holy the Firm* — and *The Best American Essays 1988*, edited, yes, by Annie Dillard. I walked around them as if they were her somehow and not her books, and left empty-handed.

I didn't buy them because, if she rejected me, they would be unbearable to own.

After I got into the class, I learned, at the first meeting, that buying her books would have been premature. She told us not to read her work while we were her students.

I'm going to have a big enough influence on you as it is, she said. You're going to want to please me just for being your teacher. So I don't want you trying to imitate me. I don't want you to write like me. And she paused here. Then she said, I want you to write like *you*.

Some people looked guilty when she said this. I felt guilty too. I didn't know her work. I just knew it had made her famous. I wished I'd had the sense to want to disobey her. I felt shallow, but I was there because my father had always said, Whatever it is you want to do, find the person who does it best, and then see if they will teach you.

I'd already gone through everyone else at Wesleyan. She was next on my list.

❖

I CAN STILL HEAR her say it: Put all your deaths, accidents, and diseases up front, at the beginning. Where possible. "Where pos-

sible" was often her rejoinder. We were always to keep in mind
that it might not be possible to follow rules or guidelines because
of what the writing needed.

The accident at the beginning here is that in the spring of
my sophomore year, I fell asleep in the drawing class of the chair
of the art department and woke to her firm grip on my shoulder. She was an elegant, imperious woman with dark, short curly
hair and a formal but warm manner, known for her paintings of
clouds.

Mr. Chee, she said, tugging me up. I think you should do this
at home.

I felt a wet spot on my cheek and the paper beneath it. I
quickly packed my materials and left.

Before that, she had loved my work and often praised it to the
class. Afterward, I could do nothing right. She began marking assignments as missing that she'd already passed back to me, as if
she were erasing even the memory of having admired my work.
I left them in her mailbox with her clearly written comments, to
prove my case, but it didn't matter: a grade of B-minus from her
put me below the average needed for the major. I was shut out.

I spent the summer before my junior year wondering what to
do, which in this case meant becoming a vegan, cycling twenty
miles a day, working for my mother as the night manager of a
seafood restaurant we owned, and getting my weight down to
145 pounds from 165. I turned into a brown line drawing, eating
strawberry Popsicles while I rang up orders of lobsters and fries
for tourists. And then, in the last days of August, a school friend
who lived in the next town over called me at home.

Do you have a typewriter? he asked.

Yes, I said.

Can I borrow it? he asked. I need to type up this story for Phyllis Rose's class, to apply. Can I come by and get it this afternoon?

Sure, I said.

After I hung up the phone, in the four hours before he arrived, I wrote a story on that typewriter that I can still remember, partly for how it came out, as I now know very few stories do: quickly and with confidence. I was an amnesiac about my accomplishments. In high school, I won a poetry prize from the Geraldine R. Dodge Foundation, and a play of mine was honored by Maine's gifted and talented program with a reading by actors from the Portland Stage Company. But those felt like accidents, in a life next door to mine. For some reason this first short story satisfied in me the idea that I could write in a way that those other things had not.

I had made something with some pieces of my life, rearranged into something else, like an exercise from that drawing class that combined three life studies into a single fictional tableau. The story was about a boy who spends the summer riding a bicycle (me). He gets hit by a car and goes into a coma, where he dreams constantly of his accident until he wakes (this happened to my dad, but also, the fateful art class). When the boy wakes, he is visited by a priest who wants to make sure he doesn't lose his faith (me with my pastor, after my father's death).

The writer Lorrie Moore calls the feeling I felt that day "the consolations of the mask," where you make a place that doesn't exist in your own life for the life your life has no room for, the exiles of your memory. But I didn't know this then.

All I could tell in that moment was that I had finally made an impression on myself. And whatever it was that I did when I was writing a story, I wanted to do it again.

My friend arrived. I closed the typewriter case and handed it over. I didn't tell him what I'd done. Somehow I couldn't tell anyone I was doing this. Instead, I went to the post office after he left, a little guilty, like I was doing something illicit, and submitted the story.

I saw your name on the list, my friend said weeks later, back at Wesleyan, with something like hurt in his voice. Congratulations.

When I looked, I saw he wasn't on the list. It felt like I'd taken something essential out of the typewriter before I gave it to him, and wanted to apologize.

I didn't think I'd gotten in because of what I'd written.

I went on to get an A in that class, which I didn't understand, not even when a classmate announced he'd gotten a B. I didn't understand because it didn't feel as if I knew what I was doing. I did apply and get into Kit Reed's advanced fiction class for the next semester —twenty pages of fiction every other week—and won from her another of those mysterious A's. I next applied for and was accepted at the Bennington Writing Seminars, where I studied with Mary Robison and Toby Olson and met Jane Smiley's editor at Knopf, Bobbie Bristol, who offered to read a story of mine and then returned it with a note that said if I could turn it into a novella, she'd buy it.

I had no idea what a novella was or how to write one, and the excitement I felt as I read her note turned to confusion and then sadness.

Great and enviable things were happening for me. Another student in this situation would have gotten Mary Robison or Kit Reed to help him understand what a novella was so he could write it, and would have been published at age twenty-one, but that wasn't me. I thought I could choose a destiny. I wanted Jane Smiley's editor to tell me, Go be a visual artist and forget about this writing thing, kid. I was someone who didn't know how to find the path he was on, the one under his feet.

This, it seems to me, is why we have teachers.

2

IN MY CLEAREST MEMORY OF HER, it's spring, and she is walking toward me, smiling, her lipstick looking neatly cut around her smile. I never ask her why she's smiling—for all I know, she's laughing at me as I stand smoking in front of the building where we'll have class. She's Annie Dillard, and I am her writing student, a twenty-one-year-old cliché—black clothes, deliberately mussed hair, cigarettes, dark but poppy music on my Walkman. I'm pretty sure she thinks I'm funny. She walks to class because she lives a few blocks from our classroom building in a beautiful house with her husband and her daughter, and each time I pass it on campus, I feel, like a pulse through the air, the idea of her there. Years later, when she no longer lives there, and I am teaching there, I feel the lack of it.

The dark green trees behind her sharpen her outline. She is dressed in pale colors, pearls at her neck and ears. She's tall, athletic, vigorous. Her skin glows. She holds out her hand.

Chee, she says, give me a drag off that.

She calls us all by our last name.

She lets the smoke curl out a little and then exhales brusquely. Thanks, she says, and hands it back, and she smiles again and walks inside.

Lipstick crowns the golden Marlboro filter.

I soon know this means there's five minutes until class starts. As I stub the cigarette out, I think of the people who'd save the filters. At least one of them. I feel virtuous as I kick it into the gutter.

In that first class, she wore the pearls, and a tab collar peeped over her sweater, but she looked as if she would punch you if you didn't behave. She walked with a cowgirl's stride into the classroom, and from her bag withdrew her legal pad covered in notes, a thermos of coffee, and a bag of Brach's singly wrapped caramels, and then sat down. She undid the top of the thermos with a swift twist, poured coffee into the cup that was also the thermos top, and sipped at it as she gave us a big smile and looked around the room.

Hi, she said, sort of *through* the smile. One hundred thirty of you applied, and I took thirteen of you.

A shadowy crowd of the faceless rejected formed around us briefly. A feeling of terror at the near miss came and then passed.

No visitors, she said. Under no conditions. I don't care who it is.

The class had a rhythm to it, dictated by how she had quit smoking to please her new husband. We were long-distance, she told me at one of our longer smoke breaks. We met at a conference. He didn't know what a smoker I was until we shacked up. She laughed at this, as at a prank.

At the beginning of class she would unpack the long, thin thermos of coffee and the bag of Brach's singly wrapped caramels — the ones with the white centers. She would set down her legal pad covered in notes and pour the coffee, which she would drink as she unwrapped the caramels and ate them. A small pile of plastic wrappers grew by her left hand on the desk. The wrappers would flutter a little as she whipped the pages of her legal pad back and forth, and spoke in epigrams about writing that often led to short lectures but were sometimes lists: Don't ever use the word "soul," if possible. Never quote dialogue you can summarize. Avoid describing crowd scenes, especially party scenes.

She began almost drowsily, but soon went at a pell-mell pace. Not frantic, but operatic. Then she might pause, check her notes in a brief silence, and launch in another direction as we finished making our notes and the sound of our writing died down.

Each week we had to turn in a seven-page, triple-spaced draft in response to that week's assignment.

Triple-spaced? we asked in the first class, unsure, as this had never been asked of us.

I need the room to scribble notes in between your sentences, she said.

The silence in the room was the sound of our minds turning this over. Surely there wouldn't be that much to say?

But she was already on her feet at the chalkboard, writing out a directory of copyediting marks: *Stet* is Latin and means let it stand . . . When I draw a line through something and it comes up with this little pigtail on it, that means get rid of it.

There was that much to say. Each week we turned in our assignments on Tuesday, and by Thursday's class we had them back again, the spaces between the triple-spaced lines and also the margins filled with her penciled notes. Sometimes you write amazing sentences, she wrote to me, and sometimes it's amazing you can write a sentence. She had drawn arrows pointing toward the amazing sentence and the disappointing one. Getting pages back from her was like getting to the dance floor and seeing your favorite black shirt under the nightclub's black light, all the hair and dust that was always there but invisible to you, now visible.

In her class, I learned that while I had spoken English all my life, I actually knew very little about it. English was born from Low German, a language that was good for categorization, and had filled itself in with Greek, Latin, and Anglo-Saxon words, and was now in the process of eating things from Asian languages. Latinates were polysyllabic, and Anglo-Saxon words were short, with perhaps two syllables at best. A good writer made use of both to vary sentence rhythms.

Very quickly, she identified what she called "bizarre grammatical structures" inside my writing. From the things Annie circled in my drafts, it was clear one answer to my problem was, in a sense, where I was from, Maine. From my mom's family, I'd gotten the gift for the telling detail—*Your Uncle Charles is so cheap he wouldn't buy himself two hamburgers if he was hungry*—but also a voice cluttered by the passive voice, which is in common use in that part of the world—*I was writing to ask if you were interested*—a way of speaking that blunted all aggression, all direct inquiry, and certainly all description. The degraded syntax of the Scottish settlers forced to migrate to Maine by their British ruler, using indirect speech as they went and then after they stayed. Add to that the museum of clichés residing in my unconscious.

I felt like a child from a lost colony of Scotland who'd taught himself English by watching Gene Kelly films.

The passive voice in particular was a crisis. "Was" told you only that something existed. This was not enough. And on that topic, I remember one of Annie's fugues almost exactly:

You want vivid writing. How do we get vivid writing? Verbs, first. Precise verbs. All of the action on the page, everything that happens, happens in the verbs. The passive voice needs gerunds to make anything happen. But too many gerunds together on the page makes for tinnitus: running, sitting, speaking, laughing, inginginginging. No. Don't do it. The verbs tell a reader whether something happened once or continually, what is in motion, what is at rest. Gerunds are lazy, you don't have to make a decision and soon, everything is happening at the same time, pell-mell, chaos. Don't do that. Also, bad verb choices mean adverbs. More often than not, you don't need them. Did he run quickly or did he sprint? Did he walk slowly or did he stroll or saunter?

The chaos by now was with her legal pad and the wrappers, a storm on the desk, building to a crescendo fueled by the sugar and caffeine. I remember in this case a pause, her looking off into the middle distance, and then back at her pad, as she said, I mean, just what *exactly* is going on inside your piece?

If fiction provided the consolations of the mask, nonfiction provided, per Annie's idea of it, the sensibility underneath the mask, irreplaceable and potentially of great value. The literary essay, as she saw it, was a moral exercise that involved direct engagement with the unknown, whether it was a foreign civilization or your mind, and what mattered in this was you.

You are the only one of you, she said. Your unique perspective, at this time, in our age, whether it's on Tunis or the trees outside your window, is what matters. Don't worry about being original, she said dismissively. Yes, everything's been written, but also, the thing you want to write, before you wrote it, was impossible to write. Otherwise it would already exist. Your writing it makes it possible.

3

NARRATIVE WRITING sets down details in an order that evokes the writer's experience for the reader, she announced. This seemed obvious but also radical — no one had ever said it so plainly to us. She spoke often of "the job." If you're doing your job, the reader feels what you felt. You don't have to tell the reader how to feel. No one likes to be told how to feel about something. And if you doubt that, just go ahead. Try and tell someone how to feel.

We were to avoid emotional language. The line goes gray when you do that, she said. Don't tell the reader that someone was happy or sad. When you do that, the reader has nothing to see. She isn't angry, Annie said. She throws his clothes out the window. Be *specific*.

In the cutting and cutting and the move this here, put that at the beginning, this belongs on page six, I learned that the first three pages of a draft are usually where you clear your throat, that most times, the place your draft begins is around page four. That if the beginning isn't there, sometimes it's at the end, that you've spent the whole time getting to your beginning, and that if you switch the first and last pages you might have a better result than if you leave them where they were.

One afternoon, at her direction, we brought in paper, scissors, and tape, and several drafts of an essay, one that we struggled with over many versions.

Now cut out only the best sentences, she said, and tape them on a blank page. And when you have that, write in around them, she said. Fill in what's missing and make it reach for the best of what you've written thus far.

I watched as the sentences that didn't matter fell away.

You might think that your voice as a writer would emerge naturally, all on its own, with no help whatsoever, but you'd be wrong. What I saw on the page was that the voice is in fact trapped, nervous, lazy. Even, and in my case most especially, amnesiac. And that it has to be cut free.

After the lecture on verbs, we counted the verbs on the page, circled them, tallied the count for each page to the side, and averaged them. Can you increase the average number of verbs per page? she asked. I got this exercise from Samuel Johnson, she told us, who believed in a lively page and used to count his verbs. Now look at them. Have you used the right verbs? Is that the precise verb for that precise thing? Remember that adverbs are a sign that you've used the wrong verb. Verbs control when something is happening in the mind of the reader. Think carefully—when did this happen in relation to that? And is that how you've described it?

wtf?

I stared comprehendingly at the circles on my page, and the bad choices surrounding them and inside them.

?

You can invent the details that don't matter, she said. At the edges. You cannot invent the details that matter.

I remember clearly, in the details that matter to this, going to the campus center on a Thursday morning before class in the middle of that spring to pick up my manuscript from campus mail. This particular essay I'd written with more intensity and passion than anything I'd tried to do thus far. I felt I finally understood what I was doing—how I could make choices that made the work better or worse, line by line. After over a year of feeling lost, this new feeling was like when your foot finds ground in dark water. Here, you think. Here I can push.

I opened the envelope. Inside was the manuscript, tattooed by sentences in the spaces between the lines, many more than usual. I read them all carefully, turning the pages around to follow the writing to the back page, where I found, at the end, this postscript: I was up all night thinking about this.

The thought that I'd kept her up all night with something I wrote, that it mattered enough, held my attention. Okay, I remember telling myself, if you can keep her up all night with something you wrote, you might actually be able to do this.

I had resented the idea of being talented. I couldn't respect it; in my experience, no one else did. Being called talented at school had only made me a target for ridicule. I wanted to work. Work, I could honor. Annie felt the same.

Talent isn't enough, she had told us. Writing is work. Anyone can do this, anyone can learn to do this. It's not rocket science; it's habits of mind and habits of work. I started with people much more talented than me, she said, and they're dead or in jail or not writing. The difference between me and them is that I'm writing.

Talent might give you nothing. Without work, talent is only talent—promise, not product. I wanted to learn how to go from being the accident-at-the-beginning to being a writer, and I learned that from her.

4

BY THE TIME I was done studying with Annie, I wanted to be her.

I wanted a boxed set of my books from HarperCollins, a handsome professor husband, a daughter, a house the college would provide, teaching one class a year and writing during the remainder. I even wanted the beat-up Saab and the houses on Cape Cod. From where I stood, which was in her house on campus during a barbecue at the end of the semester, it looked like the best possible life a writer could have. I was a senior, aware that graduation meant the annihilation of my entire sense of life and reality. Here, as I balanced a paper plate stained by the burger I'd just eaten—I had given up on being a vegan, it should be said—here was a clear goal.

If I've done my job, she said in the last class, you won't be happy with anything you write for the next ten years. It's not because you won't be writing well, but because I've raised your standards for yourself. Don't compare yourselves to each other. Compare yourselves to Colette, or Henry James, or Edith Wharton. Compare yourselves to the classics. Shoot there.

She paused. This was another of her fugue states. And then she smiled. We all knew she was right.

Go up to the place in the bookstore where your books will go, she said. Walk right up and find your place on the shelf. Put your finger there, and then go every time.

In class, the idea seemed ridiculous. But at some point after the class ended, I did it. I walked up to the shelf. Chabon, Cheever. I put my finger between them and made a space. Soon, I did it every time I went to a bookstore.

Years later, I tell my own students to do it. As Thoreau, someone Annie admired very much, once wrote, "In the long run, we only ever hit what we aim at." She was pointing us there.

WHAT I REMEMBER FIRST is our hands, raised in the air, waving and punching like sea grass in a tide, the procession moving slowly for the AIDS- and ARC-impaired, some of them in wheelchairs. At the beginning of the march, down by City Hall, our police liaison was thrown to the street and handcuffed as he tried to identify himself to one of the cops. He had stepped off the sidewalk, where we were confined, into the street, where helmeted motorcycle cops raced in figure eights and ellipses, in formation. Later, we will listen to him tell us about how the police refused to give him water to take his AZT, and taunted him with reports that some of us had been shot. But for now, he vanishes behind a cloud of riot shields.

We keep moving, eager not to have the march called off, as it is our bluff: at the end of it, we plan to block traffic to protest government inaction in the face of the AIDS epidemic. It is October 6, 1989. A cold, gray San Francisco day, the kind that replicates the mood of a flu, hot and cold, sweaty and chilled. The sun hides. To the bystanders, I think we must look like any theatergoers out for early tickets, except for the crowd of policemen in armor following us, all of them wearing latex gloves.

They confine us to the curb nearly the entire way, making sure we obey the stoplights and let the Friday tourist traffic through. We chant, though fairly quietly, chastened by the early arrest, the weather, and the flood of police: our count gives them two cops for every protester.

When we reach the Mint, we throw pennies painted red over the sides of the fence: blood money was the idea, and the very innocence of the gesture stings at me. I wonder if we are deranged, to be meeting these police with arts and crafts. "Spend our taxes back on us!" yells a marcher next to me, as if he suddenly remembers his anger.

At the Castro at last, the traffic makes a break in the police line like a cut vein, and we spill out across the intersection into a circle, linking arms and cutting off all four directions of traffic. Now the chanting is sure and strong. "What do we want? Health care! When do we want it? Now!" And the urgency of tone builds as the police whistle and gun their engines, blaring through their horns that we must clear the intersection or face arrest. In the back of the circle, away from the cops, we begin sitting down. The police cannot see this yet, but a group of motorcycle cops sheers off, headed to the side streets to make their way around to the back, an ancient strategy. At the corner of Eighteenth and Castro, another crowd of people billows out from the subway and finds it cannot cross the street. Some of them recognize friends in our group and wave as they sit down also. It is dusk, rush hour now, and it occurs to me that that corner of the sidewalk will get very crowded.

The police round us up onto two corners, with the exception of the sitting group, whom they start to haul off. Batons are out, extended at arm's length, batting hands to make them release, or barring our exit onto the street. When I try to get through the police, one of them tells me martial law has been declared. "Doesn't the president declare that?" I ask. He says nothing else, looking down, perhaps ashamed to be caught in a lie. Behind us, another group of subway travelers arrives to find they are now included with the demonstrators. Since I can't leave, I climb up onto a newspaper box, balanced against a lamp pole, just in time to see the last of the protesters taken from the middle of the street.

The riot police are marching up and down the street in twos. It's comical, even pathetic. They are trying to look strong. They begin to let traffic through. But there is another group prepared to replace them, and those people run in and sit down in the street, arms locked. A man on a motorcycle finds himself too close to a policeman, who whirls on him, whistle blowing, and he is pulled from the bike by two others. The first kicks the bike to the side. The biker bows his head slightly as he is thrown to his knees, and then doubles over as the blows rain down, first fists and then a baton scything through the air. "What are the charges?" a woman nearby yells. The crowd picks up the chant. "What are the charges, what are the charges, what are the charges!" She is small-boned, her hair woolly and red, and it rises into the air where it is easy for the policeman to grab, and he turns from the beating, pulls her hair, and throws her, face-first, to the ground.

Everyone is running now, and everywhere batons rise. The screams lift out of the street, and in restaurants up and down the block doors are locked and the diners are informed, You cannot leave, not right now, sorry for the disturbance. On top of my newspaper box, the air feels very still, but I am watching a boy I know walking backwards, his hands in the air, almost crossed, as people run for the curb and the V formation of police approaching them breaks as they charge. The point man swings and his baton glances off my friend's forearm to strike his forehead. My iend crumples, his face already bloody, falling on the sidewalk he was trying to reach. The policeman responsible keeps moving on, and the two coming from behind kick a newspaper box on top of my friend's legs, their legs rising slowly and in unison, like awful showgirls.

I jump down from my box. I am afraid he will be trampled. He is unconscious and not in view of the panicked crowd. I go to his side and find someone already there, pushing the box off him. I bend down and say his name softly. Mike, I say. His eyes open, and he is already crying. This is his first police riot, mine too. The blood is always heavy on any head wound, I say, remembering something random as I try to calm him. And I tear off a piece of my T-shirt to press against his head.

People surround us, and soon a medic appears. I follow them as they take my friend to the ambulance. "Are you with him?" they ask me, and I say yes, because it is the best thing for me to do. "Put your hand on the ambulance," they tell me, "so the police won't arrest you," and I do.

I stand there, my hand on the ambulance, and a television news crew arrives and asks me to describe what I've seen. As I tell the story, I keep my hand on the ambulance the entire time. After they leave, I think about how, up to now, I have thought that I lived in a different country from this. But this is the country I live in, I tell myself, feeling the metal against my fingers.

This is the country I live in.

HAIR

THE YEAR IS 1990. The place is San Francisco, the Castro. It is Halloween night. I am in my friend John's bathroom, alone in front of the mirror, wearing a black turtleneck and leggings. My face glows back at me from the light of twelve 100-watt bulbs.

In high school I learned to do makeup for theater. I did fake mustaches and eyelashes then, bruises, wounds, tattoos. I remember always being tempted then to do what I have just done now, and always stopping, always thinking I would do it later.

This is that day.

My face, in the makeup I have just applied, is a success. My high cheekbones, large slanting eyes, wide mouth, small chin, and rounded jaw have been restrung in base, powder, eyeliner, lipstick, eyebrow pencil. With these tools I have built another face on top of my own, unrecognizable, and yet I am already adjusting to it; somehow I have always known how to put this face together. My hands do not shake, but move with the slow assurance of routine.

I am smiling.

I pick up the black eyeliner pencil and go back to the outer corners of my eyes, drawing slashes there, and, licking the edges of my fingers, I pull the lines out into sharp black points — the wings of crows, not their feet.

I have nine moles on my face, all obscured by base and powder. I choose one on my upper lip, to the right, where everyone inserts a beauty mark. I have one already, and it feels like a prophecy. I dot it with the pencil.

I pick up the lipstick and open my mouth in an O. I have always loved unscrewing lipsticks, and as the shining nub appears I feel a charge. I apply the color, Mauve Frost, then reapply it, and with that, my face shimmers — a white sky, the mole a black planet, the eyes its ringed big sisters. I press my lips down against each other and feel the color spread anywhere it hasn't gone yet.

The wig is shoulder-length blond hair, artificial — Dynel doll hair, like Barbie's, which is why I choose it. The cap shows how cheap the wig is, so I cut a headband out of a T-shirt sleeve and make it into a fall.

The wig I put on last. Without it, you can see my man's hairline, receding faintly into a widow's peak. You can see my dark hair, you can tell I'm not a blond woman or a white one, or even a woman. It is a Valkyrie's headpiece, and I gel it to hold it in place. The static it generates pulls the hairs out into the air one by one. In an hour I will have a faint halo of frizz. Blue sparks will fly from me when I touch people.

John knocks on the door. "Girl!" he says through the door. "Aren't you ready yet?" He is already finished, dressed in a sweater and black miniskirt, his black banged wig tied up with a pink bow. He has highlighted his cheekbones with rouge, which I forgo. He is wearing high heels; I have on combat boots. I decided to wear sensible shoes, but John wears fuck-me pumps, the heels three inches high. This is my first time. It is Halloween tonight in the

Castro and we are both trying to pass, to be "real," only we are imitating very different women.

What kind of girl am I? With the wig in place, I understand that it is possible I am not just in drag as a girl, but as a white girl. Or as someone trying to pass as a white girl.

"Come in!" I yell back. John appears over my shoulder in the mirror, a cheerleader gone wrong, the girl who sits on the back of the rebel's motorcycle. His brows rise all the way up.

"Jesus Mother of God," he says. "Girl, you're beautiful. I don't believe it."

"Believe it," I say, looking into his eyes.

I tilt my head back and carefully toss my hair over my right shoulder in the way I have seen my younger sister do. I realize I know one more thing about her than I did before — what it feels like to do this and why you would. It's like your own little thunderclap.

"Scared of you," John says. "You're flawless."

"So are you," I say. "Where's Fred?" Fred is my newest boyfriend, and I have been unsure if I should do this with him, but here we are.

"Are you okay?" Fred asks, as if something has gone wrong in the bathroom. "Oh, my God, you are beautiful." He steps into the doorway, dazed. He still looks like himself, a skinny white boy with big ears and long eyelashes, his dark hair all of an inch long. He hasn't gotten dressed yet.

He is really spellbound, though, in a way he hasn't been before this. I have never had this effect on a man, never transfixed him so thoroughly, and I wonder what I might be able to make him do now that I could not before. "Honey," he says, his voice full of wonder. He walks closer, slowly, his head hung, looking up at me.

I feel my smile rise from somewhere old in me, maybe older than me; I know this scene, I have seen this scene a thousand times and never thought I would be in it. This is the scene where the beautiful girl receives her man's adoration, and I am that girl.

In this moment, the confusion of my whole life has receded. No one will ask me if I am white or Asian. No one will ask me if I am a man or a woman. No one will ask me why I love men. For a moment, I want Fred to stay a man all night. There is nothing brave in this: any man and woman can walk together, in love and unharassed in this country, in this world—and for a moment, I just want to be his overly made-up girlfriend all night. I want him to be my quiet, strong man. I want to hold his hand all night and have it be only that; not political, not dangerous, just that. I want the ancient reassurances legislated for by centuries by mobs.

He puts his arms around me and I tip my head back. "Wow," he says. "Even up close."

"Ever kissed a girl?" I ask.

"No," he says, and laughs.

"Now's your chance," I say, and he leans in, kissing me slowly through his smile.

MY COUNTRY

I AM HALF WHITE, half Korean, or, to be more specific, Scotch-Irish, Irish, Welsh, Korean, Chinese, Mongolian. It has been a regular topic all my life, this question of what I am. People will even tell me, like my first San Francisco hairdresser.

"Girl, you are mixed, aren't you? But you can pass," he said, as if this was a good thing. He said this as he scrutinized me in the mirror, looking at me as if I had come in wearing a disguise.

"Pass as what?" I asked.

"White. You look white."

When people use the word "passing" in talking about race, they only ever mean one thing, but I still make them say it. He told me he was Filipino. "You could be one of us," he said. "But you're not."

Yes. I could be, but I am not. I am used to this feeling.

As a child in Korea, living in my grandfather's house, I was not to play in the street by myself: Amerasian children had no rights there generally, as they usually didn't know who their father was, and they could be bought and sold as domestic help or as prostitutes, or both. No one would check to see if I was any different from the others.

"One day everyone will look like you," people say to me all the time. I am a citizen of a nation that has only ever existed in the future, a nation where nationalism dies of confusion. I cringe whenever someone tells me I am a "fine mix," that it "worked well." What if it hadn't?

After I read Eduardo Galeano's stories in *Memory of Fire*, I mostly remember the mulatto ex-slaves in Haiti, obliterated when the French recaptured the island, the mestiza Argentinean courtesans — hated both by the white women for daring to put on wigs as fine as theirs, and by the Chilote slaves, who think the courtesans put on airs when they do so. Galeano's trilogy is supposed to be a lyric history of the Americas, but it read more like a history of racial mixing.

I found in it a pattern for the history of half-breeds hidden in every culture: historically, we are allowed neither the privileges of the ruling class nor the community of those who are ruled. To each side that disowns us, we represent everything the other does not have. We survive only if we are valued, and we are valued only for strength, or beauty, sometimes for intelligence or cunning. As I read those stories of who survives and who does not, I know that I have survived in all of these ways and that these are the only ways I have survived so far.

This beauty I find when I put on drag, then: it is made up of these talismans of power, a balancing act of the self-hatreds of at least two cultures, an act I've engaged in my whole life, here on the fulcrum I make of my face. That night, I find I want this beauty to last because it seems more powerful than any beauty I've had before. Being pretty like this is stronger than any drug I've ever tried.

But in my blond hair, I ask myself: Are you really passing? Or is it just the dark, the night, people seeing what they want to see?

And what exactly are you passing as? And is that what we are really doing here?

Each time I pass that night, it is a victory over these doubts, a hit off the pipe. This hair is all mermaid's gold, and like anyone in a fairy tale I want it to be real when I wake up.

ANGELS

JOHN AND I ARE PATIENT as we make Fred up. His eyelids flutter as we try to line and shadow them. He talks while we try to put on his lipstick. He feels this will liberate him, and tells us, repeats, how much he would never have done this before. I realize he means before me.

"Close your eyes," I tell him. He closes them. I feel like his big sister. I dust the puffball with translucent powder and hold it in front of his face. I take a big breath and blow it toward him. A cloud surrounds him and settles lightly across his skin. The sheen of the base is gone, replaced by powder smoothness. He giggles.

John pulls the wig down from behind him and twists it into place. He comes around beside me and we look at Fred carefully for fixable flaws. There are none. Fred opens his eyes. "Well?"

"Definitely the smart sister. Kate Jackson," John says, and turns toward me, smiling. "I'm the pretty one, the femmy one. Farrah. Which one are you, girl?"

I shake my head and pull the lapels of my leather trench coat. I don't feel like any of Charlie's Angels and I know I don't look like one. I look more like a lost member of the *Faster, Pussycat! Kill! Kill!* gang. Like if Tura Satana had a child with the blond sidekick. Or just took her hair out for a ride one day.

"You're the mean sister," John says with a laugh. "The one that makes you cry and breaks all your dolls."

Outside John's apartment, Eighteenth Street is full of cars, their headlights like footlights for the sidewalk stage in the early night. I can see my hair flashing around me in the dark as it catches the light. Doing drag on Halloween night in the Castro is an amateur but high-level competitive sport. Participating means doing drag in front of people who do drag on just about every other day of the year, and some of these people are my friends. I am most nervous at the thought of seeing them. I want to measure up.

According to the paper the next day, 400,000 people will come into the Castro tonight to see us. They will all try to drive down this street, and many will succeed. Some will have baseball bats, beer bottles, guns. Some of them hate drag queens, trans women, gender queers. They will tell you they want their girls to be girls. If they pick you up and find out the truth, they will beat and maybe kill you. Being good at a blow job is a survival skill for some of my friends for this very reason — though men are unpredictable at best.

"Most men, when they find out you have a dick, well, hon, they roll right over." This is something a drag-queen friend tells me early on in my life here. "Turns out, their whole lives all they ever wanted was to get fucked, and they never had the nerve to ask for it."

I think about this a lot. I find I think about it right now, on the street, in my new look.

John, Fred, and I walk out in front of the stopped cars. They are full of people I will never see again. John swivels on his heels, pivoting as he walks, smiling and waving. He knows he is why they are here from the suburbs, that he is what they have come to see. I smile at a boy behind a steering wheel who catches my eye. He honks and yells, all excitement. I twirl my hair and keep walking, strutting. In the second grade, the boys would stop me in the hall to tell me I walked like a girl, my hips switching, and as I cross this street and feel the cars full of people watching me, for the first time I really let myself walk as I have always felt my hips wanted to. I have always walked this way, but I have never walked this way like this.

The yelling continues from the car, and the boy's friends lean out the window, shouting for me. John is laughing. "Shit, girl, you better be careful. I'm going to keep my eye on you." Fred is walking quietly ahead of us. From behind, in his camouflage jacket, he looks like a man with long hair. His legs move from his thin hips in straight lines, he bobs as he steps, and the wig hair bounces gently at his shoulders. He has always walked like this also, I can see this, and here is a difference between us. I don't want him to be hurt tonight, however that happens — either for not being enough of a girl or for being too much, not enough of a boy.

The catcalls from the cars make me feel strong at first. Isn't beauty strong? I'd always thought beauty was strength, and so I wanted to be beautiful. Those cheers on the street are like a weightlifter's bench-press record. The blond hair is like a flag, and all around me in the night are teams. But with each shout I am more aware of the edge, how the excitement could turn into violence, blood, bruises, death.

We arrive at Café Flore, a few blocks from John's apartment. We run into Danny Nicoletta, a photographer friend. He sees us but does not recognize me. I see him every day at this café; I have posed for him on other occasions. He has no idea who I am. I wave at him, and as he looks at me, I feel him examine the frosted blond thing in front of him. I toss my hair. I already love the way this feels, to punctuate arrivals, announcements, a change of mood with your hair.

"Hi, Danny," I say finally.

He screams.

"Oh, my God, you look exactly like this girl who used to babysit for me," he says. He takes out his camera and snaps photos of me in the middle of the crowded café, and the flash is like a little kiss each time it hits my retinas.

We leave the café and I move through the Halloween night, glowing, as if all of the headlights and flashes have been stored inside me. I pause to peer into store windows, to catch a glimpse of myself. I stop to let people take my picture, and wave if they yell. I dance with friends to music playing from the tower of speakers by a stage set up outside the café. A parade of what look to be heavily muscled prom queens in glistening gowns and baubles pours out into the street from one of the gyms nearby. They glow beneath the stage lights, their shoulders and chests shaved smooth, their pectorals suitable for cleavage. They titter and coo at the people lining the streets, affecting the manner of easily shocked women, or they strut, waving the wave of queens. As they come by, they appraise us with a glance and then move on.

.   This power I feel tonight, I understand now — this is what it means when we say "queen."

GIRL

MY FASCINATION WITH MAKEUP started young. I remember the first time I wore lipstick in public. I was seven, eight years old at the time, with my mother at the Jordan Marsh makeup counter at the Maine Mall in South Portland. We were Christmas shopping, I think — it was winter, at least — and she was there trying on samples.

My mother is a beauty, from a family of Maine farmers who are almost all tall, long-waisted, thin, and pretty, the men and the women. Her eyes are Atlantic Ocean blue. She has a pragmatic streak, from being a farmer's daughter, that typically rules her, but she also loves fashion and glamour. When she was younger, she wore simple but chic clothes she often accessorized with cocktail rings, knee-high black leather boots, dark sunglasses with white frames.

I kept a secret from my mom, or at least I thought I did: I would go into her bathroom and try on her makeup, looking at myself in the mirror. I spent hours in front of that mirror, rearranging my facial expressions — my face at rest looked unresolved to me, in between one thing and another. I would sometimes stare at my face and imagine it was either more white or more Asian. But makeup I understood; I had watched the change that came over my mother when she put on makeup, and I wanted that for myself. So while she was busy at the makeup counter, I reached up for one of the lipsticks, applied it, and then turned to her with a smile.

I thought it would surprise her, make her happy. I am sure the reddish orange color looked clownish, even frightening, on my little face.

"Alexander" was all she said, stepping off the chair at the Clinique counter and sweeping me up. She pulled my ski mask over my head and led me out of the department store to the car, like I had stolen something. We drove home in silence, and once there, she washed the lipstick off my face and warned me to never do that again.

She was angry, upset, she felt betrayed by me. There was a line, and I had thought I could go back and forth across it, but it seemed I could not.

Until I could. Until I did.

I was not just mistaken for a member of other races, as a child. I was also often mistaken for a girl. What a pretty little girl you have, people used to say to my mother at the grocery store when I was six, seven, eight. She had let my hair grow long.

I'm a boy, I would say each time. And they would turn red, or stammer an apology, or say, His hair is so long, and I would feel as if I had done something wrong, or she had.

I have been trying to convince people for so long that I am a real boy, it is a relief to stop, to run in the other direction.

Before Halloween night, I thought I knew some things about being a woman. I'd had women teachers and read women writers; women were my best friends growing up. But that night was a glimpse into a universe beside my own. Drag is its own world of experience — a theater of being female more than a reality. It isn't like being trans, either. It isn't, the more I think about it, like anything except what it is: costumes, illusion, a spell you cast on others and on yourself.

But girl, girl is something else.

My friends in San Francisco at this time, we all call each other "girl," except for the ones who think they are too butch for such nellying, though we call them "girl" maybe most of all. My women friends call each other "girl" too, and they say it sometimes like they are a little surprised at how much they like it. This, for me, began in meetings for ACT UP and Queer Nation, a little word that moved in on us all back then. When we say it, the word is like a stone we pass one to the other: the stone thrown at all of us. And the more we catch it and pass it, it seems the less it can hurt us, the more we know who our new family is now. Who knows us, and who doesn't. It is something like a bullet turned into something like a badge of pride.

Later that night we go to Club Uranus. John and Fred have removed their wigs and makeup. I have decided not to. Fred was uncomfortable—a wig is hot—and John wanted to get laid by a man *as* a man. I wasn't ready to let go. As we walked there, we passed heterosexual couples on the street. I walked with Fred, holding his arm, and noted the passing men who treated me like a woman—and the women who did also. Only one person let on that he saw through me, a man at a stoplight who leaned out his car window to shout, "Hey, Lola, come back here, baby! I love you!"

My friend Darren is at the club, a thin blond boy done up as Marie Antoinette, in hair nearly a foot tall and a professional costume rental dress, hoopskirts and all. On his feet, combat boots also. He raises his skirts periodically to show he is wearing nothing underneath.

Soon I am on the go-go stage by the bar. On my back, riding me, is a skinny white boy in a thong made out of duct tape, his body shaved. We are both sweating, the lights a crown of wet bright heat. The music is loud and very fast, and I roll my head like a lion, whipping the wig around for the cool air this lets in. People squeeze by the stage, alternately staring at and ignoring us.

I see very little, but I soon spot Fred, who raises his hand and gives me a little wave from where he is standing. I want to tell him I know the boy on my back and that it isn't anything he needs to worry about, but he seems to understand this. I wonder if Fred is jealous, but I tell myself he is not, that he knew what he was getting into with me — when we met, he mentioned the other stages he had seen me on around town. Tonight is one of those nights when I am growing, changing quickly, without warning, into new shapes and configurations, and I don't know where this all goes.

In that moment, I feel more at home than I ever have, not in San Francisco, not on earth, but in myself. I am on the other side of something and I don't know what it is. I wait to find out.

REAL

I AM PROUD FOR YEARS of the way I looked real that night. I remember the men who thought I was a real woman, the straight guys in the cars whooping at me and their expressions when I said, "Thanks, guys," my voice my voice, and the change that rippled over their faces.

You wanted me, I wanted to say. You might still want me.

Real is good. Real is what you want. No one does drag to be a real woman, though. Drag is not the same as that. Drag knows it is different. But if you can pass as real, when it comes to drag, that is its own gold medal.

But mostly I'm still too aware of how that night was the first night I felt comfortable with my face. It makes me wary, even confused. I can feel the longing for the power I had. I jones for it like it's cocaine.

The little boy I used to be, in the mirror making faces, he was happy. But the process took so much work. I can't do that every day, though I know women who do. And that isn't the answer to my unhappiness, and I know it.

When my friend Danny gives me a photo from that night, I see something I didn't notice at the time. I look a little like my mom. I had put on my glasses for him—a joke about "girls who wear glasses"—and in that one picture, I see it all: the dark edges of my real hair sticking out, the cheapness of the wig, the smooth face, finally confident.

I send a copy to my sister and write, This is what I would look like if I was your big sister.

I can't skip what I need to do to love this face by making it over. I can't chase after the power I felt that night, the fleeting sense of finally belonging to the status quo, by making myself into something that looks like the something they want. Being real means being at home in this face, just as it is when I wake up.

I am not the person who appeared for the first time that night. I am the one only I saw, the one I had rejected until then, the one I needed to see, and didn't see until I had taken nearly everything about him away. His face is not half this or half that, it is all something else.

Sometimes you don't know who you are until you put on a mask.

❖

A FEW MONTHS AFTER HALLOWEEN, a friend borrows my wig. He has begun performing in drag on a regular basis. I have not. I bring it to the bookstore where we both work and pass it off to him. It looks like a burned-out thing, what's left in the wick of a candle after a long night.

I go to see my friend perform in the wig. He has turned it into the ponytail of a titanic hair sculpture, made from three separate wigs. He is a hoop-skirted vision beneath its impossible size, his face whited out, a beauty mark on his lip. Who was the first blond to dot a beauty mark on her upper lip? How far back in time do we have to go? It is like some spirit in the wig has moved on, into him.

He never gives me the wig back, and I don't ask for it back. It was never really mine.

AFTER PETER

In memoriam, Peter David Kelloran
17 December 1961–10 May 1994

I slept but my heart was awake.
—Song of Songs 5:2

I AM A MINOR CHARACTER in Peter's story. Peter David Kelloran—Peter D. Kelloran, as he liked to appear in print—was a
painter. He died in his bed at the age of thirty-three on the afternoon of May 10, 1994, at the Maitri Hospice in San Francisco,
where he had been admitted after deciding he could no longer
care for himself in his apartment at the edge of town. There was
a solar eclipse that day, and his passing occurred during it. He
had spoken with his mother that morning on the phone. His dementia had parted enough for him to tell her that he loved her.
"And then he started to go," his friend Laura Lister says. The
room was full of women friends of Peter's and they laid hands on
him in a circle. Laura recalls the phone ringing, and she took her
hands off him to answer it. "He lunged up off the bed." He went
slowly. "I begged him to go, begged him to let go at that point.
He needed to go. He wouldn't go, though," Laura says. "And then
one of the male volunteers came in and he took Peter's hand in
his. You could see the change. Like a light came over him. And
he was gone."

"All the people there with him at the end, I can never thank
them enough. They were all so beautiful, so strong," his mother,
Jill Kelloran, says from her home in Chicago. "They did what I

physically could not do. Peter's death was tearing me apart and I literally could not be there. They cared for him to the end. And I will always be grateful to them for that."

"We were there until he grew cold," Peggy Sue, a friend who was present, says. "Maitri being a Buddhist place, you lie in state. So we sat with him."

◈

I FIRST SAW HIM when I worked in the Castro at A Different Light, a gay and lesbian bookstore that in those days doubled as a reference library and community center. I was twenty-two years old then. Peter was twenty-eight, tall and broad-shouldered and thin. He had a wide Irish frame and usually wore leather: a motorcycle jacket, boots. A dyed blue tuft of hair glowed across his forehead. I'd seen him walking through the Castro, and I'd seen him at demonstrations. A year would pass before I'd hear his voice, speaking to me.

The store was the first in the country to have a section devoted entirely to AIDS/HIV issues; it was located at the front of the store, beside the cash register. I supposed, the first day I saw Peter, he'd either seroconverted recently or had recently decided to do something about it. I saw many people in this way, on their first few days, and I was forever inventing some story about them, never mentioned to anyone, simply to fill the hours. I was often the first person they had to deal with after being diagnosed, a bookstore clerk who would show them the short shelf of books, expanding weekly but still short.

That day he just ran through the books and selected a few on strengthening the immune system, and then paid when someone else was at the register. I saw him leave. His blue eyes had a searchlight intensity, and it seemed clear what he saw and what he didn't. He didn't see me. I felt called and commanded by him immediately, and to this day I cannot say why it was, only that it was immediate, and thorough. I was surprised by how much I wanted to be seen by him.

That day in the store, after he didn't look at me, he moved quickly back out onto the bustling sidewalk, the afternoon sunlight making long, crowded shadows. I didn't know his name or anything about him, except that he was handsome in a way that made me lose my breath, and he was hurrying away. And that he was possibly, probably, positive.

In fact, when I first saw Peter he had been positive for three years. "He wrote to me from Morocco," Laura says, of a trip he'd taken in 1986. "And he could only write about how sick he had been. And after he got back and he tested positive, that was when we figured out, that was his onset."

He would keep it a secret for years, not telling anyone besides Laura, who kept his secret as well. "A lot of people were angry at me for that," she says. "But people thinking about your death, that'll put you in the grave. And besides," she adds, "if you didn't get your business dealt with when someone dies, that's your own fault. You had every day before then to deal."

I was not part of the group that was called when Peter died. I found out three months after his death, in New York, with my friend Choire, who had also moved east by now, and we were speaking about our friends back in San Francisco when he said, "Well, after Peter died . . ."

I felt like he had been cleaning a gun and it had emptied into me.

"Sorry," Choire said. "Thought you knew. Hate that, when people don't know."

❖

WHEN I ARRIVED IN SAN FRANCISCO, there was no way to find
the Castro on any map. People were forever calling the bookstore for directions to the neighborhood. In my group there was
the sense that we were a wave arriving on the West Coast from
the East: postcollegiate youngsters seeking and finding a paradise of cheap apartments and thrift stores bursting with the old
athletic T-shirts and jeans and flannel shirts we all prized. I remember when I put the empty clothes together with the empty
apartments, on an ordinary sunny afternoon walking down the
sidewalk to work: there on a blanket stood a pair of black leather
steel-toed boots, twelve-hole lace-ups. They gleamed, freshly pol-
ished, in the light of the morning. As I approached them, feeling
the pull of the hill, I drew up short to examine the rest of the
sidewalk sale. Some old albums, Queen and Sylvester; three pairs
of jeans; two leather wristbands; a box of old T-shirts; a worn
watch, the hands still moving; a pressed-leather belt, western
style; and cowboy boots, the same size as the steel-toes. I tried the
steel-toes on and took a long look at the salesman as I stood up,
feeling that they were exactly my size.

This man was thin, thin in a way that was immediately familiar. Hollowing from the inside out. His skin reddened, and his
brown eyes looked over me as if lightning might fall on me out of
that clear afternoon sky. And I knew then, as I paid twenty dollars for the boots, that they'd been recently emptied. That he was
watching me walk off in the shoes of the newly dead. And that all
of this had been happening for some time now.

I lived in San Francisco for two years, arriving right after I
left college in 1989. When I say I was part of a group, I mean I
was part of a group of activists who divided our time and energy

among a number of organizations and affinity groups: ACT UP and Queer Nation were the seeds of a great deal of what happened there, and what happens there to this day. We engaged in direct-action protests, spent our free time discussing new protests and the ways in which our past protests had been perceived. We thought about politics and its relationship to our personal lives, to the point the personal was political, because that was all there was. We had bitter feuds and disputes, we had angry meetings, we had raucous celebrations. We had vigils and parties, made mistakes and made amends. The average member was twenty-three, HIV-negative, white, and college-educated, usually gay or lesbian and from another part of the country.

I was twenty-two, HIV-negative, Amerasian, college-educated, and from another part of the country. Pictures of me at the time show a thin, dark-haired young man who seems inordinately happy for someone who spent a good deal of his time wanting to be dead. They all show me smiling. This young man I was drove a motorcycle, worked at a bookstore, hung out with drag queens who didn't attend meetings of any kind, and was known to dance on a bar or two. He was a member of ACT UP/SF before the bitter split of the group, a member of Queer Nation, and a pesky intern at *Out/ Look,* a queer academic journal. He was on the media committee of ACT UP and had a reputation at first for dating no one, and then for having dated everyone. He hollowed his desire to die with the knowledge that other people were dying who wanted to live, and this was the single strongest motive for his participation in direct-action AIDS activism. Being an activist meant, among other things, never being alone, and being alone was when he got into trouble. And so he made sure he was never alone.

AT THIS TIME IN SAN FRANCISCO, it seemed that the world might either go up in flames or be restored in a healing past imagining. The world seemed ripe for fixing and rescue. I think now, twenty years later, this feeling might always be true. Those of us who were in ACT UP and Queer Nation then were accused at one point of "gay Zionism," and if it was true, I think it was true only in that, in a way similar to Jewish thought, we believed we could repair the world and do it by staying together, working together.

Why am I telling this story? I am, as I've said, a minor character, out of place in this narrative, but the major characters of all these stories from the first ten years of the epidemic have left. The men I wanted to follow into the future are dead. Finding them had made me want to live, and I did. I do. I feel I owe them my survival. The world is not fixed, and the healing is still just past my imagining, though perhaps it is closer than it was. For now, the minor characters are left to introduce themselves, and take the story forward.

❖

MY NEXT CLEAR MEMORY of Peter is seeing him at five in the morning on Market Street, under the giant Safeway sign there in the middle of the city, where our ACT UP activist affinity group had gathered in the parking lot for a "non–ACT UP–related action," which is to say, we were some of the same people, just acting under a different name for this occasion—if you couldn't reach consensus on an action, an affinity group could do what the group itself would not. I was a participant in a handful of these sorts of actions. This morning, we were going to wrap false newspaper fronts over a thousand copies of the *San Francisco Chronicle.*

9,000 DEAD IN THE CITY, read the headline on the false front page we'd created. Clever group members had imitated the font and layout, and the false front wore the name *San Francisco Chronic Liar.* Anyone reading closely would see that 9,000 was the number of people who had died thus far in the AIDS epidemic, but the cover photograph, a shot of the city from the sky, was meant to evoke a natural disaster or terrorist news story, which, to us, the AIDS death toll story was. The action's purpose was to increase the accurate coverage of AIDS in the media.

About thirty or forty of us were gathered there, and we split up into groups, dividing the bales of false fronts. Each team was assigned a neighborhood. The plan was to wrap the false fronts over the papers after sneaking them into our cars. Each car had a squad of three. One of us had coins to get the newspaper boxes open, one of us drove, one of us was on lookout. As we took the bales of papers from each box, we felt we were doing something dangerous. But when we wrapped the fronts it only seemed tedious, or silly, or funny. My team, after we wrapped the last one up, sat and waited for twenty minutes to see the effect of our work. Finally a pedestrian came up to the paper box, opened it, and read the headline. This person puzzled over the paper and walked off to catch the train.

Was it all just for that quizzical look? In the morning dark, the action seemed both ridiculous and necessary. There's nothing else you can do other than everything that might work, I told myself that morning, and I often told myself that in those days. These kinds of actions were about resetting long-standing frameworks, ways of seeing the world that didn't include us or our deaths. We had to be sure people couldn't ignore us. We knew ordinary ways of protesting—blocking traffic, marching, getting arrested—were often misrepresented in the media, cost taxpayers money in police overtime, and could result in criminal records and police brutality. We weren't vandalizing the boxes that morning, for example, and even paid for one paper to open them. A quiet, quasi-legal way to do something loud. We didn't know what would work, so we tried anything we could think of. That someone wouldn't do any or all of this is what seemed extraordinary to me then.

❖

I DID NOT MEET PETER that morning. Instead, I ached as he walked in the parking lot, oblivious to me, his leathers shiny in the dark, his blue hair flashing occasionally above the perfect white of his scalp. I asked my friend Choire about him. Who was this man?

Peter Kelloran, he said. Dreamboat. Jason's boyfriend.

Jason was another member of our activist family, and a friend. He also took part in the newspaper action. He reminded me of a soldier in a poster from World War I, the same ethereal good looks, but gone punk. Jason had always had what seemed an enviable sexual success, but never more than that day. He felt to me like the blond boy I was always losing out to, and it was hard not to resent him for it. In any case, I drew a line through the possibility of ever getting Peter's attention then.

❖

PETER FELT BEYOND ME for other reasons besides Jason: too handsome, too adult, too cool to want me, and, certainly, unapproachable. But for all I tried to believe I had no chance with Peter, my desire for him was like a private horizon line, hidden inside every view I had of that morning. And after that, it seemed there was nowhere I might not see him. His electric-blue Mohawk, the blue eyes carrying the light like a filament, the way they flashed through me every time they met mine. The sight of him on the back of a friend's motorcycle, or at the wheel of his VW Thing, his head settled low as he drove by.

The next time I saw him, we were protesting the filming of *Basic Instinct.* It is not widely remembered that a leaked version of the script sparked protests about the misogynistic antilesbian story line. We had no way of knowing, of course, that in the future, the film would become a cult lesbian classic, and Sharon Stone's vehicle to fame. Peter joined me and Faustino, my boyfriend at the time, under the overpass where the crew was filming, and together we let out a discordant three-way yowl. Peter and I had both been in boys' choirs; Faustino couldn't carry a tune, but he was quite loud. The resulting sound *was* haunting, but it also filled us with joy, and I remember Peter's smile in the San Francisco night as the tone climbed the bridge's belly and flew everywhere around us.

Our shriek apparently caused so much distress on the set that Michael Douglas hit a bank of lights with his car. He was not harmed but filming was halted. A few days later, another affinity group I was a part of used fake passes and got on the set during filming. Riot police hidden inside emerged, handcuffed us, and took us all down to the precinct house, where we were held. Peter and Faustino both avoided arrest, I recall. They were technically legal observers and waited for us as we left the police garage. I remember sashaying out of the garage to the howls and whistles of my waiting friends, and that may have been the first time Peter saw me. He was standing at street level, talking to Jason. But I saw his eyes find me, smile, and go back.

Some weeks later, on a morning after we had eluded arrest for a Gulf War street action, I was having brunch at the Baghdad Café when Peter came to my table and asked for my phone number. He waited as I wrote it, grinning a little. He walked off after I handed it to him, looking over his shoulder and waving at me, more or less ignoring my table mates.

He never asks for anyone's number, my friend Miguel said. He's still hung up on his ex.

People change, I said.

I said this with the bravado I often felt back then. And Peter had asked in a manner so calm, so at odds with my reaction, it didn't seem like desire. It was courtly and calm.

I don't know how Peter saw me. I'll never know. How I saw him: Peter at Café Flore, sitting in a sunlit window, surrounded by friends; Peter walking a dark sidewalk, wheat paste in a bucket in his hand, putting up flyers; Peter at meetings, standing in the back of the room, scowling slightly; Peter shining, naked, in the reflection of the mirror in his apartment as he approached his bed.

◈

ON OUR FIRST DATE, Peter took me to see a concert. He picked me up at my apartment on Market Street, we went to the concert downtown, and we drove back to my place afterward. I don't remember the music. That whole night I was aware only of Peter. I asked him in, and he said sure. In my room he sat down on my bed, a lumber-and-cinderblock affair that I'd made with a friend. I did not turn on the light.

San Francisco nights are always more vivid than the days. The sunlight, for all its color and clarity, added to my sense that the city was an illusion, and the nights are when everything seems its true self and color. Peter felt much older than me that night. He wore his leather jacket, a coat I loved, and it was one of the few times when I knew him that his hair was blond, his head nearly bare. All night he'd been taking drops of astragalus, and he did again as we sat on my bed.

So, he said, as he tucked the dropper into his jacket, I normally take boys home and tie them up and whip them. He smiled as he said this.

Do you want to take me home and tie me up and whip me? I asked.

Do you want to be tied up and whipped? he asked.

No, I said, not really. Part of me thought he was joking. Part of me knew his reputation.

He lay down next to me. The two of us were in our coats and boots, and I felt alone with him for the first time. That's fine, he said, we don't have to do that. And he reached his arm around me.

Can you do me a favor? I asked him after we had lain there awhile, silent and still.

Yes, he said.

Can you lie on top of me? Just, you know, lie there?

He rolled on top of me, in a light embrace, and the weight of him pushed the breath out of me.

Am I crushing you? he asked.

No, I said. This was exactly what I had meant. The weight of him pressed me out. I felt covered, safe; something dark in me retreated and, for what felt like the first time in the arms of a man, I felt safe. I was still me — the switch was not flicked, but the terrible feeling haunting me then didn't reach me. Which is one of the things that love can feel like. Peter stayed there for some time. He may have fallen asleep at some point. And so it is that when

I hear stories of how thin he became, I can't reconcile them with the weight of the boy who pinned me to myself, made me feel the place in me where I attached to the world.

Eventually he got up to go home. We made a plan to see each other again. I was with him in a way that I had been with no one else, and from what I understand, this was also true for him. It isn't just that you fall in love with someone — you each allow yourself new identities with each other, new skins, almost like a cocoon to who you'll be next. Strange to ourselves and to each other; only the feeling of the room, the silence of it, was familiar. All over the city, people were strung into slings, dancing on tables, walking down alleys following strangers, but on my doorstep it felt like we were a young couple out of *Happy Days*, out of the fifties, mild as milk. I watched him go and then turned and went back upstairs to bed.

I wouldn't know until years later that he had just told his mother of his illness. He had shaved his head after returning from his sister's wedding, for which he had grown out his hair. In pictures from that day, "he looked gorgeous," his mother says. But his grandmother Paula Morgan thought otherwise. "He's sick," she said after seeing him. She knew before he had told them what was wrong. "He was a very special young man," she says of him now. "It seems to me this happens to special young men."

❖

I WAS BREAKING UP WITH FAUSTINO at the time I met Peter, or, really, what we had was falling apart.

I was as in love with Faustino as I had ever been with anyone. Once, when I told him I had trouble sleeping, he made me a ring with *zzzzzz* circling the band — he was a metalsmith. No one had ever made anything just for me. We both drove motorcycles and used to cruise the long avenues at night, then lock them up together at home. But once we were inside, undressed and in bed, it seemed like a switch had been flicked, turning off the lights. I would freeze, and feel as if I were replaced in the room by someone else. I didn't know how to stop what was happening to me; I didn't know what the problem was. I was at the age, I would one day learn, when memories and feelings related to childhood sexual abuse usually return. I thought it was peculiar to me, but it was all too ordinary; I just didn't have anyone to explain it to me.

In any case, I'd asked Faustino for a break while I figured it out. During that break, he found Jason.

This felt like another failure to me. It was not lost on me that in our circle of activists, we were the only couple composed of two men of color. All of the other gay men of color in our activist group were with white men. All of them had a tendency to date white men and had even commented on it with each other. I still remember one young white man at an activist party who came up to me and asked what it was like to date his future husband.

Want to see the ring he made me? I said, and flashed it at him.

Faustino had driven his motorcycle out of West Texas for San Francisco. Shortly after, by his account, he had walked into the bookstore where I worked. I remember it distinctly: the sunlight on the backs of his legs, the shy smile on his face as we locked eyes and fell in love. Our first kiss was at a Queer Nation kiss-in, at a straight bar downtown. Our whole story together was, before this, about dreams come true and the pursuit of justice. It was love at first sight also, but with someone who had fallen for me, too. I didn't want to lose it. But I didn't have any way to stop what was happening to me either, and I didn't know how to explain.

It may be that Peter approached me that day because he knew Jason had started seeing Faustino. This kind of drama wasn't really like him. But it doesn't mean it wasn't true. I could have been a point he was making.

Jason and I were otherwise opposites of a kind, me the dark to his light, or, as I experienced it, me the invisible to his visible. That we would end up having not one but two men in common was strange. That I would feel I had lost both of them to Jason — this was what I had always feared would be the story of my life. That I would always lose in love to any blond white man.

Faustino eventually asked me for the ring back, and I did return it after I moved away to New York, by then in love with someone else. And Jason and Peter got back together and had a commitment ceremony, before breaking up again.

After their next breakup, Peter, in the grip of his dementia, would sometimes believe, right up until his passing, that Jason, who visited him regularly, was still his boyfriend. No matter what I'd said to my friend Miguel, Peter had not changed: he still loved Jason, and would until he died.

Peter would die first; Jason, shortly after I interviewed him to write this. Faustino remains alive, but we don't speak. I hope someday we can.

I left this tangle. Peter's story continued without me, to its end.

❖

HERE IS EVERYTHING I never knew about Peter:

He was born in Albuquerque, New Mexico, and had grown up in Washington, first on Mercer Island and then in Bellevue, where he went to Newport High School. He was a skier and a swimmer in high school, but "not competitive in that way people wanted from athletes," his mother, Jill, adds. Intelligent, quick-minded, he never had to study hard and school came easily to him. "He used to love to bug me," his sister Lisa says of him. She remembers that when she would come downstairs in the morning in what he considered inappropriate clothes, he would take her back upstairs to re-dress her. He could get away with a great deal of mischief. "He used to leave the house undetected all the time," Jill recalls. "I didn't know for years that he would get out of the house through his window and go out all night. He started doing it as a child."

He graduated from the University of Washington with a degree in graphic design and left for Europe, where he lived for a year in Spain and Portugal. He had been a kind of art prodigy, good at ceramics, drawing, design. In college he had made a ceramic relief so large there was no kiln big enough to fire it, so the relief stayed at his home in Washington until his father, Tom, sold the house. Jill still has a set of plates he made in the shapes of fishes, and one Christmas, she recalls, he sent her copper candlesticks that had once been table legs; he'd wrapped each one in brown paper and arranged the group into the shape of a star. "I didn't want to open it," she says. "It was like, that was the gift itself, it was so beautiful."

He worked as a bartender at the Paradise Lounge in San Francisco and made all its event posters, using a psychedelic style that soon became its trademark. They were the kind of posters people stole to take home. "So beautiful," says his friend Laura, who bartended there with him. Peter created images for ACT UP's Marlboro boycott, and was proud to see earnings reports that showed Marlboro had lost money in the quarter the boycott began. He also wanted to be a musician, and before he became too ill to do so, he had plans to record. "He had a beautiful voice," Lisa says. "Yes, he had a beautiful voice," his mother says.

He is remembered as consistent by all who knew him, steady with everyone, but still a study in contradictions. He was immensely private, and yet he would say, without provocation, to anyone, "I'm a homo." Serious and grave, he would give in occasionally to a jig, a little hopping dance. Extremely quiet, he could, when he wanted, be the center of attention. "I was called to school by the principal when he was in the fifth grade," his mother recalls, "for a show. A talent show by the students. And out came this little boy, my boy, so self-possessed. And he emceed the entire show from start to finish, totally confident, a little Johnny Carson." Peter attended his high school prom in a black tuxedo he splattered with shocking-pink paint to match his date's pink dress and the pink shirt he wore with the tux.

In San Francisco, after college, he became part of a punk-rock scene that centered on a place called the A-hole, where he befriended the painter Pasquale Semillion, whom he and Laura cared for until his death from AIDS. Peter had turned to photography but still painted abstract canvases. No one is sure who has what pieces of his art now. His sister has three of the Paradise Lounge posters framed in her home; his mother, the plates that he made and paintings and a sketch he had titled *Three Dogs and a Pig*, though it actually depicted four dogs. Jill likes to remember this as an example of his humor. Laura has paintings and pictures and tapes. Before he died, Jason had memories only, but only after he became ill. "I can't really remember him from before he was sick, don't really remember the art," he says. "Isn't that terrible?"

His favorite musicians: Yello, Adam Ant, and Einstürzende Neubauten. His favorite article of clothing: a belt buckle shaped like a bullet. His favorite author: Kurt Vonnegut Jr., in particular the story "Welcome to the Monkey House," in which Billy the Poet, a lighthearted sexual rhymer, stalks a futuristic America with plans to make Americans enjoy the sex they now all deny themselves.

Jill has a picture of him, framed, that she looks at regularly: Peter on the beach in Portugal, waving from the sand in front of a tent he had made from debris—flags, old jeans, sails—where he lived for a good part of his time there. His father has framed a five-page letter that Peter sent from that Portuguese tent.

When an artist dies young there is always talk of the paintings unpainted, the books unwritten, which points to some imaginary storehouse of undone things and not to the imagination itself, the far richer treasure, lost. All of those works are the trail left behind, a path across time, left like the sun leaves gold on the sea: you can see it but you can't ever pick it up. What we lose with each death, though, is more like stars falling out of the sky and into the sea and gone. The something undone, the something that won't ever be done, always remains unendurable to consider. A permanent loss of possibility, so that what is left is only ever better than nothing, but the loss is limitless.

I can't help but long for Peter still, the sight of him, as I once did, love-struck and young, a star in my eye. The top corner of it dyed blue. My personal pantheon of heroes from that time— Peter, Derek Jarman, and David Wojnarowicz—inspired me to be an artist, to protest, to live as queerly, as confidently, and as openly as I wanted. Their deaths, from AIDS, from intentional government inaction—we were not believed to be worth saving —took them from me, from all of us, far too soon. They still inspire me. And so I stand here and balance what I've learned from them on the tip of a crush two decades old, the only communication possible.

In some strange way, more than my other heroes, and more than my other boyfriends, Peter and I were alike. Both oldest brothers, both with family money, both with a sense of political responsibility. Both of us got away with all sorts of misbehavior as children, both of us liked to shock with the way we dressed, both of us liked science fiction. Both of us' sang in boys' choirs as children. Both of us studied ceramics in college. Both of us skied and swam and eschewed team sports, competitive behavior in general. But in the end I wonder if it is a mistake to think about what was lost. If it isn't better instead to think about what he gave me.

❖

WHEN I FELL IN LOVE with Peter, I fell in love with what I wanted to be next. Peter was a member of what was jokingly known at first as the BART 9, a group of nine activists who had handcuffed themselves to the pole at the center of a BART train when the doors were open, stopping the train in the station. This same group had also disrupted opening night at the San Francisco Opera and blockaded the Golden Gate Bridge. They'd done a lot of protests like these over the years, and while many of them were in ACT UP, for most this was simply another in a series of protests designed to draw attention to the AIDS pandemic and the various ways in which companies were looking to exploit the dying. The BART 9 protest had ended quickly, with the group arrested and taken away. The train was delayed but still left the station. Peter missed his medication that day as a result of his arrest, Laura recalls. "It was a nightmare." Missing their medication was a constant risk for AIDS activists who had the illness. The police who denied them their pills, out of whatever rules the jail followed, were murderous.

Peter felt the risk was worthy. We have nothing to lose, the HIV-positive contingent of ACT UP would say in those days. We have nothing to lose, having lost everything. Understand that in 1989 there was AZT and that was basically it. Understand that those of us in my generation who lived in San Francisco had to overcome the false impression that no one like us had ever existed before, because the ones who might have greeted us when we arrived were already dead. We lacked models for bravery and were trying to invent them, as we likewise invented models for loving and for activism. While writing an article about love and HIV, I interviewed many young gay people who would say, I can't imagine getting older. Most of the people who might have shown them what it would be like to be gay and alive even at age forty or forty-five are dead. What happened to me is happening again, ten years later.

In *The Odyssey,* Homer describes Poseidon Earthshaker as having blue hair. He is alternately "blue-maned Poseidon" and "Poseidon of the blue brows." Peter, now returned to the sea, makes me think of that, his blue hair a mark across his brow from the ancient god.

Peter D. Kelloran, resident of San Francisco, a town ruled by earthquakes and inhabited by people who understood some of the value of what the Greeks left for us. Peter the blue-maned, now in the arms of Poseidon Earthshaker—he belongs to a time that already we can't imagine even though we lived through it, when there was one drug, and hope was hidden so it wouldn't die.

I like to imagine him as one of the science-fiction characters he favored, in flight through the sky, roaming the night in a nimbus of blue light, a smiling rogue punk-rock angel, his wings dyed blue to match, from a heaven where everyone dresses well and mercy means love and a man you don't know will hold your hand for you when you die. A heaven where, when there's injustice, you chain yourself to a train because you know that somewhere someone feels it. Somewhere along the spirit-chain world-mind oversoul. Someone somewhere who maybe thought there wasn't a thing called strength feels how you care enough to stand in front of the passage of a train.

As children, we thought Superman was brave to stand in front of a train. That's not brave, though. Superman never stood before anything that could destroy him. Peter did.

❖

DURING HIS LAST TWO YEARS, when he was very sick, he became so thin his pants would fall off him. He went in and out of dementia, regressing. He started smoking again. He would ask Jason, "Does my father know we're boyfriends?" Or he would say, "I met you during high school, right?" One day at the hospice he went out with Janet, his aunt, to get cigarettes and burgers, and he looked around on the street and said, "These people, they're all homosexuals! Every one!" He was so thin at that point that even in the Castro, where people were accustomed to the sight of wasting, Peter attracted attention.

"He had wanted," Janet says, "to be at Maitri. And so we went and there was no room, and it looked like he was going to have to go somewhere else, and then I called and found him a space there, which was good. It was where he wanted to be." Janet had rented an apartment for Peter to spend Christmas with her down in Carmel, and it was shortly after, upon returning, that Peter called her to say, "It's time. It's my time." He had been living at home until then, getting meals delivered and having home care, and when he called Janet, he gave as his reason, "I can't take care of myself anymore. It's my time."

Imagine yourself as a pool of light and sound altering as all your days run through you, and they pass again and again. From moment to moment, you are every age you have ever been, but in no particular order. Time courses through you, the time you lived, a flume of your days. This was Peter's dementia.

"I always knew where he was," Laura says of his dementia. "God, he would say something and people would say, 'He's crazy,' but he wasn't. No, people thought it was sad, and it was, but it was beautiful, really, because he was back in the days that he loved, just all at once. I remember he said once, 'I have to give Laura a baby!' and the people at the hospice really thought he'd lost it, but I knew. We used to talk about having a child, and then, well, he got HIV, and he never talked about it again. And so he mentioned the baby again there, and I said, 'No, remember? You got sick. And so we didn't have it.' And he got quiet again."

Jason remembered him saying, "I am supposed to tell you something, Jason. They want me to tell you something." So Jason waited, and then Peter said, "It's about love. I am supposed to tell you, they want me to tell you, it's about love."

"He was so angry at the end," Laura recalls. "Before Christmas we went out to dinner for his birthday, and he had chocolate. And it made him all warm, as he wasn't eating any sugar and hadn't for a long time. And so we took him home, and I stayed with him and it was then I knew, we'd lost him. That he was going to go. He was very lucid then, very disappointed. He was talking about how he'd never been properly loved by a man, and how he wouldn't be now. He spoke of everything he wouldn't do, the music, everything. And when I heard him talk like that, I knew he wasn't going to make it."

◈

BEFORE THIS Peter had wanted to live at least until 1995. Research that he and Laura had done in astrology said that 1995 would be an important year, and it would be. It was the year of the advent of protease inhibitors, the year many people mortgaged their deaths. Laura had done so much research into trying to keep Peter alive that she was awarded a full scholarship to Mills College to study microbiology. She received the letter notifying her the Monday after he had died. "It got me out of bed," she says. She had taken to her bed for a week after Peter's passing and would later in the year be hospitalized for two weeks for severe depression. "I've had a number of breakdowns since," she says. "I just felt that I had failed him. That I wasn't able to keep him alive. And it hurt too damn much."

Laura divorced her husband later, in part because without Peter she felt her marriage reduced, and she likewise gave up her research. She has lost more friends than Peter to the epidemic, but more than that, she lost the one she loved best. "If I thought for a second," she says, "that I could love like that again . . ." Her mother and Peter's mother both had not so secretly wished the two of them would marry — Laura was a Lister, as in Listerine, and Peter was a Morgan, of the banking family, on his mother's side — but eventually both accepted the situation for what it was.

Laura and Peter were closer perhaps than if they had married.

They had divined several important concordances in their astrological charts, but for Laura the most significant was that he was Aries moon at twenty-seven degrees, and she, Aries sun at twenty-seven degrees. "Your moon sign is your relationship to yourself, how you talk to yourself," Laura says. "The way he talked to himself, that was me. And your sun, that is how you greet the world."

Peter was not buried. He was cremated and his ashes were spread on a sunny day from a catamaran that sailed out under the Golden Gate Bridge. "There's no marker," Jill says. "Just our hearts. We know where he is."

MY PARADE

WHEN I'M IDENTIFIED as a fiction writer at parties, the question comes pretty quickly. "Did you go to school for it?" someone asks. Yes, I say. "Where?" they ask, because I don't usually offer it.

I went to the Iowa Writers' Workshop, I say.

Over the years, I've received two standard reactions when I say this. The first is a kind of incredulity: The person acts as if he or she has met a very rare creature. Some even challenge me, as if this is the sort of thing people lie about (and some probably do, though that makes me sad). Some ask if I mean the famous school for writers—and there are other writing programs in the state of Iowa, excellent ones, but I know they're referring to the Workshop, and so I say yes, though instantly I feel as if I have been made an impostor, hiding in the clothes of a great man.

The second reaction is condescension, as if I have admitted to a terrible sin. To these people, I'm to be written off. Nothing I do could disprove what they now believe of me. All my successes will be chalked up to "connections"; all my failures will prove the dangers of overeducation. If they ever like a book of mine, they will say, "It's okay as MFA fiction goes."

I suppose this is just part of the price I pay for having been one of those people, the doubting kind, sure that it was all bullshit.

❖

I GOT MY FIRST GLIMPSE of Iowa City when I moved to San Francisco, after graduating from college. I told the friend I was driving with to take the Iowa City exit off I-80, and we pulled into a truck stop.

"I just want to look at it, in case I decide to go to school here," I said. This seemed safe to say sarcastically, like saying I wanted to look at the White House because I was going to be president one day. I got out, pumped some gas into the car, looked around at the truck stop, and said to her, "It looks terrible. Let's go." And we laughed as we drove away.

Even then I felt a vague premonitory knock that would haunt me: *Someday you'll eat those words.* But I pushed it away. It was impossible for me to go to Iowa. I would never go, I told myself, and they would never let me in.

At Wesleyan, the college I'd left behind, I'd studied fiction writing and the essay, and the three teachers I'd spoken to about my future offered strong opinions. Mary Robison warned of studying writing too much. "No one is doing anything like what you do," she said. "You don't want to mess that up by taking too many classes." Kit Reed was dismissive: "Don't waste your time. You just need to write, you don't need the program. There's nothing there you need. Just go write."

Only Annie Dillard made the case for an MFA. "You want to put off the real world as long as possible," she said. "You'll write and read and be around other serious young writers."

Two against one.

The real world I moved to was San Francisco during the AIDS crisis. My activist friends from college were all moving to the Bay Area, getting apartments together, going to rallies, protests, marches, direct actions, street theater. I saw the AIDS activism and queer politics movement emerging as a response to the fight of my generation, and I joined with the seriousness of a soldier. My friends and I were people who knew AIDS could kill us all, and we were fighting against those who believed it would kill only gay people. To this day, I can't tell you if we were trying to remind them of our humanity or their own. My time there felt more like a preview of the end of the world.

I would stay two years.

I MOVED TO NEW YORK in the summer of 1991, for the love of a man who lived there. I had a job waiting for me, courtesy of A Different Light, the LGBT bookstore I'd worked at in the Castro. They had a New York store as well, and arranged me an employee transfer. My new bosses set me to work cataloging the contents of a warehouse in Queens that had belonged to a mail-order gay and lesbian bookstore that A Different Light had acquired at auction. After the chaos of San Francisco, New York wasn't much quieter, but this job was: it was like going to sit in a padded room every day—a room padded with books.

If I went to San Francisco with something of the seriousness of a soldier, I left with a soldier's bitterness. I had seen friends beaten by the police and hospitalized, or arrested and denied their AIDS medication under the pretext that they were taking illegal drugs. I had been profiled by the police, baselessly suspected of plotting against them. When one of the groups I belonged to had asked me to find out if my then boyfriend was a police plant, and this hastened the end of our relationship, though I don't think he ever knew he was under suspicion—at least he never found out from me—I knew I wanted to leave.

After all that, it was nice to sit alone in a quiet room every day, surrounded by books. And there were thousands of them, books I knew alongside books I'd never heard of, spilling off the shelves and out of boxes. They ranged from pulp pornography paperbacks to Vita Sackville-West first editions to the works of the Violet Quill group. My literary heroes were mostly women writers and thinkers—Joy Williams, Joan Didion, Anne Sexton, June Jordan, Sarah Schulman, Audre Lorde, Cherríe Moraga, Christa Wolf—writers who were political as well as literary. Their work was in this room, as well as that of their predecessors and teachers: Muriel Rukeyser, for example, whom I discovered in that warehouse and whose poetry I still love. I hoped, like them, to find a way to fuse my work with my belief in the possibility of a better, more radicalized world.

Slowly I became aware that for me, a young gay writer who wanted to write, well, everything—poetry, fiction, essays—this time in the warehouse was an education I could never replicate. And that the catalog I was creating was a catalog of what kinds of gay writing had succeeded and failed—what the culture allowed and what it did not.

For every writer like Gore Vidal, Gertrude Stein, James Baldwin, or Susan Sontag, there were so many others no one knew. The fame of the well-known writers seemed to me a protection against the void, and thus, worthy of study. How had they managed to survive against whatever it was that had erased so many others? Two of my literary heroes, the artist David Wojnarowicz and the filmmaker Derek Jarman, were quite publicly dying of AIDS at the time, facing another, newer kind of erasure in the process, and I feared increasingly, from the work I'd been doing, that nothing was likely to save them except posterity. It was clear their impending deaths, the result of the epidemic, were in some way welcomed, if not wanted, by the government. AIDS was not God's punishment, but the government inaction around it certainly was the government's punishment—a kind of de facto death squad composed of the conservatives who were, incredibly, in charge of these public health decisions instead of the medical establishment, though the medical establishment had its own problems, in the form of for-profit health care. Those exposed, those in danger of exposure, all seemed likely to die because it was too expensive to save us.

Structural death: a preview of the approach conservatives would take for the next thirty years.

Back in San Francisco, a certain Beat poet used to come into the bookstore and move his books from the poetry section in the rear to the new-books table up front. After he left, we'd move them back. Sometimes I'd let them stay awhile; other times what I thought of as his pettiness angered me. But here in this warehouse, I understood him. Fame seemed like a terrible, even a stupid thing to want, but it also could protect you from vanishing forever, especially if you were a gay writer, already disadvantaged when it came to publication, much less posterity. Fame would push your book to the front table whether you were there or not.

The question was, as always, how do you become famous?

The best and only honorable way, to my mind, was to write things people wanted to read. I'd made some progress on that front since arriving in New York. An editor at a publishing house invited me to lunch, because he was interested in whether I had a novel, based on a travel feature I'd written for a magazine.

I was also interested in this question of whether I had a novel, and had shown up to that lunch cocky, with my hair in a blue James Dean pompadour, wearing a ripped black T-shirt and black jeans. My tweed-jacketed new friend smiled in the dark pub as he sipped his water, and we somehow got onto the topic of the Iowa Writers' Workshop, which he had attended. Underneath my performance of San Francisco queer punk cockiness, I took mental notes as he told me stories about Michael Cunningham, one of the few male writers I admired. His story "White Angel," which had appeared in *The New Yorker*, a part of his novel *A Home at the End of the World*, was the stark marker against which I measured my own ambitions. The dishy story I still treasure from this chat is how Cunningham would go running at Iowa and smoke Gauloises afterward by the track, and how this led the other students to call him "French Cigarette."

"After we graduated, we all moved back to New York," the editor said. This I especially stored away as important: all these writers from New York heading to the Midwest to study writing, and then returning afterward. I knew Cunningham had punctured what I thought of as the gay glass ceiling, all too visible to me there in that book warehouse. I began to wonder whether his going to Iowa was part of that—and if it was, if it would work for me also.

Such were the calculations of a young man who didn't yet know that gay men had been publishing in *The New Yorker* before him. That it guaranteed nothing. That there was no guarantee except the one possible if you wrote it, and got it in front of at least one other person. Everything was possible then.

❖

FOR YEARS I had mocked the idea of applying to MFA programs, but after that lunch, I became interested in a way I wasn't prepared to admit. I still made snide remarks about how no one was going to force me to write to a formula. I still said I didn't want to write fiction that said nothing about the world for knowing nothing about the world (unspoken: like all those MFA students), and so there I was, out in the world — wasn't that better? I made a point of saying, whenever possible, that I refused to spend two years being made to imitate Raymond Carver.

This wisecrack about Carver was the supposedly damning critique of the biggest criminal of them all, Iowa. If it sounds familiar, that's because the formula for making fun of MFA programs, and Iowa in particular, hasn't changed much in the past twenty years. The fantasy of the haters is of a machine that strips away all originality, of people who enter looking like themselves and emerge like the writerly version of Barbie dolls, plastic and smooth and salable, an army of attractive American minimalists.

I was writing fiction without my MFA then and getting along fine without it, and I'd just written a story I was pretty sure was my best yet. I was also pretty sure it would never get published, for being a mix of too many strange things, some of them gay. I did not feel like a New York writer, despite being there and writing, and worse, I had to work a lot to afford New York. My bookstore salary was so low I sometimes had to choose between taking the subway and eating. A subway token cost as much as a bagel or a slice of cheese pizza, and so it was always a question of which would win. Some of my friends from college, whom I would see periodically, proceeded with a self-assurance that I didn't feel into careers that seemed beyond my reach. I told myself I didn't have the connections they had, to get jobs at *The New Yorker,* the *Paris Review, Grand Street,* the various publishing houses — and I didn't realize that, if I knew them, it meant I had connections too. Wesleyan had been my entrée into this world, but it was a world they had entered eighteen years before, here in New York or somewhere nearby. I was from Maine, the state where they had all gone to camp together, but I had never been to that camp. "You're not really from there, though, are you?" they used to ask, incredulous, as if I'd told them I cut a canoe out of the woods and rode it down the Connecticut River to college.

I was only subtly aware of getting an education in social class in those moments, which usually just felt like embarrassment that I had to hide. While I didn't have their background, what I did have in these social settings were my looks, a sharp eye, a sharper tongue, and a penchant for making a spectacle of myself, which I would then use to observe people's reactions, learning about them and me at the same time. I could do this and be amusing enough that most people didn't mind. Also, the schools where all these people who knew each other went to had at least a few people like me around — which is to say, gay, political, and an activist.

When these connections I didn't know I had led to an offer of a job as assistant editor at a start-up magazine called *Out*, I took it. The job was the best way for me to take my mind off of obsessing about whether I would get into an MFA program, because I had, by then, applied.

❖

MY REASONS FOR APPLYING were not particularly noble. My boyfriend, the man I'd moved to New York for, had also applied. We'd met at a Queer Nation meeting in San Francisco and begun an intense correspondence that turned out to be our way of falling in love. He was a writer also, and I liked the thought of us as two young, talented gay writers going it alone together outside the system. But my talented boyfriend was working temp jobs he hated, and while he made more money than I did, he didn't feel as talented as I thought he was, and he felt his education had gaps: he'd been a communications major, not an English major like me, and he wanted to know more about novels, poems, and stories. He'd never taken a writing class. He thought a program might help. And so, one night after I finished a shift at the bar beneath his apartment, where I worked to be able to afford to ride the train to my own apartment and still eat, I went upstairs to find him on his bed, covered in MFA brochures.

"What are these?" I asked. I felt betrayed but didn't want to say so. I knew what they were.

He replied defensively—he'd heard me crap all over MFA programs—and our short conversation made me understand how differently we saw ourselves and each other. In his eyes, I had a future without an MFA degree, and he wasn't sure he did.

I was afraid this was his way of saying he was leaving me, a sign of some secret dissatisfaction. In the end, I chose three schools to apply to, three schools he had also applied to, based on which schools had produced the most faculty appearing in the brochures—the schools whose students were hired the most after graduation. These were the University of Arizona, the University of Iowa, and the University of Massachusetts at Amherst.

I applied as a cynic, submitting the story I was sure was my best, the one I was sure wouldn't be published, sure they would reject me. "If they're going to have me," I said, "they need to know what kind of freak I am." In the story, a young clairvoyant Korean adoptee helps the police find lost children and is the only actually psychic member of an ad hoc coven. He has penetrative sex with his high school boyfriend, who's also in the coven, and is possessed by a ghost during an informal exorcism ritual. The plan was that a program devoted to the creation of minimalist realism would have

to reject me and I could go on my way, my beliefs about everything confirmed. But that's not what happened.

My first letter of acceptance, to UMass Amherst, came with
an offer of a fellowship and a note from John Edgar Wideman. A
day later, I got a phone call at work from a woman whose voice
I didn't recognize. "It's Connie Brothers, from the Iowa Writers'
Workshop," she said. "A letter is on the way, but I'm calling to
offer you a place in the fall class and a fellowship." She named a
sum of money.

I was stunned.

"This is great," I said, remembering to speak, and then blurted
out, "UMass Amherst is offering the same amount."

"Did you say anything yet?"

"No," I said, appalled at my indiscretion.

"Give me a day," she said, and hung up. I hadn't intended to
begin a negotiation—I wasn't aware that negotiation was possible. I was only meaning to be literal: how could I decide between
fellowships of equal amounts? I wanted to call back and apologize, but the next day she phoned and offered twice as much, and
seemed entirely unconcerned.

"Thank you," I said into the phone. "I'll speak to you soon."
I hung up and announced the news, and my coworkers cheered
and shook my hand.

❖

BEFORE I GAVE NOTICE at *Out,* I spent a night walking the East
Village, thinking about my decision. I ended up at Life Café, an
East Village institution, where I splurged and ordered an almond-
milk latte and a veggie burrito. I had some copy to edit, an aspara-
gus recipe in fact. I was still not sure I would leave New York. If I

moved to Iowa, I thought, I would vanish forever, unrecognizable to myself and others. And the amount of money in the fellowship, even after they'd doubled it — was that really enough to live on? I wasn't rich here in New York, but if I stayed at the magazine, I knew I could get by. I could afford, for example, this meal I was having. I could make my way up the New York magazine-world ladder, a thought that instantly felt hollow.

At the next table, a conversation about the new Versace leather skirts broke out, if a conversation is people all saying the same thing to each other. They were so heavy, they kept saying. *So heavy.*

I wanted out, I knew then. I wanted cheap rent and a fellowship and people who were talking and thinking about fiction. A time would come again when I would kill to hear people talk about Versace again, but it was not then. Anything you did that was not your writing was not your writing, and New York provided a lot of opportunities to write, but also a lot of opportunities not to write, or to write the wrong things. There were things I wanted, like being a contributing editor instead of an assistant or managing editor, and you didn't get there by working your way up. Contributing editors swoop down from above, made fabulous by the books they've finished, which they didn't write while chasing after other people's copy.

My boyfriend didn't get accepted to Iowa, which disappointed us both greatly, but him more than me — it was his first-choice school. But he was offered a fellowship by the University of Arizona, which was my first choice, the school where one of my heroes, Joy Williams, taught, and where I'd really envisioned myself, until . . . they rejected me. We'd both been accepted to UMass Amherst, but my boyfriend's offer was without aid. We drove up to Amherst as we thought about it and had lunch with John Edgar Wideman, who was, well, John Edgar Wideman: a profoundly intelligent, decent man, and a legend. But we knew, by the time we left, what we would do.

We had been long-distance before, and were prepared to be so again. We each chose our careers over being together, which seemed best for our relationship as well as for our futures. We packed up our little apartments and had a last dinner, where our friends sang "Green Acres" to us over a cake at Mary's in the West Village, and we made our way onto I-80 West, to drop me off first.

❖

THAT YEAR, I lived alone in an apartment that was once ROTC housing for married officers at the edge of town, up by the grave-yard and the Hilltop Bar. This lent the whole project the air of a failed military mission. The floors were linoleum, and a couch, desk, and table were part of the deal.

The Iowa I found was a gentler place than the one my editor friend had described. Under Frank Conroy, the director when I arrived, the list in the student lounge ranking students from 1 to 50 had disappeared, and with it the fierce feuds the list's posting engendered.

Conroy was said to reread the rejected stories first, because he believed that real genius is often rejected at first. This rumor endeared him to me when I eventually heard it, but in those days he was only the legend, sitting in his peculiar way—he could double-cross his legs—in a room full of the incoming class, giving the speech he always gave.

"Only a few of you will get to publish," he said. "Maybe two or three."

I remember looking around the room and thinking, *I bet not. I* had no way of knowing, of course, but I was right: of the twenty-five students in my class, over half have published a novel or collection of stories. But the talk was not meant to discourage us. If anything, it was a bravura dare, like a whack on the shoulder the Zen teacher gives to awaken a drowsy meditator.

I never studied with Conroy, but he taught me one lesson I still remember. I was featured in *Interview* magazine that year as an emerging poet, and I showed him the page, with my face huge and my poem tiny, almost hidden in my short hair. He smiled, congratulated me, and then said, "You succeed, you celebrate, you stop writing. You don't succeed, you despair, you stop writing. Just keep writing. Don't let your success or failure stop you. Just keep writing."

◈

BY NOW, I knew the Iowa City truck stop was not the town, and that the town was a pretty university town away from the highway, populated with Victorian houses that had been built from plans sent there from San Francisco, the result being that I would experience occasional uncanny moments, passing houses I knew first from that beloved place.

Not only did no one try to make me write like Ray Carver, no one tried to make me write like anyone. No one even tried to make me write. The only thing I really had to do was figure out whether my ideas were interesting to me, and then, in workshop, I discovered whether those ideas were interesting to other people. I was surprised to learn attendance was, mysteriously, not mandatory. It's an occasionally controversial part of the Workshop. But the policy acknowledges a deeper truth: if you don't want to be a writer, no one can make you one. If you need an attendance policy to get you through, then, go — don't just skip class, go and don't come back. Writing is too hard for someone to force you into it. You have to want to run for it.

That year, the Workshop accepted 25 students from a field of 727 — now the Workshop regularly receives over 1,100 applications. In the fall of 2001, the numbers leaped upward — as did applications to MFA programs nationwide — and they've never really dropped. This fascinates me still, the idea that the September 11 attacks might have spurred people toward the institutional study of fiction.

The lore around your admission becomes irresistibly interesting once you get in, because it seems the odds are so shockingly against you. You either suspect you do not deserve to be there, or you suspect the others in your class do not deserve to be there. And whatever you think at first, it doesn't matter; at some point the projection flips. You go from being suspicious of everyone else's talent to suspicious of your own, or vice versa, until finally you get over it. Or don't.

Soon I was walking around town with people I barely knew as if I'd known them forever. The conversations were long and passionate and exhausting, punctuated by strong coffee and the huge, strangely fluffy midwestern bagels. I was reading and writing, and doing a fair amount of drinking, for the alcohol was very cheap, and we were writers in the bars of Iowa City, bars that had been frequented by writers for decades. Something was happening to us all, and it felt as if we were all a part of it, even the ones who wouldn't speak to each other. It was a little or a lot like a family.

My first professor for workshop was Deborah Eisenberg. She often dressed in head-to-toe black clothes, familiar from my previous life in New York City, and walked across campus in the impossibly high heels she favored, an ocean of flip-flop-wearing undergraduates around her. She was the kind of woman I had idolized in New York, and finding her here made me feel I'd made the right choice. She was at once a walking memory of the life I'd left behind and a vision of the life I wanted, and I fell head over heels in love with her. I volunteered to drive her home from workshop after the first class, eager to impress her in this puppy dog way I had, and when she asked when I'd started writing, I answered that I'd started late, in college. She laughed a little into the car door as I said this and then straightened up. "I didn't start until my late thirties," she said. "I consider *that* starting young."

Driving her became a regular routine for us, one that thrilled me. I forgot my unhappiness about not getting into Arizona and dove into her mind as much as I could, at first through the short stories — her two (now four) collections. I took her seminar also, and read anything she suggested, from Elfriede Jelinek to James Baldwin to Mavis Gallant, and like all of her students, hung on her every word.

My first workshop with her was a revelation. I'd put up my application story — most of us did at some point in our first year, usually in the first term — still living with the idea that it was the best I had. She saw straight through it, into the way it was a mix of the autobiographical (I really had been in a coven in high school, with my high school boyfriend) and the fantastical (I did not ever help the police find lost children with clairvoyant dreams). I had tried, crudely, to make something out of a Dungeons & Dragons group I'd been in back in high school, but I hadn't done the work of inventing a narrator who was whole and independent of me. Deborah drew lines around what was invented, and what was not, with a delicate pencil, and patiently explained to me how what we invent, we control, and how what we don't, we don't — and that it shows. That what we borrow from life tends to be the most problematic, and that the problem stems from the way we've already invented so much of what we think we know about ourselves, without admitting it.

She sometimes sat down at the beginning of class and would look out at us, smile, and say, "I don't know how you do it. I could never stand it." Unlike us, she had never attended an MFA program, and had ideas about radicalizing it, like making financial aid a random lottery instead of merit-based, or everyone getting the same amount. In our workshops, she listened carefully to each of us talk about the stories, and then, as a way of closing the discussion, delivered her very deliberate remarks, and it would be as if everyone had been arguing about how to turn the Christmas lights on, while she simply walked up to the problem bulb and fixed it and all the lights would go on. She also gave us some of the best advice I've ever heard about how to work with workshop advice. It was, approximately, as follows:

> Listen to your classmates' comments and try to listen to them in the round. Someone will insist if you just fix X on page 6, all will be better, and someone else will say no, it's page 13 that needs your attention, and then you will change something on page 10, give it back to them, and they'll all say, "It's so much better, that's exactly what I meant." The problems are not where they think they are.

This taught me a valuable lesson. It is a rookie workshop mistake to go home and address everything your readers brought up directly, and if there is a problem inherent to workshop, it is that some people credulously do that. A reader experiencing what they called a pacing problem could be experiencing an information problem—lacking information that would make sense of

the story for them about the character, the place, the situation —
and problems with plot are almost always problems that begin in
the choice of point of view. I learned to use a class's comments as
a way to sound the draft's depths, and as a result had a much better experience of the workshop overall.

One common complaint about workshops is that the people
who take them end up in some way alike, and that the class en-
forces this alikeness on one another's writing in the workshop.
But that was never what I experienced. Instead, I think of a great
line from one of Deborah's short stories: "You meet people in
your family you'd never run into otherwise." It's true of families,
and true of workshops also: you meet people there you'd never
otherwise meet, much less show your work to, and you listen to
them talk about your story or your novel. These are not your ideal
readers per se, but they are ideal in that you can never choose your
readers in life, and this is a good way to get used to it. Listening
to their critiques forces you past the limits of your imagination,
and for this reason, also past the limits of your sympathies, and in
doing so it takes you past the limits of what you can reach for in
your work on your own. Fiction writers' work is limited by their
sense of reality, and workshop after workshop blew that open
for me, through the way these conversations exposed me to other
people's realities.

I will never forget the classmate who said to me in workshop,
about one of my stories, "Why should I care about the lives of
these bitchy queens?" It angered me, but I asked myself whether
or not I had failed my characters if my story hadn't made them
matter to someone disinclined to like or listen to them — someone like him. A vow formed in my mind that day as I listened to
him, which has lasted my whole career: *I will make you care.*

If his reaction sounds too harsh, well, the criticism you receive in your workshop is as nice as it is going to get in your writing career. I never tolerated abuse, racism, or homophobia in workshop back then, and I was in Connie Brothers's office so often that first year, she offered to place the entire Workshop in sensitivity training. I turned this offer down. It seemed to me the more reactionary people in the program would make me the target, instead of their own racism or homophobia. I decided to focus on confronting what I found, as I found it, regularly.

I now think of an MFA as taking twenty years of wondering whether or not your work can reach people and spending two years finding out. It is not an escape from the real world, to my mind, but a confrontation with it, even if it also felt, in my case, like a fantasy in which it was my good fortune to study with Marilynne Robinson, James Alan McPherson, Margot Livesey, Elizabeth Benedict, and Denis Johnson, as well as Deborah Eisenberg. I had left a job, and a man who loved me, whom I loved, to be there. That's as real as anything.

The man and I broke up finally in 1994, the year I finished at Iowa. He'd applied to the Workshop again during our first year apart, and when he was rejected a second time, it ate at him, and he resented me. When he canceled our plans to spend the summer together, saying, "You're going to be the famous one, the one everyone remembers," I tried to give him room for his disappointment, but it felt like he was punishing me. He's since had a lot of success as a writer, so in that sense he was wrong. I think disappointment, and the desire to revenge oneself on that disappointment, can be an enormous motivator. Being rejected from an MFA program can push you as much as getting in can.

❖

THE FIRST THING my MFA meant to me, when I finished, was that I seemed to have become unfit for other work, though this proved to be an illusion.

I was fit for writing and for teaching. That I knew. I also knew the only teaching job I wanted was the sort you could get if you had published a book. As I was newly single, and as New York seemed like a good place to be single and gay and a young writer, I moved back, the words of that editor—*After we graduated, we all moved back to New York*—echoing as I did so.

That first summer, I went on interviews for jobs in publishing, but everyone who interviewed me, on seeing that I'd just come from Iowa, assured me I didn't want to work there. "Writers shouldn't hear the way publishers talk about them," one publishing friend said by way of advice. "Also, the pay is crap." I've since known several successful writers who had publishing careers, but it takes a canniness that I couldn't fake, to go into publishing and act as if I had no interest in being an author.

I ended up being a waiter—first a cater-waiter, and then I waited tables at a midtown steakhouse. Deborah Eisenberg had been a waitress, I told myself when the possibility came up, and I remembered the story she often told of her time as a waitress, and I even let it be something of a guide. Joseph Papp, of New York's Public Theater, approached her to commission a play and was surprised to find her reluctant to leave her job. She didn't want to lose valuable shifts. He asked her what she made on those shifts, and that was partly how the price of the commission was set.

I could live that way, I told myself. And sure enough, a few months after taking my first waiting job, I set plates down between an editor and a newly hired editorial assistant and overheard the figure quoted as they discussed a promotion, almost half of my annual income. I was waiter rich, as we called it then, and I stayed at that job for four years while writing my first book.

During those years of waiting tables, I was not above bragging about having gone to Iowa in moments of insecurity, but I always reproached myself afterward. The white shirt, black bow tie, and apron came to feel like a cocoon for the novel, or the writer, or both. I wrote that novel on the subway, going back and forth to the restaurant, and sometimes I wrote it while at work—I still have a guest check with an outline that came to me while I waited for my section to be seated.

The year after that novel was published, I was invited to teach at Wesleyan. I congratulated myself on a completed plan on that first day of classes. I know some people condescend to me when I mention that I was once a waiter, but I will never regret it. Waiting tables was not just a good living, but also a good education in people. I saw things I never would have imagined, an education in life out past the limits of my own social class. Your imagination needs to be broken in, I think, to become anywhere near as weird as the world.

❖

IT'S A STRANGE THING to teach at your alma mater. I have done it twice, at Wesleyan and at the University of Iowa. You learn that students and faculty are kinds of insiders at such places, but within realms that keep each hidden from the other. When you teach as an alum, then, gossip soon illuminates the old myths— the gossip that only the faculty has combines in your head with the gossip only the students had when you were a student, and your own students add to that.

At Iowa I learned to talk about Raymond Carver, because he

so often comes up if I mention Iowa. He is part of the lore, but not, as everyone seems to imagine him, as the so-called high priest of minimalism. That is not—was not—him. He was not especially celebrated for his writing while he was a student at the Workshop, we learned as students there. And his famous minimalism grew out of his relationship with the editor Gordon Lish—a very New York sort of story, not at all a midwestern one. The extent to which Lish cut himself into Carver's work is a source of jokes now, a punch line. I am more concerned with what I see as Carver's real legacy, as a professor: Carver was known for being drunk much of the time, at least in the stories I've heard. His generation of writing professors—most of them literary writers given jobs because of their published work alone—resulted in the reputation that *all writers are like this!* That has followed all writers now in academia.

The boom in the MFA, whatever you might think of it, didn't come about because young writers wanted to imitate Carver's work, as is sometimes alleged. It came about because too many of them imitated Carver's life, and administrators of writing programs began to demand some sort of proof that the writer hired to teach have the skill and the will to teach, to be a colleague, and to participate in the work of the department. You can sniff all you like that a book is the only credential that matters, but chances are you haven't met a provost. In the aftermath of these unaccredited greats, the rest of us are now required to present our degrees.

With this, ironically, comes the complaint that even our sins are on the decline, that more and more we are too well behaved, domesticated creatures writing domesticated fiction, and the MFA is also blamed for this situation, created by, well, writers who don't have MFAs.

It may be that you, like many, think writing fiction does not require study. And not only that: that it is not improved by study. That talent is preeminent, the only thing required to become a writer. I was told I was talented. I don't know that it did much except make me lazy when I should have worked harder. I know many talented people who never became writers, perhaps because they got lazy when they were told they were talented. Telling writers this may even be a way to take them out of the game. I know untalented people who did become writers, and who write exceptionally well. You can have talent, but if you cannot endure, if you cannot learn to work, and learn to work against your own worst tendencies and prejudices, if you cannot take the criticism of strangers, or the uncertainty, then you will not become a writer. PhD, MFA, self-taught — the only things you must have to become a writer are the stamina to continue and a wily, cagey heart in the face of extremity, failure, and success.

❖

"I AM TAKING THIS PARADE down the middle of the road," I wrote in a letter to a friend from San Francisco soon after arriving at Iowa. I had the sense of being given a place inside an American tradition, and I decided I would make the best of it. I would queer it.

A favorite photo from my time as a student in Iowa is of me at a Halloween party, dressed in short shorts, fishnets, a black motorcycle jacket, a yard-long blond wig on my head, applying lipstick in front of a bull's-eye, studiously not looking at the camera, aware that it was on me. I was eventually crowned the Queen of the Iowa Writers' Workshop Prom, an event that saw me appear at the Veterans of Foreign Wars hall in that same wig, wearing a red leather coatdress slit up the sides, makeup, and heels. I remember the hush as I stepped into the bar area where the veterans sat, the saloon doors swinging, to go to the restroom, and the pause as I realized I had to decide which one to use.

I am still, I think, that prom queen, caught in the doorway.

Going to Iowa was one of the best things I ever did for my writing life. If the myth about the Workshop was that it tried to make us all the same, my experience was that it encouraged me to be a writer like no other before me. Whether I did that was up to me. I applied because I was afraid of losing something I lost anyway, and I went because I got in. I hoped to find some protection from oblivion, from my own shortcomings, from the culture's relentless attack on the stories of people like me. I don't know if I've found that, or if I ever will. I still fear those things. I still face them. And for now, I'm still here.

MR. AND MRS. B

HOW COULD YOU? my friends would ask when I told them. How could you *work* for someone like him? Do you ever want to just pick up a knife and stab him in the neck? Poison his food?

You would be a hero, one friend said.

I did not want to stab him, and I did not want to poison him. From our first meeting, it was clear, he was in decline. And as for *How could I*, well, like many people, I needed the money.

And besides, *he* didn't really matter. I loved *her*.

❖

BEFORE I WORKED AS A WAITER for William F. and Pat Buckley, I knew them the way most people did: from Page Six of the *New York Post* and its editorial page; from *Vogue*, the *New York Times,* and the back pages of *Interview.* When I first moved to New York, in 1991, Pat Buckley was the preeminent socialite if you were looking in from the outside — and I was.

Like many ambitious young New Yorkers, I had ridiculous fantasies that involved how one day I would run into Pat Buckley in the rooms I saw only in those pictures. Reading the *Times* on the train on my way to work, I imagined walking into the dimly lit salons where the rich and powerful met and determined the fate of the culture, if not the world.

When I say I really didn't think of William F. Buckley, I mean I didn't read what was referred to by her friends at their parties as "his magazine," the *National Review,* though I sometimes read part or all of his column in the *Post.* I tried to read him when I did because I thought of him as the opposition, and I wanted to know what the opposition said and thought, or I thought I did, but too often it was too awful, too enraging, to finish. I knew civilized people were supposed to read the ideas of people who disagreed with them and at least think about them. In this way I was not so civilized.

When I met him finally, he was not as vigorous as she was, perhaps from drink or cigars or both, though she certainly drank and smoked as well. He was shorter and more rumpled, as if one day he had gotten tired and then never quite rested enough. She was very tall, tanned, and animated, with a wild shock of carefully highlighted hair. She wore a painterly face of makeup that at times resembled the portrait of her that hung in their home. She had the habit of filling the room, and then you might notice him somewhere in it, holding court in a quieter way. It was easy to imagine the woman she'd once been, handsome though not manly, a natural leader. And for those of us who worked in their house, it was her we watched, always. For it would be her we answered to if anything went wrong.

❖

IN 1997, when I began working for the Buckleys, I was the picture of a New York cater-waiter: five foot ten, 165 pounds, twenty-nine years old, clean-cut. I liked cater-waiting because I looked good in a tuxedo and couldn't stand the idea of office work unless it was writing a novel. It was the easiest solution to my money problems when I returned to New York after getting my MFA at the Iowa Writers' Workshop. Cater-waiting paid $25 an hour plus tips and involved working everything from the enormous galas in the Winter Garden at the World Financial Center to *People* magazine lunches to openings at the Guggenheim Museum. The tuxedo and the starched white shirt—and the fact that each assignment was at a different, often exclusive place—made me feel a little like James Bond. Sometimes my fellow waiters and I called it the Gay Peace Corps for how we would go to these places, clean them up, make them fabulous, throw a party, and leave. And I liked that when I went home, I didn't think about the work at all.

As part of my writer's education, being a cater-waiter allowed me access to the interiors of people's lives in a way that was different from every other relationship I might have had. When you're a waiter, clients usually treat you like human furniture. The result is that you see them in unguarded moments—and that I liked. There was the Christmas buffet dinner where the host and hostess served their visiting family wines given to them by various friends that they considered unworthy of being cellared. Or the Christmas party where the host took a friend into the coatroom to beat him in private (so badly he had to leave), to punish him for being a jerk to us, the waiters. Afterward the host handed out his friend's cigars to us and said, "My friend said to say he was sorry." There was the party on the Upper East Side where we changed into our tuxes in a spare apartment we jokingly called Daddy's Rumpus Room: the walls were padded with gray flannel and the windows frosted so that no one could see in or take a photo of whatever it was our host did in there. And then there was the Upper East Side party for some wealthy closeted gays and lesbians who, to hide their sexuality and protect their fortunes, had paired off and married so they resembled straight couples. They looked on with a placid mix of despair and happiness at their sons and daughters, many of them openly gay and lesbian, who were there with their same-sex lovers.

The best thing I'd done for myself as a waiter was to have the cheap polyester tux we all had to wear tailored shortly after starting. I soon caught the eye of a private-client captain, who eventually brought me to the Buckleys. He was a funny, boyish, older gay man whose expression could change from a warm smile to an icy stare in less than a heartbeat. He had an English face and complexion, with a last name that didn't match. I interviewed with him and left, certain I'd failed. If he liked you, he never let on right away.

He worked for some of the wealthiest clients in New York City. I recall helping Martha Stewart pick out a favorite petit four in the home of the entertainment lawyer Allen Grubman while the fashion designers Vera Wang and Tommy Hilfiger looked on. I learned, as I washed up after the party, that the plates had cost $3,000 a setting. "Don't drop them," the captain said. "They're worth more than you." I became used to climbing, at high speed, the back stairs at prominent homes up and down Fifth and Park Avenues, and washing plates and glasses that cost more than my yearly rent.

The moment I describe next was not at the beginning any different from any of those other jobs, but I remember it because of a word: maisonette. It started with a phone message on my answering machine: "Come to _____ Park Avenue. It's a maisonette. Don't go to the front, come around the side. But don't ring the bell. I'll be in front and take you in the service entrance. Tuxedo, plain shirt, bow tie. I want a fresh shirt — no stains on the cuffs or collars. And be sure to shine your shoes, as she'll know."

And then, after a pause: "When I say she'll know, I'm talking Pat Buckley. You're working at the *Buckleys'*. Look your best."

❖

I KNEW William F. Buckley in the same way that every gay man of my generation knew him: as an enemy. On March 18, 1986, the *New York Times* published an op-ed column by him that advocated for the tattooing of people with AIDS on their buttocks and wrists. He initially proposed something more visible, but then rejected it as an invasion of privacy.

A part of my history made me an unusual figure in the Buckleys' home. I was a former member of the San Francisco chapter of ACT UP. In 1991 I had driven to Maine along with thousands of other protesters to lie down in the street in front of President George H. W. Bush's house in Kennebunkport, for a die-in protesting his inaction on AIDS. I still had episodes of PTSD whenever I saw policemen, after being attacked by them during a riot in San Francisco in 1989. I had been a committed member of the group's media committee and occasionally appeared on television, determined to make a difference in the fight against a disease I was sure was going to devastate the world. This was an era when it was still shocking to hear that ten thousand Americans had contracted AIDS. But in just the six years between the die-in at the Bush house and the day when I walked up to the Buckleys' entrance, I'd watched the number of infected grow exponentially each year, past all imagining. The World Health Organization report for 1997 es-

timated that 860,000 Americans had HIV at the time of this story's events, and 30.6 million were positive worldwide.

So when I tell you that I thought of William F. Buckley
as the opposition, I mean specifically because he had given a
powerful public voice to the belief that the illness revoked your
basic humanity and placed you beyond help. The tattoo he suggested was to make sure you knew it. Whatever you might think
of my friends who joked of my killing him, you may better understand the sentiment as a reaction to his denying that they
were even *people.*

On the day I arrived at the service entrance of his Park Avenue maisonette with a waiter's tuxedo on my shoulder, I knew
that we bitterly disagreed on the question of what it means to be
human. I had never imagined meeting William F. Buckley at all,
and so when my first day in the Buckley house began, the reality
of what I was about to do set in. I walked to Park Avenue from
the subway and looked up at the enormous stone and brick tower
in disbelief. I wondered briefly whether they ran background
checks on the waiters, whether they knew of my past, whether
someone like me could really work there. I drew a breath and put
all of that out of my head.

And then the door opened and I was let in.

❖

A MAISONETTE, if you don't know, and I didn't, is a house hidden inside the walls of an apartment building. The owners share
services with the rest of the building but have their own door.
In the entrance to the Buckleys' maisonette sat a small harpsichord of the most delicate gold and brown wood. I was told that

Christopher, their son, could play it very well. A portrait of him when he was young hung on the wall on the right, near the entrance, and in it he looked preternaturally beautiful, like the child of elves. Next to the harpsichord was a tree made of metal, with what looked to be cut glass or semiprecious stones for leaves, set in a bed of rougher stones in a low vase. There were trees like this all through the downstairs, chest-high, and the effect was like entering a forest grove under a spell, where the elfin child from the painting might appear and play a song. The forest was also populated with expensive rugs, cigar ashtrays, lamps, and chairs covered in chintz. The house gave the appearance of having been decorated once in a particular style and then never updated again. Between the dark reds on the walls and the glittering stone trees, it felt warm and cold at the same time.

I was being auditioned, the captain told me. If I succeeded at this, one of his most difficult assignments, I would be a regular. "Mrs. B will watch you like a hawk," he said, "in general, but especially for this first one. So you have to be on your very best behavior if you want to be asked back." As the door closed behind us, he said, "That's what we call them: Mr. and Mrs. B."

I was then introduced to a kind older gentleman who, in my memory, ran their household. I don't recall his precise title or his name, but if it had been a palace, I think he would have been the chamberlain. He impressed me instantly as one of the sweetest and most elegant men I had ever met, with a full head of white hair and a wry look in his eyes that stayed whether he was regarding a martini or a waiter. He was busy with showing the cooks around the kitchen. The waiters were brought upstairs to change in a small room that sat at the end of a hallway near the entrance to the back stairs, which led from the second floor to the kitchen. The room contained a single bed, made up with a torn coverlet, and a treadmill covered in wire hangers and books. Dusty sports trophies lined dusty bookshelves.

"Whose room is this?" I asked the captain.

"Mr. B's," he said.

I stared, waiting for him to laugh.

He said, "Oh, honey. Sure. She's the one with all the money, after all. Canadian timber fortune, I think. Her friends call her Timberrr because of that and because she's tall and when she's drunk she falls over, because she won't wear her shoes." I thought of Mag Wildwood in *Breakfast at Tiffany's*. I laughed, he laughed, and then his face came over serious and flat, and we both stopped laughing at the same time.

"Don't you dare write about any of this," he said, "or I'll have to hunt you down and kill you. With my bare hands. Because I love them dearly."

❖

THE PARTIES THE BUCKLEYS HAD IN NEW YORK were typically attended by a strange mixture of her friends and his, which is to say, I remember holding out a tray of scallops wrapped in bacon to the socialite Nan Kempner and the conservative writer Taki Theodoracopulos, both of whom looked down at it as if it had insects on it, and then I moved on to the magazine people, who swarmed the trays quickly, eating everything. It was her very rich society crowd mingling with the young writers Buckley was fostering, and they had very little to say to each other, often drifting to different sides of the room, yet never hostile.

Despite the way the writers condescended to me, I knew I made more money than they did. But it wouldn't matter. I was holding the tray they were eating from. The food was always from another era: the terrines, for example, which I never saw anywhere else I worked. The scallops wrapped in bacon. Gravlax slices on Melba toast. The Buckleys did not go in for the new trends in cooking. There was never going to be a piece of charred tuna, pink on the inside, on those trays. The only pink was in the roast beef appetizers. There would never be coconut-crusted shrimp. And dessert was often, perhaps even always, rum raisin ice cream, a favorite of theirs. I found that endearing.

On my first night there, when I was not supposed to make a mistake, I did. I remember very clearly being in the dining room and making my way through the thickets of chairs around the tables. Someone was speaking to the room for some reason as the courses were being changed—we waiters had to bring in one plate and leave with another, swapping them out very quickly, working in rows. I cleared from the wrong side and served from the wrong side, and while the guests didn't seem to notice, I was helpless as I looked up and saw Mrs. B glaring at me as if I'd personally done it to hurt her feelings. Her dark, thickly lined eyes barely held in her fury.

I went to the captain immediately. He swore and glowered at me. "Chee . . ." he said, trailing off. And then he said, "It's okay. I mean, you're in for it now. But there's only one thing for you to do."

That one thing, it turned out, occurred at the very next party, and it was a part of my probation. Instead of passing food or drinks, I looked after her. Mrs. B typically sat talking to someone animatedly, her cigarettes, lighter, lipstick, glasses, and cocktail beside her on a small table. She drank Kir Royales, but with a light blush, not too dark. She would take off her shoes, setting them to the side. And when she leaped up to speak with someone she recognized on the other side of the room, she left everything behind.

Your job at that moment—should you have screwed up as I had screwed up—was to go immediately to the back and emerge with a fresh Kir Royale, prepared as she liked it. You never brought her the one she'd just abandoned. You then grabbed her lipstick, glasses, cigarettes, and lighter in your other hand, bent down to retrieve her shoes, and went over to where, by now, she was in conversation again. You did not interrupt, but waited until she looked at you, and then you said, "Mrs. B, you left these," and she would exclaim, take them from you, and sure enough, if the color of the Kir Royale was right and you were appropriately chastened in your manner, and you did all of this exactly right each time she moved, you survived.

As I handed her shoes over that first time, I blushed a little, like someone in love. → why does he write this w/ women? be.g. prof.

◆

I HADN'T READ Mr. B's famous column on the AIDS tattoo before I worked for him. After I began working for him, I still did not read it. I felt it was somehow safer not to, because once that friend had asked me whether I'd ever imagined stabbing Buckley in the neck, it then flashed through my mind whenever I was in the house. I remember serving him and watching his neck as I set the plate down. The single thing I forbade myself to think of became, of course, impossible to ignore. I felt a little like the narrator in Chekhov's *Story of an Unknown Man*, who pretends to be a serf in order to work in the home of the son of a politician he opposes. It's an act of political espionage that uncovers nothing, and soon the narrator despairs of what he's done. He eventually runs away with the neglected mistress of his employer.

This is not what I did.

For as much as William F. might have done to undermine the situation of people with AIDS, Pat seemed to do in their favor. In 1987 alone, for example, a year after his famous column, she was involved in raising $1.9 million for the AIDS care program at St. Vincent's, a hospital at the epicenter of the epidemic in New York. Today it might be easy to underestimate the value of that gesture, but at the time, no one wanted anything to do with people with AIDS. Pat was one of New York's greatest fundraisers for charity, and however many lives her husband may have put at risk, it seems to me she may have saved many more. If it was ever glamorous to raise money for people with AIDS, it was partly because she helped to make it so. And while the finances of their family were known only to them, it seems to me that Mr. Buckley would never have condoned the types of donations Mrs. Buckley made. If there is a question as to whose money it was, perhaps the proof is there. She could afford to go against him.

And if it seems strange to you that one of America's most famous homophobes was married to a woman who was a hero to many gay men, if it seems strange to you that the household where she lived with him was sometimes full of gay men serving food and drink to her guests despite his published beliefs, well, it *was* strange. It was what we used to call complicated. And yet the times were such that we, her waiters, experienced the millions of dollars she raised for those who were abandoned to their fates as a kind of protection and affection both. Money raised for people with AIDS was not for us per se, but it could easily have been us next. For gay men in the 1990s, that thought was never far from our minds. And so I think we could joke about killing him. But never, not even a little, about doing even the slightest thing to hurt her.

❖

I REMEMBER being in the back of the Buckleys' limo, headed to their home in Connecticut for a party there. Their driver, our captain observed to me, kept a gun under the seat. A VW Cabriolet convertible pulled even with the limo, and the driver gave three short honks to get our attention. It was Nan Kempner, waving wildly, girlishly, her hair held back in a scarf tied at her neck, the convertible top down. This was just a few years before her death.

"She thinks we're them," one of the waiters said.

I didn't think so. I was pretty sure she knew we were the waiters. Why wouldn't she know Mr. and Mrs. B were already in Connecticut? She was a good sport, is the thing. It made no sense, of course, but it was easy to believe she was happy to see the men who carried around the food she so routinely ignored.

The Connecticut party invitation was a sign you'd arrived, both for the guests and for the waiters. To be asked to work there meant they trusted you the most. What I remember chiefly about the party is the roses, everywhere, carefully maintained. I had a rose garden myself in Brooklyn, and well-cared-for roses have always impressed me. I first pictured Mrs. B tending them, before my imagination conceded to who she was and replaced the image with that of a gardener. The Connecticut place was a large, if somewhat unassuming house in Stamford, a city quickly becoming notorious for gang activity across the tracks from seaside places like the Buckleys'. As Nan Kempner had sped away earlier, I wondered if she knew to worry about being carjacked in her convertible. Perhaps she had a gun under her seat too.

We changed clothes this time in an attic room with a view of the grounds and the pool, before hustling down and attending to the needs of the hundred or so guests swarming the lawns. The party passed in its usual bustle, and was entirely unremarkable until the evening, as we went upstairs and changed to go. From the window, I saw Mr. Buckley head to the pool with a dark-haired young man we could see only from the back. I raised an eyebrow, and one of the waiters said to me, "It's a tradition. He always invites a male staffer to a skinny-dip at the end of the night when there are parties up here."

"Really," I said.

We heard the splashes. My coworker smiled. "Really. That's how they used to swim at Yale, after all," he said. Before I could absorb this, Mrs. Buckley appeared in the doorway.

She was, as I've said, very tall, and she loomed there like a ghost. We all froze. We were in various stages of undress. I had my pants on, but my shirt and jacket were hung up, and I wore just a V-neck undershirt. She had never before come to where we changed. Her eyes were half lidded as she looked down at me. I was nearest to the door of all the waiters, who stared as she gave me a long, long look and walked slowly ahead until she was right in front of me. "Thank you," she said, very quietly, looking at me. "Thank you so, so much." And as she said this, she set her long fingers down into the hair on my chest.

"Thank you," I said. It was clear she couldn't see me very well. She didn't have her glasses on, and she was drunk.

I could only think I was very good with a Kir Royale. I wondered if perhaps Mrs. B had decided it was time for her to invite a male staffer of her own. Why was she there that night, when she had never come to us like that before? Was that party somehow unbearable, when all the others had been bearable? Whatever the reason for her arrival in the room, all of us were shocked to see her.

There was a terrible loneliness and sadness in her expression, and then it was gone, and she seemed to come back to herself. "Thank you, thank you all," she said, and turned and left the attic.

We finished dressing and started back to New York in the car before the swimmers returned.

❖

IN THE DAYS AFTER, when I thought of this evening, I could barely believe it. And then months went by, and years, and I could still barely believe it. I knew that, yes, if I ever wrote of it, my captain would throttle me — at the least. But more important, I'd lose my job. And for what? Waiters and escorts both know that indiscretion is a career-ending move. You reveal a secret only if you are never going back again. At the time, I knew I had reached one of those accommodations one finds in New York — I had carved out a little place I could make a living, in a city where finding and keeping a job has always been an extreme sport. I was also supporting my younger sister with this money as she made her way through college. I couldn't afford, in other words, to risk it — to become famous as a waiter who spoke of all this and then be blacklisted by New York publishing in the process. They were *monstres sacrés*, and I was not. Everything in my life would change, but nothing in theirs — I wouldn't be a hero, just an example, the briefest object lesson. And so it soon became a story that I told instead, to which people listened in disbelief, and at the end we laughed as if it were only funny.

All these years later, the moment itself has come to represent some sort of peak, the climax of my life as a cater-waiter. It's as if I never did it again after that night, though of course I know I did. I'm sure I was back at the Buckleys' at least once more, for example, in New York. But in the way of these things, there was no goodbye. I didn't know in advance the moment I would leave, and there was no presumption of intimacy such that I would have written a note saying, "Thank you for the time in your service." I left the business, having finished and sold the novel I'd been working on. I transitioned to living off a mix of grants, advances, and teaching writing. I remember arriving as a guest at a party in Chelsea after the publication of that novel and finding my captain holding a tray. He smiled at me, we spoke, he congratulated me. Unspoken between us was that I still should never write of that time and place.

And now Patricia Buckley is dead, William F. Buckley is dead, and the Buckley maisonette has been sold by the beautiful son. Even St. Vincent's Hospital is gone. The building is being slowly converted into a nest of luxury condos.

When I knew I would not return — could not return — I finally did find and read the famous column. And when what he'd written was there in front of me, contending that people with AIDS should be tattooed as a matter of public safety — in the *New York Times Book Review* of all places — I had a number of reactions. I was surprised to see he wanted not one tattoo but two, one on the forearm and one on the buttocks. I wondered if he knew, before he died, that this column would be mentioned in his obituary, along with the names of his wife and son and his place of birth — that it would, in fact, tattoo *him*. And I couldn't help but imagine him in that pool in Connecticut with the young male staffer, swimming underwater, the walls glowing with light, their naked bodies incandescent, just like at Yale, and — maybe — wishing there was some mark on the boy he could easily see.

100 THINGS ABOUT
WRITING A NOVEL

1. Sometimes music is needed.
2. Sometimes silence.
3. A novel, like all written things, is a piece of music, the language demanding you make a sound as you read it. Writing one, then, is like remembering a song you've never heard before.
4. I have written them on subways, missing stops, as people do when reading them.
5. They can begin with the implications of a situation. A person who is like this in a place that is like this, an integer set into the heart of an equation and new values, everywhere.
6. The person and the situation typically arrive together. I am standing somewhere and watch as both appear, move toward each other, and transform.
7. Alice through the looking glass, who, on the other side, finds herself to be an Alex.
8. Or it is like having imaginary friends that are the length of city blocks. The pages you write like fingerprinting them, done to prove to strangers they exist.

9. Reading a novel, then, is the miracle of being shown such a fingerprint and being able to guess the face, the way she walks, the times she fell in love incorrectly or to bad result, etc.

10. The novel is the most precise analogy the writer can make to what was seen in the rooms and trains and skies and summer nights and parties where the novel was written, as the writer walked in moments with the enormous imaginary friend, before returning to the others, which is to say, the writer's life.

11. Or you are at a party and you hear someone call your name outside the window, and when you get there, a dragon floats in the night wind, grinning. How did you know my name? you ask it. But you already know it's yours.

12. You write the novel because you have to write it. You do it because it is easier to do than to not do. You can't write a novel you don't have to write.

13. Typically, a novelist's family will not believe the novelist to be someone who does "real" work, even after the publication of many novels.

14. It is said that families should try not to punish their writers. I am the one who said it.

15. The family of the novelist often fears they are in the novel, which is in fact a novel they have each written on their own, projected over it.

16. For the novelists in your life I have heard it said that it is better if you pretend they do something else and that it is always attended to, and doesn't need your attention in the slightest. And then when asked for support, muster an enormous enthusiasm.

17. Attempts to find out what the novel is about on uninvited occasions will meet with great resistance.

18. If I do not answer the question *What is the novel about?* or *How is the novel going?*, it is because my sense of a novel changes in the same way my knowledge of someone changes as I get to know them.

19. You are looking for an answer you can rely on later, and so am I. But my answer will eventually be the entire book, and I do not want to give any of it away.

20. If I seem cagey, it is because I am not a liar and hate being considered one, due to an accident of craft. But also, if I tell you the idea, and the description disappoints you, the novel can be lost.

21. Novels are delicate when they are being written, if also voracious. They move around my rooms, stripping half-finished poems of their lines, stealing ideas from unfinished essays, diaries, letters, and sometimes each other. Sometimes, by the time I get to them, one has taken a huge bite from the other.

22. There is usually no saving the poem in these circumstances, or at least not yet.

23. There is no punishing a novel in these circumstances either, because hunger has its own intelligence, and should be trusted. It is dangerous to be a new novel around another new novel in the years they are each being written, but they know this.

24. Once you have finished a draft, revising it turns something like laundry into something like Christmas.

25. The first draft is a scaffolding, torn down to discover what grew underneath it.

26. The first draft as a chrysalis of guesses.

27. Novels in progress have many faces, like an actor playing all the roles in the film. The novel as jailer, say—in a dark room with no answers to any of your questions and no one seems to hear your pleas, not for days, months, years. Indifferent the entire time to all requests for visits or freedom. Hard labor too.

28. Or the novel as Champagne Charlie. The limo pulls up, there's a stocked bar and an entourage. A lover you haven't met yet already mad at you for not calling enough, arms crossed, pretty face steamed.

29. Or the novel as Fugitive, arriving at night through an open window. Not quite a dream, it carries a work order signed by you, your own handwriting insantly recognizable. The factory address is your own.

30. As the work proceeds, the factory is near the roads leading back and forth to the jails, and the Champagne Charlies can be seen heading in and out. Sometimes it is clear that the prisoners and the party are trading places (the entourage fits in the cell). Sometimes not.

31. The Fugitive leans out the window, watches, has guessed the limo and the jail cell are the same.

32. Or the novel as Lover. Impatient. It wants you to know everything. And it won't stop until it's done telling you. Factory, cell, limo, it doesn't matter where you are or with whom: the conversation will not stop. It is not endless but is long, it is longer than the writer can contain, and so it gets written down and is born that way.

33. Thus you may discover the novel is a thought too long to fit in your head all at once until after it is all written down.

34. Your hats still fit. But inside you there's more room.

35. Think of a dream with the outer surface of a storm and the inside like the surface of your days as you have sometimes found them. The novel being the only way to lead anyone to the entrance of those days.

36. A stranger on the street, walking up to you, grabbing you by the lapels, and walking away with you quickly, with passports, money. You fall in love as you leave immediately, together.

37. The novel coming not from the mind but the heart, which is why it cannot fit in your head. Why, when you hear it, it seems to be singing from somewhere just out of your sight, always.

38. For the duration of the writing, your heart may believe the novel is a liberator. You will not deny it this belief, as you do at other times in your life, because you are distracted by the story. It is why you love novels more than you think you do when you read them.

39. You are in love with the unmet ending—you long for it, sometimes you even know it from the start, the novel one long path cut through the woods, right to the ending's door.

40. The heart's ruse is nearly over. This entire time, it has convinced the novel it was only following along.

41. This game it has played with the novel like the date that begins with love's possibility but ends with the memory of the other, the one you lost or who lost you and who you fooled yourself into thinking was gone from your heart forever, but instead, reappears in a mask, that of the stranger you kiss against the wall in the street at night.

42. Of course, a novel is also a mask.

43. Not for the novelist. Not for the reader. But for some-

thing else the novelist brings in from the back of the tent like a lion on a chain.

44. Do not notice the slashes in the novelist's shirt, the welts along the arms and legs. Do not try to decipher them. If the lighting is right you will see them only when you have the chain in your hands and you are ready to let go. You will remember then. The cuts will write another novel in you, about what the novelist went through. You will not write it down, and it will leave on the wake of your next thought.

45. Unless, of course, you are also a novelist, and then sometimes it is your next novel. You wake to realize you are in the back of the tent.

46. I think of them like a visitor from another planet, the sentences being like the circuits of a vast and beautiful machine that communicates the creature. A creature of pure meaning.

47. Or a distant relation I've never met, from another country and with a language barrier between us. We try charades. He tries on clothes and wigs I give him, hops on one leg, imitates strange animal noises, and soon I have the wig. I am hopping, hopping, hopping.

48. With my other hand I am taking notes.

49. Everyone has a novel in them, people like to say. They smile when they say it, as if the novel is special precisely because everyone has at least one. Think of a conveyor belt of infant souls passing down from heaven, rows of tired angels pausing to slip a paperback into their innocent, wordless hearts.

50. If it is like the soul, it is a soul you can share, like the gnostic one, externalized, with a womb.

51. What if the novel in you is one you yourself would never read? A beach novel, a blockbuster, a long, windy, character-driven literary drama that ends sadly? What if the one novel in you is the opposite of your idea of yourself?

52. The novelist as a circus attraction with many limbs, a horse with eight legs or three faces, or two heads.

53. Now we are back in a tent, but another tent altogether, that of a circus.

54. We discover we are the animal made to learn tricks in order to please something with a whip.

55. Kneeling in the sawdust, juggling plates, we hope the crowd cheers, though we cannot see them past the lights.

56. All the while, we know in some cultures we would be revered as gods. Others, put to death.

57. Of course, this almost never happens.

58. And then sometimes, it does.

59. The novel for which you can be killed is a picture someone is trying to hide of what is inside whoever it is threatening to kill you for writing it.

60. You did not know this was what you were doing, you were only trying to take a picture of the landscape. You thought of yourself as a bystander, you saw something you thought you should try to say this way. In the corner of the photo, something you do not quite recognize, not right away.

61. When you look closely at the picture, in it is a map left behind by a stranger who says, This is the way to the treasure, and then this is the way o—

62. The piece that is missing, hidden somewhere but call-

ing, describing itself to you from behind the walls of your days.

63. Would it be beautiful or devastating to write the one novel if it was the only one you had? And what then, to discover that was the one?

64. Perhaps sometimes the angels are tired and out of their hands slips not one novel but five, twelve, one hundred, one thousand. A library for a soul.

65. They will never come back for them, but when the novels appear, the tired angels will smile quietly instead, and pass invisibly through the bookstore, remembering.

66. Remembering that in fact no one has only one.

67. The novel and God are always being declared dead. Both are perhaps now indifferent to this, if either really can be said to exist.

68. Imagine for now they pass the time in the Kitchen of Life, telling jokes, each trying to tell if the other's feelings are hurt.

69. God feels confident He is having a comeback. Also the novel. Each is jealous, does not want to say this to the other, not directly.

70. The novel is being sold in vending machines in airports. God points out there are no vending machines for God.

71. Are you sure, though? the novel asks. And then adds, I feel like you could do something about that.

72. Tell me about it, God says. This being one of the things the novel can do.

73. Sometimes it is the ship, sinking, and you, you are the captain, running around the deck, having decided not to go down with it, but to save it, to head for land all the same.

74. The ship, moved, returns from its fascination with the deep.

75. It would be easy to forget that sometimes the shipwreck saves the ship or the captain. Sometimes one or the other remembers this at the touch of the rock.

76. Think of Nemo in his submarine, touring the submerged treasures of all of the failed voyages in all of history. A library of unfinished novels could be like this.

77. Or like the buckle of a belt, worn by an islander who found it in a reef, and seen years later by the original owner's friend when he comes to land. Where did you get this? the explorer asks, and then asks to be taken to the wreck.

78. It is like the language the explorer must learn even to ask the question.

79. What is it you want from me? the novel asks.

80. What is it you want from me? the novel tells you.

81. Everything in here is about you, the novel says.

82. This feels like a trick to keep you reading it or writing it, a lie that is also true. And this is another thing a novel is.

83. In the novel, the true things often run around like children under sheets, playing at being ghosts. Otherwise we would ignore them. Not now, we would tell them if they arrived without their sheets.

84. Go to your room, we would say, and wait for me. And then we sob when we get there, to see they are gone.

85. Novels do not take orders well, if at all. They are not soldiers, usually, or waiters. They do badly at housework and will not clean silver.

86. Novels do not wait. They are poor chauffeurs.

87. Novels are good with children but are considered un-

trustworthy tutors for the young. And yet there we are, as soon as we can crawl, pulling them off the shelves.

88. Cheever said of the novel that it should have the direct and concise qualities of a letter. To whom and by whom, I wonder, as I think also of how I feel this is true. I want to argue briefly — it is not a letter from the author to the reader — and then I stop. It is not a letter, just like a letter. This being the kind of question — to whom, from whom — that, if you sat with it, could begin a novel.

89. For most, novels are accidents at their start. Writers lining the streets of the imagination, hoping to get struck and dragged, taken far away. We crawl from under the car at the destination and sneak away with our prize.

90. This is because the novel begun deliberately is so often terrible, with the worst qualities of a bad lie, or a political speech given during a campaign. The writer turned into something like a senator.

91. In your room after the successful accident, you wake. Something is left in your hand.

92. It is a letter. Or, like a letter.

93. Beside your bed is you, the one who writes the novel, in disguise, funny hat and all. Hoping to understand. Do not look too closely at the ridiculous mustache. Listen. Surreptitiously, against your hand, write down what is said. In its elaborate disguise it acts out the answers.

94. The novel then a letter from the novel to the reader, and dictated to the writer by the writer.

95. But what is it about? you might ask, and then the novel recoils.

96. I just need to get a drink, I'll be right back, the novel says. Do you want anything?

97. Days later the novel returns. I wasn't with anyone else, the novel says. There's only you, the novel adds, even as the writer fears it has taken up with others. Imagining pages across the other desks of the neighborhood.

98. There's only you, the novel says again.

99. You are out in the street, outside the novel's window, screaming into the wind. Please, you say finally, finally quiet, uncertain of how to go further.

100. The novel is already at the door. Waiting, but just for a little. It is the lover again, impatient again. Wanting again for you to know everything.

THE ROSARY

I

IN DECEMBER of 1995, I am shown an apartment in Brooklyn by a broker who apologizes for it as soon as she opens the door.

"It's small," she says, looking away, as if the sight of such a small place offends her. We walk into a large studio and kitchen with high ceilings, the wood floor buffed to a high gloss. Beyond that, a sliding glass door shows a small wooden deck that leads to a yard at least as large as the apartment, a mud slick striped by a stone walkway. Wooden seven-foot-tall picket fences line the sides, and a chain link fence closes off the back.

I don't respond to the broker right away, because as I enter the apartment and the sun fills the back window, I see, like an apparition, roses tossing in the air like a parade, pink, orange, red, white, all lit up by the sun. They appear and then are gone by the time I am fully inside the apartment, as if painted on a curtain someone drew back. As if an entire garden could be a ghost, together, or a premonition, or both.

I follow the broker into the yard and back into the apartment while she talks through the apartment's qualities, a short list: The rent is cheap. There is a garden. That's about it. As she does so, the winter mud, the dead grass, the snow, these all seem like lies after the strange vision I've just had. I notice a rubble-strewn yard next door, visible through three missing teeth in the wooden fence. A black-and-white mother cat nurses black-and-white kittens on a board someone left in the sun.

The rent is so cheap. I ask why.

"Too many people moved in and out, raising the rent too high, way above market, and so this lease has a rider attached giving it a five-hundred-dollar discount," she answers. This seems like a lie. She says nothing else, and the silence is out of a horror film, a silence that tells the audience, I will later discover, that anonymous, unspeakable murders have happened here.

As the broker moves me to the front door, I don't want to leave. I feel like I am already home.

I go with her to see a second apartment, out of some idea that it will make it less strange when I decide on the first, but am nervous the whole time that I could lose the first to someone else. The second apartment is a little larger, a little more expensive, on the second floor, with four rooms. It feels large and lonely. "It's too much room," I tell her, and she raises an eyebrow.

"Are you *sure*," she asks me as I fill out the application for the garden apartment.

"Yes," I say. Impatient to move in and open that ground.

❖

PREVIOUS TO THIS, I had no talent for gardening that anyone knew about, ever, including me. As a child I helped my mother garden, but recall very little of it except for placing pine needles and Styrofoam cones around her roses at our home in Maine, insulating them for winter. One winter, I struck a buried rose with a shovel as I built a tunnel through the snow, and I tried to see into the darkness where it slept, afraid I'd killed it. I felt so terrible I was unable to tell her what I'd done, and covered the hole with snow. When the spring came, I avoided finding out if it had survived.

The single clue that I had any future as a gardener was the long hours I spent in the woods alone, so much so that my neighborhood nickname was Nature Boy. I hunted for the wild orchids called lady's slippers, sitting and visiting with them, in awe of their beauty and their status as rare and endangered. I picked bouquets of black-eyed Susans, lilacs, and Queen Anne's lace to bring home for my mother—whatever I found. But I did not grow anything, which I think is why my sister said, "I would have thought you'd kill anything you planted," when I told her what I had planned.

In my family, I am not known for patience. I was the one who yelled, slammed doors, who had confrontations. And at the time, I was not known for living anywhere more than a year—usually six months.

The only explanation is that it was some gift of the apartment's, an otherwise unmystical, unmagical place. An ordinary, even miserable apartment, renovated once in the eighties and then once more before I moved in. It was a blank white box, with a small kitchen and a small bathroom, that special lowered rent, that single window that was also a back door, cross-ventilation possible only when I opened the front door as well. And if not the apartment, then it was a gift of the garden, given when I looked through that window, into the space the garden would fill. Given before it existed at all.

◆

IN THE FIRST DAYS after I move in, I read books on garden design. They agree that proper gardens are planned to give something to the gardener in each season, even in winter. The spring garden should have early color to revive the eye after the long, colorless winter; in the summer, a circus of full blooms; the fall, a harvest of deeper colors. The winter garden is a shape under the snow, or evergreens and the occasional mahogany red of a rose cane. Many gardeners try to match the colors and ground types and sun exposures, others compose with the scents in mind as well, in the manner of a perfumer. One book instructs on how to layer bulbs at different depths, so that the crocus is replaced by the tulip, then the lily, iris, canna, and so on, with a last set of lilies to emerge in the fall, a plot like a holster of bulbs. Some are rarefied and planted to be seen at night, with white foliage and night-blooming flowers, and fragrances that appear only in the evening. Too much of a single variety of plants, the books warn, will make the garden dull outside the season of the chosen variety's blooming, and draw a dense number of pests—as if the pests are drawn to dullness.

I begin to make my plan, sketching out the garden, and then my original idea, of roses everywhere, asserts itself. I discard the plan for a careful garden I do not want.

"I am planting a rose garden," I tell a friend at what I choose as my local bar, shortly after moving in, testing out saying it. The month is January, dark and cold.

"Do you have a lot of sunlight?" he asks me.

"Yes," I lie, unsure.

The next day I don't have to work. I stay home all day and watch the sun move across the ground. One of the books recommends keeping a garden diary, tracking the sunlight exposures, the rains, the seasons starting and ending.

The first sunlight hits my windows at seven-thirty and touches the ground in the back around eight. The sun leaves the last patch of dirt at four p.m. It is January, so the summer promises to have more. All roses, a guidebook says, need a good six hours of sunlight. I have more than enough.

The next morning, I turn back to my record of the sunlight and begin another entry. And this is how this essay begins, on that day.

◆

EACH DAY I wake to the new apartment, still full of sealed packed boxes and a scattering of furniture: a small table that I use as a desk, a chair, and a futon. I take a few of my books out and pile them against the wall, reading some, browsing others. I enjoy the silence. I worked extra jobs like a demon in the previous months to get the money together to move, and it's as if the effort has burned off all conversation. I do not get a phone installed immediately, as I do not know what I would say if it rang and I answered. I make calls only when I need to, from a pay phone. When I am questioned by police, who suspect I'm a drug dealer because of this behavior, I get a line installed, but it feels like a concession.

The center of this block is an H of adjoining yards, variously planted and tended or, as in the yard on my right, abandoned. By spring, it will be clear the bare wintry trees in the back will remain like this all year. The black branches pinch the sky like the trees in an Edward Gorey cartoon.

"They were root-poisoned by the landlord," my neighbor tells me when she emerges one day and introduces herself. Their taproots had endangered the pipes and foundations of the buildings as they made their slow push through the ground below us. The trees will stay like this the entire time I live here, branches occasionally falling into one or another garden. My yard is full of the fallen limbs of the poisoned trees.

My neighbor is a young woman, roughly my age, living off of SSDI due to AIDS, she tells me. I like her right away. She is new also, and almost always at home. She has plans for a lawn and vegetable garden, and keeps a compost pile in the back corner of her yard, but she worries about the poison in the ground used to kill the trees. "I'm testing the soil," she says. "You should too."

A beehive is back there also, wild but, as she points out, useful: the bees will pollinate our gardens. She will not remove it. This strikes me as both wise and foolish.

The only living tree remaining is a silvery magnolia, still dormant and inexplicably alive amid its dead cousins.

The yard to my right is all trash bags of dead plants, an old bicycle, and a smashed fence, and home to those feral yard cats, the mother cat and her new brood. The three yards, when viewed together, my young neighbor's, mine, and the abandoned one, are like a declension, variations on the theme of habitation: my neighbor's yard is the neat one; mine, half spoiled; the last, a ruin.

What appear to be metal ladders ascend from the yards, several stories high, notched with pulleys to hold laundry lines, strung over the yards with panties and sheets and towels hung to dry. Occasionally a sock or a panty falls into my garden. No one ever comes to ask for them, and I do not ever know whose these are, and inevitably I throw whatever the stray item is away. The only other neighbor I see for the first few months is an older woman opposite me, her hair a combed and brassy hat. She occasionally appears and leaves large metal bowls of cat food for the yard cats, who tumble nightly through my garden in yowling fights.

I have a dream of a garden, my first ever, and in the dream

there are grass leaves as thick as sword blades, and flowers, indistinguishable by type, of the deepest red and blue and pink. I walk through the garden and that is the entire dream.

2

IN THE INTRODUCTION to the British horticulturist Ellen Willmott's *The Genus Rosa,* a brief story:

> The Persian poet Omar Khayyám, who flourished in the eleventh century, has much to say about Roses. A hip from a Rose planted on his grave at Nashipur was brought home by Mr. Simpson, the artist of *The Illustrated London News.* It was given to me by the late Mr. Bernard Quaritch, and reared at Kew. It proved to be *Rosa damascena,* and a shoot from the Kew plant has now been planted on the tomb of his first English translator, Edward FitzGerald.

A rose travels from Omar Khayyám's grave to Willmott to the tomb of his late translator. Willmott declines to say if she is the source of this planting, but her knowledge of it is such that I can only imagine her digging the hole herself, smiling to think of the same bloom watching over both men's graves.

Willmott's two-volume *Genus Rosa* is one of the grander dames of rose culture, published in between 1910 and 1914. Willmott walks the reader through the various mentions of roses in classical literature and the Bible, always calling it the Rose, with a capital R. She mentions rose garlands found in ancient Egyptian tombs dating to AD 300, takes us to the aforementioned Khayyám anecdote, and duns Linnaeus for his "scant attention" to the genus and the confusion that resulted from it for those who came after, even somehow knowing, like a spy, that there were roses in his herbarium that he neglected to mention: *"Rosa mochadi, Rosa agrestis (sepias)* and *Rosa multiflora."* She then reels off the attempts to gather the roses that have appeared between her and Linnaeus, concluding before she fully begins, without fanfare, that "the *Index Kewensis* gives specific rank to 493 Roses, with additions in the first, second and third Supplements amounting to about 50." Around 543 roses, then, or Roses, as she would put it.

David Parsons, in the revised edition of his *Parsons on the Rose*, published about the same time as Willmott's book, in America, notes more than 2,000 varieties. At present there are around 3,000, though there remain approximately 150 species commonly grown.

Every book on roses I have ever read begins in some way like Willmott's. For example, the *Rosarum Monographia*, a lovely and rare volume of roses, praised by Parsons as among the finest and published in 1820 by a young Dr. John Lindley, who dedicates it to one Charles Lyell, Esq.: "Although the number of publications on the present subject is already too considerable, and their authors, in many instances, men of established reputation; yet nothing is more notorious than the almost inextricable confusion in which Roses are to this day involved."

Lindley accuses some of the authors of the aforementioned confusing works of having used dead and dried flowers as specimens, and reveals his book to be inspired by the "considerable private collection of living plants" that has occupied him for years. His new book is meant as a corrective to those who haven't had the advantage he has, which is to say, the advantage of his own garden. And this is because all rosarians, I think, find their own garden to be not just a wonder, but a messenger, from a place of secrets that other rosarians cannot know.

From Lindley we learn the rose was a bribe given to Harpocrates, the god of silence; that there is a custom in northern Europe of hanging a rose from the ceiling above a table if what passed beneath it was meant to be secret; that the red of roses comes from the blood of Venus, whose feet were cut by roses as she attempted to protect Adonis from the rage of her husband, Mars. Or, per Theocritus, the red is the blood of Adonis himself. Or it is Cupid, who spilled a bowl of nectar while dancing, staining the rose red. Or, per Ausonius, it is Cupid's own blood. Or it is the sweat of Muhammad, according to the Turks.

Perhaps all of it is true. The rose as love gift, stained by the gods, no matter the god or the giver, the first secret of them all.

In any case, the lesson we can take, I think, is: Plant a rose, wait for a message. Be it earthly or divine.

3

A GOOD PLACE TO BEGIN a garden is to undo whatever appear to be the clear mistakes of previous owners.

I tear up the stone walk. It occupies patches of ground feasting on sunlight, a feast of no use to a rock. The mother cat looks at me skeptically as she nurses her kittens, as if she has seen this happen before. I make a figure-eight path, irregular in the manner of handwriting, hollowing out the spaces for the stones before I water them into place and hop on them as they set, in a method I invent as I go.

I wander out to the chain link fence and back again. Shattered glass and ceramic shards cover the ground in my yard, and I consider using the larger pieces to make a mosaic of some kind, but discard that idea quickly. Most gardens are palimpsests of previous gardens, and the first spring usually has surprises, but it is already clear someone before me planted mint—a newbie mistake, my neighbor points out, as mint spreads rapidly, choking out everything else with long, fragrant rhizome ropes just under the surface of the dirt.

The woman who lived here before me, according to the neighbor, had vegetables, some herbs, some flowers. My neighbor and I have conversations over our fence, each of us standing on benches; mostly we talk about getting the yard cats adopted. The tomcat suitors of the mother cat pass through the missing teeth of the fence at a high run, and we discuss whether repairing the fence will slow them down. One tom seems to be the neighborhood king: he has a giant head and is so heavy that when he climbs down the fire escape and drops to my deck, he sounds like the full sack of a burglar.

My neighbor is concerned about what pesticides and fertilizers I will use. I assure her I will not use chemicals without consulting her. She tells me she has planted dandelions, and I studiously do not laugh at her, instead quietly remembering summers spent pulling them out of my mother's yard.

❖

I HAVE TWO MORE DREAMS about gardening during my first year of living in this place, and then never again to this day. In the first, I take a train ride, much like the one I once took from London to Edinburgh, and meet, at the station, my grandfather Goodwin, my mother's father, a man who farmed every day of his long life in Maine. He takes me in his pickup, quietly, and shows me a beautiful forest of parti-colored leaves, each of them as big as the shield of a Templar. Behind the leaves are flowers as big as faces.

It is the same garden, I understand after waking, that I

dreamed of when I moved in, though in the way of dreams, there is no resemblance, just an inner knowing.

In the second dream, I am walking through Brooklyn and flowers fill the streets like a river, roses that climb several stories high, foxglove and lupine like missiles. So many flowers that we Brooklynites must walk on catwalks set along the top stories of buildings, built especially to accommodate those garden streets.

❖

ROSES, I discover in my research, appear delicate but have adapted to most climates. They can be made to bloom all through the year until winter. The more they are cut back, the faster they grow and the stronger they are. My role models at last, I think, when I read this.

I will have the dull garden with just one type of plant, I decide, but the variations on the theme seem enough.

I begin with just ten roses. Shrubs and climbers, a few floribundas and everbloomers. All are chosen for being described with words like "hardy" and "disease-resistant."

As I wait for the order to arrive, I go into the yard and gather all the dead wood and giant dead stalks left from the sunflowers of the previous inhabitants. I bundle the wood branches with the idea I'll use them to stake the roses, until I remember they're poisoned and take them out.

The roses arrive, bare roots wrapped in a brown paper bag, looking like the sticks I cleared from the yard, except, touching the bag, I can feel they are alive, a fierce halo of living force against my fingertips. I understand immediately why people speak to plants, as I draw a bath of cool water for them per the instructions that accompany them. I set the roots in the tub and step back, feeling crowded out of the bathroom.

People talk to plants because they're alive.

I get into bed and can feel them still, in there, drinking the water. In the morning, I rush to put them in the ground.

❖

BEFORE THE PLANTING, I walk around the garden with the tags of the various roses and set them in different spots as I try to decide on the final design. I use the pictures and the projected measurements to imagine a sort of ghost garden amid the straw-colored dead plants.

I then dig three of the holes in quick succession. With the fourth, my spade hits cloth, and I put it down.

Briefly, I imagine the possibility that I am in a very different story from the one I believed myself to be in. A murder mystery, for example. This is perhaps the moment when I discover the murders that made the rent cheap.

I go back and dig until I pull from the ground what turns out to be a pale blue cotton housedress, flecked with a flower-bud print and stained from the pale mud tea soaking the wet ground. It is light, the size of a small pillow. I set it down gently and with the spade's blade push the folds of the dress back. At the center is a small crucifix and rosary, wrapped around a pile of small, thin bones. Among them are sharp fang teeth, one still attached to a piece of jawbone, reassuring me this was once a cat or small dog. I place it all carefully into a trash bag, go to the corner bodega, and look for a saint's candle, settling on Our Lady of Guadalupe, the avatar of the Virgin Mary, always painted surrounded by roses. I've always liked this story: A campesino asked to prove he saw the

Virgin Mary returns to where he saw her, and she tells him to go to the top of a hill in winter to collect flowers he can take back as proof. He arrives to find a rose garden blooming in winter.

I light the candle, set it by the hole, and finish digging it. As I go through the rest of the garden, I find more bones — it is like a boneyard — ox tails thrown here after making soup? Some look to be birds, others, the remains of a hundred feral cat feasts. A dead rat is under the deck — I use the spade to remove it. I uncover piles of magazines that seem to have been put in the ground as landfill and carry these to the curb. I let the candle burn for hours, in the manner you're supposed to, and when I put it out, I consider the possibility I've disturbed some kind of spell. I've never heard of a cat being given a Catholic burial — I imagine a small girl or boy doing such a thing. A private religion, a child's insistence on the animal's soul. Much like me, the nonbeliever who goes to the corner to buy a saint's candle, just in case.

That night I go out for a beer and meet up with a friend, a Brooklyn native and contractor. He tells me that in Brooklyn, as late as the 1950s, Italian and Irish Catholic families buried their dead in their yards if they were too poor to afford a grave site. The houses often had a room used only for wakes, a dead room, which are now used as the small bedroom in apartments shared by roommates. "You're lucky it was just a cat," my friend says, and he puts his beer down.

"It *was* just a cat, right?"

I think of the fangs staring up at me, and nod.

4

THE MORE I THINK about the word "rosary," the more I understand it must be related to "aviary," "topiary," and so on. When

I check the definition, I see the first meaning is for the prayer and then, in italics, that it once meant "rose garden" in Middle English.

How did a word for a rose garden come to mean a prayer? "Bimbo," for example, used to refer to a man. The French word *rien*, which means "nothing" now, in ancient French meant "something." But the story of this word is not a journey from one meaning to its opposite.

"Rosary" was once a term for rose garden, until it was not.

The cultivation of the rose in gardens, as we know it now, was firmly established in Europe by Empress Josephine of France in the eighteenth century, and was further refined in the nineteenth century, until we arrived at the tea rose type we all know today from all of those Valentine's bouquets. Rose tea is not derived from this rose, though, and predates it considerably. The rose's flower is the blossom of the rose hip fruit, a relative of the blackberry and the raspberry, and is likewise edible. There are recipes for cooking with roses, using chicken or chocolate. Tea can be made from the fruit as well as from the petals, and rose tea is used in Indian Ayurvedic medicine to calm the drinker's constitution. But it was never grown primarily for these uses.

The meaning of "rosary," as we know it now, comes to us from the thirteenth century. As the story goes, Saint Dominic, greatly concerned for the future of the Roman Catholic Church in France, prayed at Notre-Dame in Prouille for guidance. At the time, the Albigensian dissidents were teaching an interesting heresy: that the body belonged to the devil, and the soul to God. So there was no need to worry about the body's sins, as they belonged, with it, to the devil. The Albigensian heresy quickly spread, and thirteenth-century France was soon in moral turmoil.

When Dominic prayed to the Virgin Mary, she appeared to him and instructed him on what was first called the Angelic Psalter, and told him he was to use this weapon against the heresy. At the time, a rosary was only a rose garden, though in England, "rosary" was also the name for the equivalent of a penny.

The turmoil of the Albigensian heresy was rivaled only by the demand from the thousands of believers returning to the Church for the Angelic Psalter, a popular spiritual practice, and Dominic, who had been a studious young man given to ostentatious penances that made the older members of his order nervous, was now a hero and eventually made a saint. The young man who had once tried to sell all his books for money to feed the poor had invented — or, say, was given, by the Virgin Mary — a system of memorized and recited prayer, useful to a young man who'd sold all his books to feed the poor.

It was Thomas of Cantimpré, a Dominican scholar in Flanders and a contemporary of Dominic's, best known for his multivolume work *Opus de natura rerum*, who, in a book he wrote on the lives of bees, was moved to consider the Angelic Psalter within it, and described it as being like a circlet of roses to be offered up to the Virgin Mary. Shortly after the publication of Thomas's book on bees, "rosary" earned and kept its current meaning. So the story of the word "rosary," coming to mean prayer, is, in the end, a story of the power of metaphor.

Mary and roses have been linked since her death. On the third day after her burial, mourners who went to her tomb were said to have found her body gone and her shroud full of roses. The scent of a rose where none should be is now formally one of the signs of Mary's presence — in one of her twentieth-century appearances, for example, the visitant's mother said she believed her daughter's vision of Mary was manifest because of the scent of roses in the surrounding air. One result of this connection is that contemporary rose culture was for some time dominated by Catholics, who tried to keep the number of varieties limited to 150, the number of beads on a rosary and the number of psalms in the prayer.

I like the story of Mary's tomb and think of it sometimes in graveyards. I'm not a Catholic, but I like to imagine a God moved to grief by her death, taking her from the tomb and filling her shroud with roses as He left. In any case, the dead are often honored with roses, either left at their graves or planted there, and the result is that cemeteries are often home to some of the best of the heirloom varieties. It's an old rose gardener's trick, one I haven't tried yet, of taking cuttings from these graveyard roses, but I still can't allow myself to leave a cemetery with anything I didn't bring in.

5

DURING THE FIRST WINTER, at night, I sometimes feel as I imagine they do, as if the part of me that is exposed is plain, stripped of all ornament, and the part that isn't seen is growing, spreading. Roots cast like a net through an ocean of silt.

I now know this is also what it feels like to write a novel. Which is exactly what I was doing.

"Your grandmother grew roses," my mother tells me. "Do you remember that?"

I don't. I recall walking with her through her canning garden in Maine, her pulling a potato out of the ground for me to eat. She would rub off the dirt on her apron and bite hers like an apple as we entered the house. If I flinched at the dirt on the potato, she'd say, "You'll eat a peck of dirt before you die." We spoke very little, she and I, but we loved each other.

My grandfather showing me the garden in my dreams now

seems more like someone welcoming me to a place I could have found only by searching, as in that test of virtue in every legend.

❖

THE ROSE I PLANTED in the spot where I dug up the cat bones gives me no flowers for the first two years. In the catalog it was listed only as "special climber," and so I wonder if it is a mutant dud sold on the cheap, but I do not pull it up. I rename it, jokingly, the Voodoo rose, after its first mute year. For two years it only grows stalky and huge, until it seems almost demonic, whipping the wind with seven- and eight-foot canes. The absence of blossoms feels like a sulk at the garden's corner.

In the third year, when it finally buds, I feel forgiven. Thick clouds of teacup-sized pink blossoms appear. My neighbor stares. "They're so beautiful," she says. "What did you do?"

I shrug. I do not feel at all responsible.

The Voodoo rose soon becomes the garden's bully, beauty, alluring and cruel, often looking as if it is reaching for the Climbing Blaze I planted at the garden's center, or whipping at the Thérèse Bugnet next to it. Its thorns are especially long, and sometimes I find clots of cat fur on it. Occasionally, working in the garden, it smacks my head lightly like it is mocking me, and sometimes draws blood.

❖

THE RELATIVELY MATURE GARDEN, then, at age three years: When I stand on the deck, the Voodoo rose is on my near left, and on my right, two *Rosa rugosa*s, the sea roses I grew up with in Maine, their canes furred with thorns. A Thérèse Bugnet is in the near center. In the middle, the Fairy is on the left and the Climbing Blaze at the center. Behind the Climbing Blaze is the Joseph's Coat, and behind that, another Thérèse Bugnet. A Golden Showers climbs the far back left.

Together they are a slow concert. Each year, the twin Thérèse Bugnets, planted at the back and front of the yard, push up first, and though they are also delicate, the blossoms softer than eyelids and poor for cutting—they belong in the garden, that is to say—these dress themselves before the rest, like haughty sisters, head to toe in crisp green and, when the blossoms come, pretty-girl pink, flashing at the top of new dark maroon canes. The far one, at the center of the back wall, grows tallest first, and every year offers a single pink blossom at the top, like the opening note of a song. From there, the other blossoms open and spread down, like the slowest possible flamenco dance, extending over several weeks. Her sister follows suit a few days after that first blossom. Then the Joseph's Coat lights up from behind the far Thérèse, with golden blossoms tinged by red stains, as if someone has touched them all with a brush. These blooms change color as they open.

In the center, the Climbing Blaze is a little fire pit of red blooms, and if I prune regularly, I have roses until December. In the winter, it often has frozen buds, as if surprised every year that there is a winter. The Golden Showers never does very well, more like a well-meaning trickle, though the blooms are nice when they arrive, a perfect bright yellow. I think it needs a longer, hotter season—years later, I will see the variety in Texas during the spring, massive yellow clouds everywhere I look. The Fairy rose, the one I thought would be so delicate, blooms through the summer and into the fall and winter, keeping the Blaze company, blithely tossing out a froth of pink blossoms and shrugging off any mildew or fungus, heavy rain or cat landings. The two *Rosa rugosa*s seem to have perpetual indigestion on the rich diet I feed them in my yard, perhaps more accustomed to the briny stones of any beach in Maine: they have long, woody, spiny stems, with a kind of hat of blossoms at the top. They always seem to want to leave.

They are on my mind when I head to Maine by car at the beginning of my first summer. I go back for a week with my brother and sister and her husband, and they laugh when I poke the window, asking to stop at plant nurseries. We are going to celebrate our cousin's wedding and visit my aunt, a lifelong gardener who has become a florist and landscaper in Rangeley, near the border of Canada. My aunt's yard is full of plantings, many vigorous roses among them.

I explain to her what I'm doing in my garden and ask for her help. She offers me a ten-pound bag of manure to take back with me. "Roses love manure more than just about anything," she says. My siblings refuse to allow it in the car. "I'll mail it," she says to me, and laughs, and then sends me home instead with something called seaweed tea, a noxious brew of seaweed and what I grew up calling "gurry," down on the Portland waterfront: the remains of gutted fish.

"It has a smell too," she says, "but not until you put it in the pail. And this might be the one thing roses love more than manure."

We stop at the beach on our way back to New York, near our mother's new place in Biddeford. I stroll the boardwalk of Kennebunkport, the beach lined with sea rose hedges. These are the sea roses of my childhood, the ancient variety that seems to me the hardiest of them all. I follow a line of greenery out along a spit of sand and rock to a sandbar, where I come across a sea rose perched on, or really around, a granite boulder. The roots wrap the boulder like the ribbon on a present and probe for chinks.

Erosion has taken away the ground around it and the rock has tumbled into the beach, so the rose is growing at an angle, reaching for the sun, new buds flourishing. They lift along the side of the rock and over it, as big as a single bed. The ocean and the rose compete in a slow race to break the boulder apart, though it looks as if the rose flew down to grab the boulder, and having caught it, won't fly off and won't let go.

You might think a rose was something delicate, but you'd be looking in the wrong place.

When I return from Maine, home again, I open the door to my apartment, afraid my roses will be withered, fainting, dead. No rain for four days. I rush to the back, where I find them giddy, hurling color up from the ground like children with streamers at a parade.

❖

I TRY THE SEAWEED tea my aunt gave me. It has the rank, terrible smell of a fish left out in the sun not quite long enough to dry, but for months. Not even the feral cats come to the yard while the scent is in the air.

I test everything I hear about a rose. I plant garlic and onions at the feet of two bushes to try and make the roses too bitter for aphids, and when the hot summer arrives they smell hotly of garlic and onions, and the aphids continue eating them all the same. I use soda water for some of the feedings, to aid the greening, and it seems to work. I take a pitchfork and stab at the earth to aerate the roots. Every so often I pee into a pint glass and take it outside to shake it along the garden's perimeter, to keep the worst of the cats at bay. Or at night, alone, or seemingly alone, I leave it there myself.

The cats do seem to come less, as if this is a fence they understand.

I pull weeds from the ground that grow a yard in a single week. How did I not hear them pushing their way up? Afterward the earth looks stark and bare. When I am done cleaning up, I walk around the corner and come to a full stop in front of a white tea rose in front of a flower shop. It is called Great Century and seems exactly right for the bare spot in my yard. I had decided against tea roses, thinking them hard to grow. Tea roses are the reason the rose has a reputation among nongardeners as being too difficult to raise. But the bloom there on the bush is a pretty one, and the florist selling it has no idea what it is worth, so the price is very low. The rose is too large for the pot it sits in, and so this, in the end, this elegant creature's pinched feet, is the reason it comes home with me.

Come, I tell it as I carry it. Soon you'll have a place where you can stretch your feet.

At home, I pull and cut at the balled gnarl of its roots. When, in late summer, it offers me roses, despite being planted so late, it feels like a cat laying a catch by its owner's door.

6

MY NEIGHBOR peers over my yard to check my progress. "Gorgeous," she says. I wonder if she really means it. Her yard is impeccably neat, whereas the kindest thing you can say of mine is that it is an untidy cottage garden, a mix of what I meant to plant and what was left behind by others. But she is really amazed, like a child at the fair. Sunflowers have come up, also apparently hard to grow, uninvited guests from the previous tenants, along with a miraculously large phlox and peppermint flowers, pearly tines at the end of the hearty, fragrant spirals of green I still have to pull from the ground every week. At the back of the garden in midsummer, I smell what I think is cinnamon or clove, and find lavender, roasting in the late July sun. There's marjoram hanging down, funny round flowers, a sort of ocher, that crumble to my touch, and summer savory and hyssop, the savory blue, the hyssop blue-white. The hyssop is strangely vigorous, and the rosemary planted near it shies away, as if afraid. I planted a "wildflower" mix compulsively, scattering the seeds haphazardly, and snapdragons, cosmos, and poppies grow from that, red, white, and pink.

From where I stand on the deck in the morning, I admire the blossoms' whirl. It is not yet as high as I'd like. I want to feel surrounded by them, to feel that someone left me a hundred bouquets in my yard while I slept. Still, I'm gratified by the second round of blooms appearing, the summer blossoms after I deadheaded the spring ones—cutting off the fading blossoms makes the rose grow more of them. I notice the Joseph's Coat roses at the back of the garden and decide it is time to see those new blossoms up close. As I get near, the largest bloom quivers and the shiny backs of nine Japanese beetles emerge, combing the petals with their horned mandibles, oil black and oil green, chomping hard. I run to the house and return with my pyrethrin spray, foaming the rose until the beetles slide to the ground. Pyrethrin is my favorite bug killer. Nontoxic to humans, it is a paralytic agent. The bug cannot move and dies as its metabolism burns its very spare stores of energy, starving it to death.

I never had the urge to kill a thing, it occurs to me as I sweep the beetles up from the ground, until I started growing roses.

◈

AFTER THE ATTACK of the Japanese beetles, I am protective of the garden in a whole new way. I take out my copy of *A Year of Roses*, by Stephen Scanniello, and read about all the terrible things there are that seem to live just to eat a rose. Aphids, sure, and Japanese beetles, but also rose mites and, worse, the cane borer.

The cane borer drills down into the cane to plant its larvae, hollowing it as they emulsify the cane's center and killing the rose as they go. The borer leaves a tiny hollow tunnel behind, as if someone had taken the lead out of a pencil.

I put the book down and with a growing sense of alarm rush to the garden and begin inspecting it for borers. I check the far Thérèse Bugnet first.

The hole is there.

I go to the hardware store and buy lop-handled shears and then, at the pharmacy, nail polish, per Scanniello's instructions. I am to cut the stems back until the cane is smooth again and cauterize the wound with the lacquer. I buy a pale, frosted green color, so it blends in with the foliage.

Much of what I must cut off are the second-round blooms this rose has given me, and what is left looks like the bush was prepped for surgery. I walk inside to let the canes dry a little and then come out again, painting each cut stem.

❖

AT THE BEGINNING of the second spring, as I prepare to leave for a month at a writers' colony in Virginia during the month of March, when I would do much of the gardening preparation for the season, I go to wake the roses from their winter sleep by pruning them. I have the proportions wrong in my head, however, and

I cut them back by two thirds instead of one third. When I finish, I am startled at the sight of all the sticks, a picture of pain, the cut stems wet with fresh sap. After I take the trimmings to the curb, I lie down on my bed, horrified.

The trip to Sweetbriar, Virginia, is a long but simple one. I arrive to a town with fields full of giant wild roses. They climb up trees, spill down the other side, filling the grounds of the colony, where I find rose bushes the size of cottages, bristling with thorns and buds. Sweetbriar, I learn, is named such for the roses planted by cattle ranchers who tried to save on cow fencing. It didn't work —the cows ignored the roses—but the town is surely the proof of what my aunt said about how much roses love cow manure.

I am here to work on my first novel, and I do well. I spend five weeks among these enormous roses, and write 120 pages.

On the morning of my departure, I discover a black-snake skin, shed whole and without a tear. Its former owner had spent the previous week sunning itself on the fence near my studio and left its coat across the walkway to my door. I imagine the snake using the thorns to shed its skin, but I see no holes in it anywhere when I hold it up to the light. Instead, it glows in the sun, the scales light up, and blue sky shows through the holes for its mouth and eyes.

I climb into the car of the man giving me a ride back to New York, and show it to him. He laughs and tells me he has been writing about the traditions of the area's indigenous people, and that according to them, this would be a powerful omen of good luck. The snake, he tells me, leaves the skin with you as a sign of its respect and good wishes. I am awed, but can't imagine living with it, so I give it to him to give to his son, as payment for my ride.

When I return to my garden, the roses I feared would be dead or dying are instead huge, the canes thick and new, the leaves a sturdy dark, and the buds firm to the touch. I can feel them surging under the surface. My cutting them back by two thirds would seem to have made them more powerful than ever.

Perhaps it was the gift of the snake. The lesson for me at least —and this I think of as the gift of the garden, learned every year I lived in that apartment: you can lose more than you thought possible and still grow back, stronger than anyone imagined.

◈

I STAY FIVE YEARS MORE past that spring.

In those years, I take roses with me to dinner parties, usually the Voodoo roses, as the plant seems able to provide the vast amounts of roses needed to make such gifts. A flower shop opens next door, and when I go by with some, the owner is shocked, and asks me where I got them. Soon I am providing her with a bucket of them to sell.

I throw my own parties, and the garden fills with people drinking around the roses. I have affairs, boyfriends. One summer I learn about garden feng shui, and map my body onto the garden. Shortly after, an outbreak of cane borer seems to predict exactly a case of crabs. The feng shui map like a fetish doll drawn onto the garden, one that had mapped its problems onto me. Or vice versa.

I eventually take pity on the sea roses and remove them. In an unscientific gesture that I also feel very sure of, I take them to the beach in Maine and leave them out on the rocks to fend for themselves.

After I finish and publish my first novel, I become restless, and when I talk about moving, I mention taking the roses with me, because people say, What about your garden? They arrived by truck, I tell those people. They can leave that way as well. In the end, though, when I do move, I leave the garden there with the rest of its mysterious contents, deciding they belong to the place and not to me.

I had come to this garden much like what I found in it. I was a mess, a disaster in need of a reckoning. That backyard was my perfect mirror, and the dream of the garden was in its own way a dream of myself. I arrived there after many years of self-abandonment, sure only that I did not know myself, but certain that I needed to believe I had a future. I did not know what the garden could do, and I did not know what I could do. If my garden was a messenger, the message was in the silent moments when I was sure I could hear it growing toward me through the earth. That more was coming. But I did not know this then. I knew only that it was time for me to leave. I had done what I came to do.

Whenever I am back in the neighborhood, I sometimes pass my apartment from the street. I like to believe, stupidly, that if I were to open the front door again, in the back I would find my roses, huge from their seaweed tea and the many days of six hours' sunlight, perhaps growing legs, ready to push down the building and walk out to the street, striking cars out of their way and slicing the blacktop to ribbons. I want to think that they would miss me, their erstwhile tormentor, the one who pushed them so hard to grow, cutting and soaking them in the blazing sun from spring to winter. From the street, from across the river, where I live now without them, I can feel them still, the sap pulsing in their veins, pushing their way to the sky.

But the creature that grew legs and walked away from the garden was me. I was not their gardener. They were mine.

INHERITANCE

IN 2000, I became, somewhat by accident, the director of All Souls Unitarian Church's Monday Night hospitality program for the homeless, on the Upper East Side of Manhattan. The former director had a medical emergency and had to leave her responsibilities immediately, and so the next week when I went in for my volunteer shift, I was asked if I would consider running the program, at least until someone else could be found. I would be acting director for three years.

On my first day, I went to Western Beef, a low-cost butcher shop and grocery store where the program did its shopping, the week's dinner budget in an envelope of cash. And even though I had previously gone along with the director, as her assistant, I was nervous that first day on my own. The program fed one hundred guests on a first-come, first-served basis—more, if more showed up. Some diners even took leftovers back to their shelters for those who couldn't leave. This was a big responsibility. I planned the meal, bought the food under budget, and returned to the church, and I did the job for three years. Gradually the program expanded, especially after September 11, 2001. I was proud of the work we did.

The calm with which I did this every week was not visible in the rest of my life. In the apartment I returned to after those volunteer shifts, my closet was full of stacks of boxes of files and receipts going back fifteen years. Many were unpaid bills, missed payments, or collection notices. Letters from the IRS. A personal organizer I had hired a few years before had said, looking them over, "Oh, wow, you don't need these," then she laughed and told me to throw all the papers away. But I could not. When I eventually moved out in 2004, I moved with those boxes.

In some way I wasn't quite aware of, I had imagined the problem was receipts. But I did not feel that pain when I shopped for the church's program and put the receipts in an envelope before turning them over to the office. The more I kept a steady hand on the program, the more I was aware I was in the presence of a revelation about myself. The ordinary transactions contrasted with the pain I faced, almost supernatural, every time the money was mine.

❖

THE PAIN WAS THERE in every transaction. Whenever the question came, "Would you like a receipt?" I never *wanted* it. But I took it, knowing I should, and would put it quickly in my wallet instead, until the wallet bulged like a smuggler's sack.

I had no system for the next steps. The receipts stayed in there, usually too long, sometimes fading to meaninglessness. Or I emptied the wallet into the pocket of a backpack, or I stuffed them into an envelope, always with the promise of getting to them later. Then I put them in the boxes. There they fluttered around like some awful confetti, saved for a celebration that never came.

I knew they represented, in part, money that could come back to me, but for me they mostly represented money lost. Pain is information, as I would say to my yoga students at the time, and my writing students also. Pain has a story to tell you. But you have to listen to it. As is often the case, I was teaching what I also needed to learn.

❖

THE PAIN THESE RECEIPTS REPRESENTED was not particularly mysterious to me then. I had just never examined it. I hadn't even felt I could. I simply thought everyone had these difficulties. But this was a lie I told myself, a way of accommodating the pain instead of facing it.

In a file I still have from 1989, there is a letter from my sister, when she was fifteen and I was twenty-two, asking me to send my tax form to my mother so she could give it to our accountant. This is in a folder with the tax return from that year, completed after I sent the form. I can see the earnings from the sandwich shop I worked at in Middletown, Connecticut, while a student at Wesleyan; earnings from my first months at A Different Light, the bookstore where I worked in San Francisco just after college graduation; and the taxes paid on the stock certificates I sold from my trust in order to pay off my tuition bill at Wesleyan.

Asking my younger sister to write and ask me to send the tax form was my mother's way of communicating, off-kilter and indirect. To this day, she will ask one of us to communicate something to the other, though she could just as easily call directly. I have tried my whole life to change this in her, as I have tried to change my own relationship to money and pain, which are forever twinned in my mind. The anxiety about receipts was anxiety about money, but also much more than that.

Underneath that anxiety was the belief that there would be an accounting demanded of me, one that I would fail. After reading Joan Didion's *The Year of Magical Thinking*, where she describes keeping her late husband's things as if he might return for them, I understood it a little better: I imagined someday having to tell my father about everything I had bought with the trust fund I received after his death. And having to explain how I'd failed him.

◈

MY FATHER WAS SO YOUNG when he died, forty-three years old, that he hadn't made a will, due in part to the faith the young have that a will can be written and notarized at some later date, because surely death is far away. As a result, the State of Maine divided my father's estate four ways, among my mother, myself, my brother, and my sister—my mother receiving, by law, the majority. I was given a trust that would be vested to me when I reached the age of eighteen.

Just three years earlier, at the time of his death, three years after the car accident had rendered him paralyzed on the left side of his body, my mother had confessed to me she was repaying his medical bills, which totaled more than a million dollars, and this was after what was paid for by medical insurance. He'd had repeated surgeries over those three years, home care, physical therapy, and experimental treatments. My father's family was wealthy enough to have helped us out, and for one year they had, but they'd held the cruelly contradictory belief that my mother should both be able to pay the bills and also not have to work

—to stay home and take care of my father. I can only think they believed the money would magically appear out of my father's business, a mistaken notion born of a mix of sexism and parochial privilege so extreme as to be laughable, if the price of it were not so steep. My father's father had worked very hard, but his family had mostly never worked, or if they had, they did not understand the structure of my parents' financial lives. My father's family have been, in my experience, people who believe something is wrong if the world is not the way they imagine it to be. And so they treated us as if my mother was lying, or deceitful.

This was unexpected and difficult. My mother did the only thing she could do. She put in fifteen-hour days to turn the assets of the business, now the assets of the estate, into something that could meet the scope of the problem, leaving me to cook for my siblings, to drive them to sports practices, to grocery shop, and even to shop for her clothes while she did this. She was soon able to pay off my father's medical debts, and did.

And now we had arrived here.

My mother told me the trust was, first and foremost, for my education and anything related to it, and I should spend it wisely. "Your education is the one thing you can buy that no one can take away from you," she said portentously. Also: "I wouldn't have given you control over that much money at age eighteen." But the state had decided it, and she had to allow it. I rankled at the thought, but it was also true that for me to be presented with money enough for college after years of worry over mortgages and my father's medical bills felt like an unearned luxury at best.

As a result, the first thing I did with my money was part rebellion, part panegyric. My father had loved fast cars and expensive ones, both, and so I bought what I thought he'd want for me, a black Alfa Romeo — a Milano, the first year they were available in the United States — a sort of cubist Jetta with a sports car's heart.

I drove off to college with my younger brother literally along for the ride — he wanted to see how fast it could go. He was the king of auto shop in high school, and had saved up the regular gifts of money given to him by our relatives over the years until he could buy the cars he rehabbed in autoshop, and then he sold them for more money. He has always had a gift for making more out of what he was given. He had taught me how to drive stick shift on his red 1974 Corvette 454, a car so beautiful the police would pull him over just so they could look at it.

My brother had been reading the Alfa Romeo manual, and after he looked at the speedometer, he said, "It says this car tops out at 130 mph," and he gave me a little smirk.

I nodded. The highway ahead of us was oddly empty, and so I floored it. For a brief moment on the Massachusetts Turnpike, we flew, pushing the speed as far as I dared, a 130 mph salute to our father.

❖

I DROVE THE CAR for the nine years the trust lasted, except for when I lived in California, during which time my mother, despite her objections to the purchase of the Alfa Romeo, drove the car and enjoyed it, in what amounted to a truce on the subject. I used that money not just for my tuition costs, but to turn myself from a student into a writer. I paid for my college and left with no debts — an extraordinary gift. This gave me the freedom to intern at a magazine that published my first cover story, and to take a job at an LGBT bookstore that let me read while at work, meet authors, and even help with the planning of the first LGBT writers' conference, OutWrite. And while I went to graduate school on a fellowship with a tuition waiver, I had no health insurance, and so the trust money paid for my regular dental work and a trip to the hospital back in New York, where I lived before and after grad school. I know this freedom looks ordinary to many, but I also know all too well that it is rare when the children of Korean immigrants are given this kind of latitude from their family to pursue the arts.

Besides the car, what I thought of as my excesses at the time now seem more or less pragmatic to me. My clothes were usually secondhand, my books also, or purchased with an employee discount. I bought a used Yamaha 550 motorcycle, which I drove while I lived in San Francisco, where there were four cars for every parking space. I made a trip to Europe in the fall of 1990, to Berlin, London, and Edinburgh, which I took to investigate whether I could live somewhere other than the United States. And while I ended up staying in America after all, the trip was its own education. My greatest indulgences were probably during a long-distance relationship while in Iowa: phone bills that regularly cost as much as the plane tickets for said relationship, not otherwise affordable on a graduate student's budget.

For those nine years, I felt both invulnerable and doomed, under the protection of a spell that I knew to be dwindling in power. The Alfa broke down finally while I was driving from Iowa to New York City. I left it where it stopped, in Poughkeepsie, on a block in front of a friend's apartment. That summer, newly released from graduate school, with no job and no prospects, I had no money to repair it or move it. Eventually the car, covered in unpaid tickets, was impounded and sold by the state to cover the towing and storage costs. My money gone, I surrendered to life without either the trust's protections or the car. I know it was all stupid, and I was ashamed, and felt powerless in the face of the problem and ashamed of that powerlessness. But I was also tired of being mistaken for someone who was rich when I felt I had less than nothing.

I had believed I would feel lighter without the money, free of the awful feeling of having it but not having my father. And yet spending the last of it was not just like failing my father. It was like losing him again.

◈

WE LEARN OUR FIRST LESSONS about money as children, and these shape much of our ideas about it. We learn these lessons from our parents, but from others also. But I feel as if I have always been taught about money by everyone, every day of my life a lesson, whether I want it or not, in what money is and does.

The lessons my life had provided until the point I describe were that money is conflict, strife, grief, blood. Money is necessary. Money divides families. Even the promise of it, hinted at. And that nothing destroys a family like an inheritance.

My mother likes to tell a story of me at age two. We were living in my grandparents' home in Seoul in 1968, and three of my father's siblings were still of school age—two uncles and an aunt. The three-story house was surrounded by a high wall, covered with nails, barbed wire, and broken glass, that I would later come to expect on houses like this all over the world—the homes of the rich, living amid great poverty. The house is near the Blue House in Seoul, the presidential residence, and the Secret Garden, formerly a palace where the king kept his concubines, is visible from the third floor. For years it was one of the most privileged of neighborhoods, exempt from development.

The reason we were living in Seoul at the time this story happened is that my parents could not afford me on their own. When I was born, my father was a graduate student in oceanography at the University of Rhode Island. A favorite photo I have of him from that time shows him posing with his URI classmates, holding a whale rib. My mother taught home economics at the local public school, and since women were not allowed to teach while pregnant, married or not, when she started to show, she was dismissed, and the economic crisis that I was began. My birth was unplanned; my parents were not financially ready to start a family. In the first photos of my father holding me in his arms, he looks tired and dazed, and the expression on his face is one of amazement, love, and frustration. He seems ready to agree to his father's offer of a job back in Korea, which came soon enough.

My father's siblings had lined up to ask for their lunch money, and after the youngest had taken her turn, I went and asked for my lunch money, as they had. My grandfather was so charmed —he was worried I would never speak Korean—that he came downstairs, laughing, and gave me some money, just the same as he did them. I was then allowed to spend the money across the street at the small market, to get a treat.

I did the same the next day, and the next, as it made him laugh, and he gave me money for treats. Soon he gave me the money daily.

My father's siblings still resent me, I think, because of it. I became just another sibling to compete with for attention, approval, and money.

I was born slightly premature, and so at age two, because I was underweight, I was allowed to use my daily allowance to buy a chocolate bar at the snack stand across the street. This is the context for the next story my mother likes to tell about me from this time: She decided one day to punish me for something, and told me I could not go to the stand. Later, she found me eating my chocolate bar. Confounded, even alarmed, she asked me how I had done this.

The maid explained that I had sent her with the money I'd been given.

My mother tells this story as an example of my shrewdness in the face of an obstacle, also my devilishness. And I do like to think the story is about my improvisational mind. But it also shows that even at a young age, I understood how power worked. I was adapting to my sense of the class I belonged to, as all children do. That this class would change, that I would become a class traitor — as all writers are, no matter their social class — was all ahead of me. Perhaps this was preparation for that change: reading context clues for signs of how to get around the stated rules — how to find the real rules, in other words, that no one ever tells you but that everyone obeys.

However it happened, my relationship to money began before I can remember it, and it seems it started that way.

❖

I WAS A TRICKSTER CHILD, whether by accident or fate. My first Korean words were "Obi Mechu," the name of a beer (the Korean Budweiser, really), spoken as I sat on my mother's lap and saw the sign over her shoulder while we were driving in a car through downtown Seoul.

I am still someone who absent-mindedly reads aloud from any signs I see, as if it is some way of learning where I am.

I was also a regular source of anxiety during my time in Korea, most of which I was not aware of. Biracial Korean and white Amerasian children in Seoul in 1968 were typically thought to be the children of American GIs and Korean women, and were often kidnapped and sold, as, for some time, your patrimony was your access to personhood. Put another way, if your father was a white GI, no government authority automatically thought of you as a citizen. My mother was warned never to let me out of her sight in public, and I did have a knack for disappearing. My eyes had been blue when I arrived, alarming my father's family, my grandparents especially, but they quickly settled into hazel, green coronas with brown rings, which was seen as more acceptable. As the eldest male child, certain responsibilities and privileges accrued with that status: during the first months I lived there, until my eyes changed, the family struggled with the idea that a blue-eyed half-white boy might become the *jongson* of the forty-first generation of Chee.

My father liked to joke that, as a part of my status, a house in Korea would be mine when I got older, and only as adults would my younger brother confess to me just how unfair this had struck him. I used to wonder sometimes if this was why he went into private equity. But in truth, his first distressed assets were those cars he'd refurbished in auto shop. And being the *jongson* was not exactly a prize to be jealous of.

The *jongson* does typically receive a greater share of the inheritance. He does not always get a house, but he often does, because when he becomes the *jongga*, the head of the family, he is supposed to care for his parents in their old age, hold the *jesa*—a ceremony held annually to honor one's ancestors—and tend the graves of the family's ancestors. In the most conservative families, he isn't supposed to live anywhere but Korea. He looks after the entire family, the living and the dead. My brother and sister and I now joke that Korean traditions like this exist only to create conflict and pain—and that has certainly been our only experience of it. Brothers turn against each other; sisters feel invisible and powerless. Most of what I know about my nonmonetary, spiritual responsibilities came to me from people who were outside the family.

My father, the middle child, was forever settling disputes between his siblings, and they were always over money and patrimony. After he died, no one was left to settle these fights, and after the death of their father, the siblings sued one another for a decade. I will forever remember my oldest aunt, a respected translator and professor in Korea, when she reflected on the long battle over my grandfather's estate, saying, "My sisters were so talented. And yet they did nothing with their lives except this—this fight over money."

She said this, though she had joined in too.

❖

MY PARENTS did not give me lessons in money so much as they enacted them. My father spoke of money only rarely. He explained his absences from church on Sundays by saying, "My church is the bank, and I'm there five days a week." He dressed for work in well-tailored suits from J. Press, wore handmade shoes from England, and was uninterested in cutting a low profile. He was the first nonwhite member of his golf club and the Kiwanis and Rotary clubs, and he never looked less than sharp. That this sort of dapper dressing was something he had to do—that his appearance, as an immigrant, required him to be tailored, impressive, to project wealth or at least comfort, just to be treated with respect—would not be visible to me until much later. I remember he said, "I'm treated better when I fly if I wear a suit jacket," and each time I put one on to fly—and he's right, I am treated better —I feel close to him.

Both of my parents had worked hard for what they had— my father, with his older brother, had scavenged for food from abandoned army supply trucks in Seoul during the Korean War. My mother had cleaned hotel rooms during the summer for the money she used to buy the car she drove away from Maine. My father believed money was for spending, and my mother believed it should never be spent. Her clothes were handmade also—for much of her life, she made them herself. She was as stylish as my father, but by her own hand.

The only time I recall hearing my parents speak of money together was the day my father came home with an antique eighteenth-century Portuguese cannon, "the only one of its kind with a firing piece," I remember my father explaining. My mother was as angry as she's ever been. He had spent their savings on it: $750 at the time. The seller was a marine who had, with his buddies, each taken one of these cannons back to the United States from Korea at the end of the war. Or so he said. Part of my mother's anger then was that there was no certification of its authenticity, but also, as she said that day, "What are we going to do with it? Declare war on the Mullinses?" It was a strange, brute artifact, out of place, and after the purchase, it stayed behind our blue corduroy couch alongside many of our father's rifles, by the entrance to our suburban two-story house. As if it were hidden there in case we ever really did need it.

After my father's death, we considered having the cannon appraised, even selling it. We also thought of selling his Mercedes. We did neither. The cannon sat behind our living room couch for years and is now my brother's. The car went into storage in Vermont during the summer of the bankruptcy. My brother may have it still. The last time I asked about the car, he never answered my question. He did recently admit to having the cannon appraised by Christie's; it is now worth $28,000. Thirty-seven times its original price, thirty-seven years later, the lesson of the cannon is at last visible: my father was right.

❖

THE EVENTUAL allowance I received as a child in America, from my own father, the first allowance I remember, was given to me to soothe the pain of the allergy shots I required, starting around age seven. There was the sharp flash of the needle's injection, and then, at the corner store near the doctor's office, my father would hand me a quarter, which I could use to buy comic books.

The cycle was pain, then money, then power over pain. A feeling like victory — if not over the pain, at least over powerlessness. And one of my earliest experiences of fatherly love.

Pain, money, power over pain. My mistake being that money is not power over pain. Facing pain is.

In the first years after the end of the trust, I had dreamed of a payday as big as the trust had been, imagining it could save me, because it was all I could imagine. I see now it never could. It was a dream that the sacrifice of the trust could return to me as a payday the size of the trust, a simple exchange that would clearly mean it had all been worth it, in the primitive religion around money and self-worth that I had made for myself. But this longing for a payday was really just a mix of two stories in my head, turning the money from the father into something that both conquers the pain and also stands in for it.

I was searching for new narratives with which to remake my relationship to money. I had several identities, whether I was aware of them directly or not: as the child of a scientist and schoolteacher; as the child of entrepreneurs; and, as a friend of mine likes to say, as a lost prince, far from his kingdom. My identity as a writer was the newest of these.

But to the extent that I identified these ways, it is because I did not want to be a *jongson*, or at least not in the way it had been described to me. My experience of that role was that it had made me a target. I wanted to belong to myself, much as my father had, and the stories I had of him, as someone who had worked multiple jobs in order not to rely on his father, inspired me also — and so, with my trust fund gone, I not only waited tables, but took any work I could get. I followed the example of my father, and not his family.

I had been raised with the idea of writing as an inherently unprofitable enterprise from which one derived token sums of money while being supported by other means, and I had to teach myself to fight this too. But my dream of a writer's payday was just as unrealistic. My mother was fond of asking me to get an MBA and write on the side. My grandfather, in our last visit before his death, said to me, "You are a poet, which means you will be poor, but very happy," and then he laughed uproariously.

I laughed too.

These allowances, this trust, had taught me one thing: money belonged to other people, not to me. I was trying to undo the spell all of this had cast on me, beginning with the lunch money my grandfather used to give me back before I could remember, which became the $100 bill he would give me whenever he visited from Korea. This was something my father's oldest brother, my Uncle Bill, did as well. And while I could never imagine myself being like my grandfather, the self-made millionaire with an international fisheries conglomerate, and the seven children who would, after his death, sue each other repeatedly for a decade, I could imagine all too well being like Bill someday.

Bill was a well-dressed man who favored a uniform that hardly ever varied: a chambray shirt with a paisley ascot, worn under a navy blazer with gold buttons, khaki pants, tasseled oxblood loafers—he was the man who taught me what paisley meant. When going outdoors, he topped this uniform with a Burberry overcoat, Burberry scarf, and a beret that hid his hair, a raffish comb-over that I always viewed tenderly, for even as a child I knew it fooled no one. He loved us deeply and was forever smiling and impish, so much so that when he was sad, it reverberated. A legal scholar, a lawyer, a professor of law, Uncle Bill had pursued a distinguished academic career in the United States before being summoned home by his father to be a good son. He began teaching law in Korea, at Hanyang University in Seoul, eventually rising to be a cabinet-level presidential adviser on international treaty law, and was the first Korean elected to the United Nations International Law Commission. In 1994, as I was finishing my graduate degree, Bill asked me to copyedit a translation of one of his books, which I still have, detailing his work on behalf of stateless Koreans inside Russia and China. He lived, until his death, in the home left to him, the house I had lived in as a child with my father's family. It was too much house for one man, but he insisted on it, despite the punishing tax burden. His mother had always dreamed the family would gather there, and he lived there in a lonely vigil, against the day the next in line would take his place.

I have always suspected that this was the house my father spoke of, the one I would have one day inherited. Bill, like me, had been an eldest son. I visit the house whenever I am in Seoul.

For years after his death, it was a ruin, open to the weather, left to a cousin he'd adopted as his heir. Now it is a Vietnamese restaurant, no doubt the cousin's decision—we do not speak, a product of the estrangement created after my father's death, when the family's disagreements over money took aim at what my father had left behind. The persimmon trees in the backyard still stand, taller than all of the new buildings built around them.

I come here to see what I know, without speaking to him, is true: that he is struggling to do, even to be, that which was denied me.

❖

IN THE YEARS after the end of the trust, which I still think of as the loss of the trust, I taught myself to do without the idea of my being *jongson*, except perhaps for the *jesa*. Two years ago in October, I made my first, but my version. I made an altar in my home with an elaborate Korean meal I made myself. I poured soju, wrote a letter to my ancestors, telling them how angry I was with them, asking them to tell me what they wanted from me. Then I burned the letter, to send it to them.

My father's rebellion against his family became more fully my own. I taught myself to live without so much as the idea that anyone would help me but me. Someday I would learn how radical it was to have a Korean immigrant father who asked only that his son become himself—with no expectations that I be a lawyer, a doctor, or an engineer, like him. It felt that I was learning to walk in a new world, in new gravity, and by the year 2000, when I was made the acting director of the All Souls Monday Night hospitality program, I had been living in that world for six years. I had joined the church with a boyfriend, and had stayed after we broke up. "We don't expect to see you on Sundays if you're here on

Monday nights," the reverend had said to me when I apologized once for missing the services—the church, on the Upper East Side, was a long way from where I lived in Brooklyn. That idea of acts of charity as service, as a way of offering something to God as well as to others—the Monday service counting as much as or more than the Sunday one—made me feel at home.

I did not cure myself entirely. I am still curing myself. I am almost through those boxes of files. I let go of the fantasy of a massive payday and taught myself instead to get by with the shepherding of sums. I came up with rules I still live by: always keep your rent low, no matter the city you live in; write for money more than for love, but don't forget to write for love; always ask for more money on principle; decide how much money you must make per month and then make more than that as a minimum; revise the sum upward year by year, to match inflation. Do your taxes. Write off everything you can.

To the extent I have survived myself thus far, it began there, when I realized I treated money emotionally. I decided that I needed to treat myself as I would anyone else I was taking care of. It was just ordinary thrift and self-forgiveness that I needed to learn, together with the payday only I could provide, but this realization was the gift of that time, and as close to a Unitarian grace as I think I'll ever get.

These small things I did saved me when nothing else could.

IMPOSTOR

IN THE SUMMER OF 2003, a friend who knew I needed a place to live asked me if I would be interested in subletting her apartment near Gramercy Park in New York. She was trying to sell it, as it was too small for her and her fiancé, but the sale had taken too long, and in the meantime, she'd moved out to Brooklyn, to Park Slope, to live with him instead. She wasn't legally allowed to rent, so the deal she offered was that I would pay only the maintenance, a more than reasonable $900 a month, and in return I would keep the place perfectly clean and organized for when the broker came by — and move out once the apartment was sold.

I agreed, though I wasn't sure I could hold up my end of the deal — I'd never been regularly neat before. But once I moved in, somehow, magically, I was. The broker would call, giving me as much notice as possible, and I'd wash any dishes in the sink, straighten out the bedspread, hang the towels, wipe down the faucets, and head to one of the cafés in Gramercy until it was safe to return. My friends who visited couldn't believe it, and neither could I. But I'd have done much more if she'd asked.

It was the sort of apartment you dream you'll have in New York before you live there but that you usually don't get: a one bedroom co-op on the nineteenth floor, with views north up

Third Avenue to where the horizon cuts off and across the city west toward the Hudson. And I watched the East River out my porthole of a window whenever I did those dishes.

Every day, the apartment felt like some just reward after a long period of hard work. I no longer needed to wait tables. The paperback of my first novel had just come out, and with that money, in addition to my income from teaching, I felt rich for the first time in my life as a writer. I knew I was not rich in a way that anyone else in the building would recognize, but I was writer rich. I had money earned from writing that I would spend on more time to write, and the cheap deal on this apartment meant the money would last longer — it even felt like the beginning of more of that money and more of that success. It was a beautiful moment, when the money and the time it represented added up to a possibility for the future that felt as vast as the edges of the known world. The apartment's views resembled the way I wanted to feel about my own future each time I looked at them.

The only sign of darkness was that I was trying to begin work on my second novel and it was not going well. Each week I abandoned it by Friday and returned to it on Monday, as if it was a bad love affair. I think I suspected even then that the novel would take me over a decade to finish. But the apartment made my despair easier to bear.

Whatever was happening with my writing, I liked to sit and watch the clouds go by over the city. It was like living in the sky. The windows were large and ancient, original, framed in black iron, and they had old latches that needed looking after or they'd rattle in the high winds and a pane might crack. There were two balconies, one quite small, suitable for standing on alone or with one other person, for a cigarette and a whiskey. The other was good for sitting down with company. These were lined with a mix of plants, some dead, some alive, but as the sun set you never saw them. Instead you saw the city, and you counted the landmarks in the view. Which, I learned when I lived there, cost money. Each landmark you could see added something to the price. It was funny to think of the Empire State Building adding, say, $15,000 to the value of your apartment if you could see it. Every time I watched the skyline light up at night, it felt like counting money.

◆

I HAD SUBLET OFTEN in this life, but this time was different. In previous sublets, I'd been around other people's things, but here I was with my own, and I found I liked my things in this apartment in a way I hadn't before. I had never been much for furniture, and had never spent more than a few dollars on any particular piece, because what was the point of having things if you couldn't write? You would only sell them in order to write, as I'd learned early on in New York, standing in line at the Strand to sell a few used books just to pay for lunch. The books on my shelf after all this time have withstood at least a thousand moments when I scanned them, deciding which ones I could or could not turn into money in order to eat, if this or that check failed to come through. A library of survivors.

I think writers are often terrifying to normal people—that is, to nonwriters in a capitalist system—for this reason: there is almost nothing they will not sell in order to have the time to write. Time is our mink, our Lexus, our mansion. In a room full of writers of various kinds, time is probably the only thing that can provoke widespread envy, more than acclaim. Acclaim, which of course means access to money, which then becomes time.

If I could be said to like things, they were books, but I had a few good things all the same, or not-terrible ones, and here they looked stylish, even a little grand, in a way they never had in my previous apartment in Brooklyn. I had a red leather couch and wingback chair that had once been in my late father's office, and that looked very rich here, alongside an antique table with corkscrew legs, bought from a friend leaving for Los Angeles. If I was going to act like a man who belonged in a co-op building, a part of the charade of living here, apparently, was having the furniture of such a man.

All of this was lit lovingly by my friend's Italian chandelier, decorated merrily with glass pears, grapes, and apples. When the news came that fall that I had won both a Whiting Award and an NEA fellowship, I began to call it my lucky chandelier. Either of these awards would be enough to make you feel you'd had a good year, but winning them together was to me a clear sign that the magic promise of the apartment was real. Surely it will be easier now, I told myself. Surely this is what it means to have made it. I think many writers pass through this. But believing trouble is gone forever is the beginning of a special kind of trouble.

◈

ONE SATURDAY MORNING a month after moving in, I went to the elevator and, when the doors opened, there was Chloë Sevigny, standing against the back wall.

I am not easily or often starstruck. But I had loved her ever since *Boys Don't Cry*, when in the course of a single movie she became, to me, one of the most important actresses of my generation. Now here she was.

Her eyes were level, focused on some middle distance, far from anything in the elevator shaft. She was wearing spectator pumps and a white Burberry Prorsum trench coat, belted, the collar up.

A hapless-looking skinny boy, his arm covered in sleeves of tattoos, accompanied her. He was dressed in a trucker hat, expensive jeans, and a wifebeater shirt, and he looked around in dismay, as if there might be some hidden exit in the elevator he could use, if only he could find it.

The elevator descended quietly, and somewhere around the tenth floor she said, without looking at him, "Did you give them my name?"

He said nothing as the elevator descended. I remembered it was Fashion Week; the Marc Jacobs show was that morning. She was likely on her way, though it could have been anywhere, anything.

"Did you. Give them. My. Name?" As she spoke each of these words, they were wrapped in fire, hanging in the air, perfectly timed to the floors flying by, the last said just before the elevator finally stopped. Her companion still said nothing. The doors opened and she flew off through the lobby, those spectator pumps flashing and echoing on the marble floor as he chased behind her.

I never saw him again. Her, however, I saw regularly. The elevator became a little theater of her. The doors would open and she would be there, sometimes dressed very elegantly, sometimes in a tank top and Daisy Dukes, a bottle of Woolite perched on her hip, going to the basement to do a little laundry. It was the best ad Woolite never had. She soon would nod when she recognized me, before the doors closed again. But I never intruded on her, never spoke to her.

We continued like this until one day in the lobby, as I got my mail, the concierge, a sweet older woman who I think had decided she didn't care that I was living there illegally, said my name. I went over to her. "Alexander, Chloë here is interested in seeing the apartment. She understands it is for sale."

I turned. There "Chloë" was, looking at me expectantly.

I don't remember what she was wearing then because my mind went white. It still seems to me she is more beautiful in person, or on film, than in photos. Something happens across moments with her that isn't apparent in a still. "Is it for sale?" she asked, her direct attention blinding me.

I tried to stay calm as I answered. "Yes, it is." I remembered a warning from my friend: "Do not show the apartment on your own," she had said to me. "Only the broker shows it."

But this is Chloë, I said to myself then. I decided to disobey my friend exactly once.

I will always remember what happened next: her walking around the apartment, saying, "I'm subletting from a friend upstairs and I think she should just buy this place and just go through the floor. I mean, it's so cheap, don't you think?"

We were both subletters, then. My affection for her quickened. I didn't think it was cheap, though, not at all. My friend was asking $579,000 for it, about a thousand dollars a square foot. A few weeks earlier, I'd stood in the bedroom of the apartment with a friend who'd asked the price, and when I told him, he outlined a square foot in the air with his hands. "Fill it with a thousand dollars and then do that five hundred seventy-nine more times, and then it's yours," he said.

Here in front of me, Chloë was like an apparition, an emanation of all of that money, ambition, and desire, glowing as she walked the rooms. My impostor self wasn't going to let her know that I was not just like her, not now, not in the face of our idol. And so I felt myself nod at the idea that it was cheap, like I agreed. But now the extent of my charade was apparent to me, and the joy of her being there was tinged with shame.

"It's a steal," she said, looking out at the view and turning back to me. "She has to buy this, don't you think? I mean, the view is so beautiful. She'd be stupid not to buy it."

I nodded—I didn't know her friend—and gave her the broker's card, and then she left.

She knew I couldn't afford it when she said her friend should buy it. This was also a way of saying she couldn't afford it, either.

There were lots of reasons not to buy in the building at the time, another friend revealed later. The maintenance fee was high. The building was brick, which can crack with age, and the mortar would eventually need repointing, never good for a long-term investment. The apartment eventually sold to a school administrator, someone with family money. Someone who belonged there more traditionally. I miss it still. But I would never move back, even if I could now. I would miss the way it was with her upstairs.

❖

I SPENT THE REST OF MY STAY there as I had before, but now, when I was on my balcony I heard Chloë on hers, wishing I had the nerve to leave a copy of my novel for her in the lobby with a note. But I never did. It felt terrible and sad to do something like that, like a compromise with someone I'd never agreed to be. Someone else would have found a way to be upstairs, I think, but that was not me. And so it was I last spoke to her, right before I moved out, in the lobby again, getting my mail. She passed me and said, "Hey, Alexander," and smiled. I paused, paralyzed by love, before saying "Hey" back, like it was any other day.

The real me, it turned out, was too shy to explain I was leaving. He was in charge again, he had his reasons, and he sometimes told me them. But I left happy she knew my name.

The chandelier I took with me. It hangs in my kitchen now.

THE AUTOBIOGRAPHY
OF MY NOVEL

I

THE QUESTION CAME amid some more ordinary ones: How long did the book take to write, and did you do any research? Seven years, and yes. And then: Were you a victim of sexual abuse yourself?

Yes.

Why didn't you just write about your experience? the reader asked me. Why isn't it a memoir?

I looked at him and felt confused for a moment. I didn't understand the question immediately. The questioner sounded annoyed, as if I were deliberately hiding something from him. As if he had ordered steak and gotten salmon. Had I chosen? I felt in the presence of conflicting, confusing truths. I was talking with a book club in downtown Manhattan, on Wall Street, a paper cup of coffee on the table in front of me. All of us were seated around a conference table, blinking under a fluorescent light that felt, along the skin and eyes, both thin and heavy at once. Like this question.

The questioner was an otherwise nice white man, a few years older than me, I guessed. He would have been in high school when it all happened to me, and I wouldn't have told him about it then. That I could even speak to him about it now was not lost on me.

The things I saw in my life, the things I learned, didn't fit back into the boxes of my life, I said. My experiences, if described, wouldn't portray the vision they gave me.

I saw the room's other occupants take this in.

I had to make something that fit to the shape of what I saw, I said. That seemed to satisfy them. I waited for the next question.

That afternoon, I tried to understand if I had made a choice about what to write. But instead it seemed to me if anyone had made a choice, the novel had, choosing me like I was a door and walking through me out into the world.

❖

I BEGAN in the summer of 1994. I had just finished my MFA and moved into an apartment with my younger brother and sister off Columbus Avenue, on the Upper West Side of Manhattan. My brother was starting his first job in finance, at a stockbrokerage. My sister was beginning her studies at Columbia University. I used to joke that we were a little like the Glass family from Salinger's novels and stories, except our mother was in Maine, alone with her own troubles. But the truth was more complicated, and more melodramatic, than the world of a Salinger novel. My mother had been betrayed by a business partner who vanished, leaving behind altered partnership agreements indemnifying her for his debts. When she declared bankruptcy, she also sold our family home. She had mostly hidden her problems from us until they could no longer be hidden, and to this day I think we three siblings moved in together in New York at the same time she was forced out of our family home because it was the single self-protective gesture we could make that was entirely under our own control.

The means by which I had made my way in the world prior to that summer were coming to an end. Grad school was over, as was my accompanying stipend. My inheritance, a fund left to me after my father's death and meant for my education, was likewise almost spent—the move back to New York would exhaust it. I had not won any grants or gotten into any of the postgrad programs I had applied for. The despair I felt as each possible future I had dreamed of dropped away with yet another rejection was the surface of me; underneath that, on the inside, I could feel my family fracturing. Myself, too.

I kept seeing reports that summer of other writers, some of them friends of mine, selling their novels, some of them, unfinished, for what seemed like outlandish sums of money. I thought it was my turn when a friend from college, who worked in the fiction department at *The New Yorker*, asked me for stories, and I sent her part of my then novel in progress, what was to be a book about AIDS activists in the late 1980s in New York and San Francisco. While she found the excerpts weren't right for the magazine, she admired what I submitted enough to send the pages to an editor she knew at William Morrow. The editor, in turn, liked the pages enough to tell me he wanted to have his house consider the unfinished novel for publication. This interest quickened the interest of a friend's literary agent, who became my first literary agent, and I spent a happy ten days hoping this was it. But the house eventually passed on the novel, thinking it would be too large to publish based on my synopsis. "They fear it will be six hundred pages long," my new agent said. Her advice: "If you finish it, then no one will be guessing how long it will be, because we'll know, and we'll just send it out then."

I tried to master my desperation at this news. What happened next was a product of my cynicism, my youth, and my anger. By now, it was clear our apartment was too expensive for us, at least based on the money we actually were earning, and that my sister, due to our mother's bankruptcy, would have to leave Columbia.

I could have finished that first novel already in progress. In just a year's time, as if to mock me, several novels more than six hundred pages long would appear, and the year after that, *Infinite Jest*, weighing in at 1,079 pages. Length was not the issue, though. I could have tried even one other publisher. But I didn't. Instead, I became obsessed with the idea that I could sell an unfinished novel and that the money might be enough to save my family. I began what would become my first published, finished novel with the idea that autobiographical fiction was as easy as writing down what was happening to me. I turned my back on the experimental novel I'd put forward, and told anyone I knew, "I'm just going to write a shitty autobiographical first novel just like everyone else, and sell it for thousands and thousands of dollars." And then I sat down to try.

❖

THE STORY OF YOUR LIFE, described, will not describe how you came to think about your life or yourself, nor describe any of what you learned. This is what fiction can do—I think it is even what fiction is for. But learning this was still ahead of me.

I knew what I thought was normal for a first novel, but every first novel is the answer to the question of what is normal for a first novel. Mine came to me in pieces at first, as if it were once whole and someone had broken it and scattered it inside me, hiding un-til it was safe for it to be put back together. In the time before I understood that I was writing this novel, each time a piece of it emerged, I felt as if I'd received a strange valentine from a part of me that had a very different relationship to language than the me that walked around, had coffee with friends, and hoped for the best out of every day. The words felt both old and new, and the things they described were more real to me when I reread them than the things my previous sentences had tried to collect inside them.

And so while I wrote this novel, it didn't feel like I could say that I chose to write this novel. The writing felt both like an autonomic process, as compulsory as breathing or the beat of the heart, and at the same time as if an invisible creature had moved into a corner of my mind and begun building itself, making visible parts out of things dismantled from my memory, summoned from my imagination. I was spelling out a message that would allow me to talk to myself and to others. The novel that emerged was about things I could not speak of in life, in some cases literally. I would lie, or I would feel a weight on my chest as if someone was sitting there. But when the novel was done, I could read from it. A prosthetic voice.

❖

PRIOR TO THIS, my sentences were often criticized in writing workshops for being only beautiful, and lacking meaning. I felt I *weird, not my take* understood what they meant, and worked to correct it, but didn't really think about what this meant until the novel was done.

I'd once organized my life, my conversation, even my sentences, in such a way as to never say what I was now trying to write. I had avoided the story for years with all the force I could bring to bear — intellectual, emotional, physical. Imagine a child's teeth after wearing a gag for thirteen years. That is what my sentences were like then, pushed in around the shape of a story I did not want to tell, but pointing all the same to what was there.

I have a theory of the first novel now, that it is something that makes the writer, even as the writer makes the novel. That it must be something you care about enough to see through to the end. I tell my students all the time: writing fiction is an exercise in giving a shit — an exercise in finding out what you really care about. Many student writers become obsessed with aesthetics, but I find that is usually a way to avoid whatever it is they have to say. My first novel was not the first one I started. It was the first one I finished. Looking at my records, I count three previous unfinished novels; pieces of one of them went into this first one. But the one I finished, I finished because I asked myself a question.

What will you let yourself know? What will you allow yourself to know?

2

THE IDEA OF AUTOBIOGRAPHICAL FICTION had always rankled me. Whenever I told stories about my family to friends, they always told me to write about my family, and I hated the suggestion so much that I didn't write about families at all.

Even so, most of what I wrote then, if not all of it, was in some way autobiographical. My central characters were typically a cipher to me — like me but not me, with one-syllable names. Jack Cho, for example, the recurring character in four of my first published stories, all a part of that rejected experimental novel. Jack was a Korean American gay man from San Francisco, the only son of a single mother, who moves to New York for love and becomes involved in ACT UP. His relationship to me was more than accidental, but not so close that I couldn't delineate his experiences from my own. Even the name, Cho, was like Chee

—a name that was Chinese and also Korean. I invented Jack to help me think through my relationship to activism and sex. Other stories I wrote at the time were investigations of various friendships, relationships, and breakups. I was, meanwhile, struggling with a different existential issue from the ones my writing peers from more normative backgrounds simply didn't have to address. Kit Reed, my undergraduate fiction teacher, first identified it. She had told me that if I was fast enough, I might be the first Korean American novelist. She wasn't entirely right: Younghill Kang was, in fact, that person, but he was, until recently, lost to contemporary literary history. And when Chang Rae Lee published *Native Speaker*, in 1995, she said, "Well, you'll be the first gay one." And she would be right.

None of this was inherently interesting to me, however, at age twenty, and felt strange, uncomfortable, to aspire to. I was by now used to people being surprised by me and my background, and their surprise offended me. I was always having to be what I was looking for in the world, wishing that the person I would become already existed—some other *I* before me. I was forever finding even the tiniest way to identify with someone to escape how empty the world seemed to be of what I was. My longstanding love for the singer Roland Gift, for example, came partly from finding out he was part Chinese. The same for the model Naomi Campbell. Unspoken in all of this was that I didn't feel Korean American in a way that felt reliable. I was still discovering that this identity—any identity, really—was unreliable precisely because it was self-made.

When people told me to write about my family, it felt like I was being told that my imagination wasn't good enough. But also that I could only write one kind of person, a double standard in which as a fiction writer I was supposed to invent characters from whole cloth and tattoo my biography onto each of them. I think every writer with a noncanonical background, or even a canonical one, faces this at some point. I was fighting with this idea, in any case, when I pulled out a binder I had promised myself I would look at once I got to New York.

❖

I HAD CREATED the binder a few months earlier, in the spring, as I was going through my papers, deciding what to save and what to throw away when I left Iowa. I discovered some pieces of writing that initially seemed to have no common denominator. There was a short story, written in college; several unpublished poems, whose blank verse felt a little too blank, more lyrical prose than prose poem; a fragment of an unfinished novel, with a scene in which a young man kills himself by setting himself on fire; and a fragment of an unfinished autobiographical essay about the lighthouses in my hometown at night. I put them all in a binder and said, out loud, "When we get to New York, tell me what you are."

I think I knew all along the process of writing a novel was less straightforward than it seemed. But thus far, it hadn't seemed straightforward at all. Perhaps out of a desire not to appear prescriptive, at no point in my education as a writer had my teachers offered specific instruction on the writing of novels and stories. We read novels and stories copiously, argued about what they were constantly, but plot was disdained if it was ever discussed, and in general I went through the MFA feeling as though I had to learn everything via context clues, as if I had wandered into a place where everyone already knew what I did not know, and I had to catch up without letting on.

The one conversation I can remember having about the conception of a novel had come indirectly, several years earlier. In college, when I was at work on my first collection of short stories for a senior creative writing thesis, I had the good fortune to be classmates with the writer Adina Hoffman, who read my collection and delivered this news: "I think that these all want to be a novel," she said. "I think you want to write a novel."

Hoffman's idea that day challenged me at first—I had been trying very hard to write stories and I felt as if I had failed. The connections between the stories seemed at best remote to me. But over time I understood: she saw the way each of them had roots that connected to one another, and also the way I'd formed a narrative in my ordering of them. Even the enjambments between sections gave the reader the pause you feel as you understand a story is about to unfold. And when it didn't go further, it felt like a mistake. This vision of my own process, and the way it has informed what I do, and even how I teach, continues to this day. That day when I asked my fragments to tell me what they were when we arrived in New York, before I got into my loaded car and drove there, I knew I was calling out to a novel. I knew these pieces had their own desire to be whole. And as I opened the binder, that summer in New York, and read through the fragments again, I could sense the shadow of something in the links possible between them, and began to write to the shape of it.

❖

THE FIRST PLOT I CAME UP WITH was drawn right from that summer. The drama of my mother's bankruptcy seemed, at the time, a good place to start: a young man returns home to help his mother move out of their family home. She's been forced into bankruptcy after being betrayed by a business partner, and the son finds her lost in depression and grief — still grieving her husband, his father, who had died eight years earlier. The son plots his revenge on the lawyer he sees as responsible for his mother's current troubles, hoping at least to find a measure of justice, and then a lightning strike burns the lawyer's house to the ground.

The main character was, of course, another cipher for me.

At 135 pages, I sent it to my agent, who said, "It's beautifully written. But it's a little hokey, in the sense that no one is going to believe this many bad things happened to one person."

I laughed. I had often found my own life implausible.

"Still, it really picks up after page ninety," she said. "Keep going."

❖

WHEN I LOOK at that first manuscript, I can see again how the plot was, well, not a plot — it was only a list of things that had happened. I also saw what she saw change on page 90. After the narrator visits his father's grave, the novel moves into the past, and into the present tense.

This is how I remember the summer of being twelve to thirteen: fog-horn nights, days on bicycles at beaches, lunches of sandwiches and soda. My mother works to get recycling made mandatory, sends me off into parking lots with hands full of bottle-bill bumper stickers as she does the grocery shopping. My hair is long and wavy and I am vain about the blond highlights at my temples that my father admires. Summer in Maine starts with the black flies and mosquitoes rising out of the marshes to fill the woods, and they drive the deer mad enough to run in the roads. The tan French-

Canadians arrive in cars, wear bikinis, eat lobsters, glitter in their gold jewelry and sun-tan oils. The New Yorkers bewilder and are bewildered, a little cranky. The Massachusetts contingent lords around, arrogant, bemused. They are all we have, these visitors. The fisheries industry is dying, the shoe manufacturing industry, the potato farms, all are dying. Our fish are gone, our shoes are too expensive, the potatoes, not big enough. The shallow-water lobster was made extinct the year I was born, quietly dropped into a pot, and now we serve the deep-water brothers and sisters. The bay no longer freezes in winter and dolphins have not visited us in decades. In a few years, cut-backs will close our naval-yards. Soon a dough-nut shop will be a nervous place to be. We can only serve the visitors and make sure everything is peaceful and attractive as we sell them our homes, the furnishings inside them, the food we couldn't think of eating.

A space break, and then:

The sun is hours from setting. I am sun-burned, tired, covered in sand. I go into the bathroom, lock the door and lay down on the floor. On my back the cool tiles count themselves. I pull down my trunks, kick them across the floor to the door. The only light a faint stream coming in under the door, a silver gleam. I look into it and wait for time to pass.

I'd moved into the present tense as I had the idea of making the novel into something like *Cat's Eye*, by Margaret Atwood, a novel I loved, told in alternating points of view from the same person at different times in her life. An artist goes home for a retrospective of her work, and memories of the scalding love of her best friend from childhood return and overwhelm her. The novel uses past tense for the sections in the present, and present tense for the sections in the past, and between the two, the reader senses what the girl experienced that the adult does not remember.

I was interested in this idea of the self brought to a confrontation with the past through the structure of the narration. I found that writing in the present tense acted as self-hypnosis. Discussions of the use of the tense speak often of the effect on the reader, but the effect on the writer is just as important. Using it casts a powerful spell on the writer's own mind. And it is a commonly used spell. The present is the verb tense of the casual story told in person, to a friend — *So I'm at the park, and I see this woman I almost recognize . . .* — a gesture many of us use. It is also the tense victims of trauma use to describe their own assaults.

The pages previous to this, in the past tense, shed a little light on what my agent meant by "no one will believe this many bad things happened to one person." The draft included my father's car accident and subsequent coma, and the suicidal rage he emerged with, and which returned in storms until his eventual death; my father's family's various betrayals of us, ranging from stealing bank statements for my father's business to suing for custody of me and my siblings to accusing my mother of infidelity while she was caring for my father; and my own suicidal feelings, and sexual abuse, which I hadn't told anyone about, because I feared becoming even more of a pariah than I already was just for being mixed. And while it had never felt like love or community, it had almost felt like not being alone.

These autobiographical events were not organized in any way. When I was helping my mother move, I'd noticed she had not moved in; she had just left everything where the movers had dropped it. I'd had the sense of being in the presence of a metaphor, and I was: my novel draft was like that. Page 90 was where my narrator's attention turned inward, when he looked away from the crisis in his mother's life to see his own.

I cut those first ninety pages and continued with the remaining forty-five, using them as the new beginning. These pages took up the problem of my narrator's silence and his urge to self-destruct, and I saw it as if for the first time.

The college story in the fragments binder had been my first attempt to write about my abuse: a story about a boy in a boys' choir who cannot speak about what is happening to him, and thus can't warn away the other boys, and so the director continues his crimes until he is arrested, and the boy blames himself for the role his silence played in the ongoing disaster. The boy wants to kill himself once the crimes are revealed—ashamed of his silence more than anything else—and is prevented by the accidental intervention of a friend, a victim also, one of the boys he was unable to protect. This, I understood, was where that story belonged. I had written my way there. And as I continued on, this would happen again and again: I would pause, find a place to insert a section from the binder, and continue.

3

IN AN INTERVIEW Deborah Eisenberg gave to the *Iowa Review*, she describes learning from Ruth Prawer Jhabvala that it is possible to write a kind of fake autobiography, and that idea—as I understood it—guided me next. I needed to make a "fake autobiography," for someone like me but not me, giving him the situations of my life but not the events. He would be a little more unhinged, a little less afraid, a little more angry. These inventions were also ethical and gave everyone else involved in the real events some necessary distance. To begin imagining the memories that drew my narrator into his past, I found I kept thinking of what that boy was looking into, in the light under the crack in the door.

There's a quote in my journals from June 4, 1998, four years into the writing of the novel: "These stories are gothics, and have in common a myth of a kind where the end result is the same paralysis." I don't remember who said this to me. There is no attribution and no context. I think I must have thought I would always remember the speaker—my hubris, and as such, a common omission in my journals. But it succinctly describes so many of my early attempts at fiction, even what I thought of as my life, and what I was reading. And the primary challenge I faced next with the novel.

The boy needed a plot. I wanted to write a novel that would take a reader by the collar and run. And yet I was drawn to writing stories in which nothing happened.

My stories and early novel starts were often criticized for their lack of plot. I was imitating the plotless fiction of the 1980s, but also, it seems, lost in a landscape where I was unthinkingly reenacting the traumas of my youth. All of my stories lacked action or ended in inaction because that was what my imagination had always done to protect me from my own life, the child's mistaken belief that if he stays still and silent, he cannot be seen, and this was wrong. And yet I had believed it, without quite knowing I believed it. In light of this insight, I knew I needed a new imagination. I needed to imagine action.

The plots I liked best worked through melodrama, the story's heart worn on the sleeve before being bloodied up: rings of power, swords, curses, spells, monsters and ghosts, coincidence and Fate. These were safe to the person I had been, as all of them were imaginary and impossible problems with imaginary and impossible solutions. They consoled, but they were not choices, emotions, and consequences based on choices, people exchanging the information they needed to live their lives. Finding a magic ring of power that would allow me to face an enemy who had won all our fights before was not the same as mastering myself for the same fight. And these stories did not often require that the hero change. The plotless, literary fiction of the eighties and the blockbuster science-fiction novels I'd read and loved until now both had in common that they had consoled me and thrilled me, but they didn't inherently offer me a way to understand how to write this novel. I needed to learn how plot and causality could be expressed in story—not one I read, but one I wrote. Stories about the most difficult things need to provide catharsis, or the reader will stop reading, or go mad.

I examined my favorite myths and operas, searching for plots I loved, with explicit action, drama, and catharsis. *Tosca*, for example, where everyone conceals a motive in their actions, and at the end everyone is dead. Or the myth of Myrrha, in which a daughter, in love with her father, poses as his concubine, becomes pregnant, and is turned into a myrrh tree. She gives birth and tree nymphs hear the crying child, cut him loose, and care for him, raising him as their own. The tree weeps myrrh forever after. Forbidden desire, acted upon, resulting in transformation, paralysis, and then catharsis. I needed to learn how to make something like this, but not this exactly. I needed to hack a myth, so it could provide some other result. To use the structures of myth to make something that was not a myth, but could be. I wanted this novel to be about this thing no one wanted to think about, but to write it in such a way that no one would be able to put the book down, and in a way that would give it authority, and perhaps even longevity.

Plots like these contained events so shocking or implausible that the reader sympathized with the emotions instead, the recognizable humanity there: loss, forbidden love, treachery. No one has ever said they couldn't empathize with Hera for her jealousy at Zeus taking lovers just because they themselves had never lived on Mount Olympus. As I remembered the way victims were met with condescension, disgust, and scorn, I knew if I told our story, or something like it, I had to construct a machine that would move readers along, anticipating and defeating their possible objections by taking them by another route—one that would surprise them. They would want to grasp for something familiar amid it all. Plot could do this.

Plot was also a way of facing what I couldn't or wouldn't remember. The gothic story that led the character—and the writer —into paralysis, that left me paralyzed and unable to write. Annie Dillard, in my nonfiction class at Wesleyan, had warned us that writing about the past was like submerging yourself in a diving bell: you took yourself down to the bottom of your own sea. You could get the bends. You had to take care not to let the past self take over, the child with the child's injuries, the child's perceptions. "All of us were picked on, growing up," she said. "Come up before that happens." I knew that my situation was different, but also the same. I would need a way to descend and return safely. Turning myself into a character, inventing a plot, turning that past into fiction, I hoped, could solve for all of this.

4

AUTOBIOGRAPHICAL FICTION requires as much research as any other kind of fiction, in my experience. I bought books about sexual abuse, the predatory patterns of pedophiles, and a self-help book for survivors, which I needed more than I knew. I bought a book about the flora and fauna of Maine in every season. I took out my old sheet music from the choir. Whether or not I could trust my memory, I was also writing across gaps, things I wouldn't let myself remember. While I had no choice except to invent my way forward, I relied on material that contained the facts I needed.

I also bought a weathered copy of Aristotle's *Poetics* at a library sale. I don't know for sure when I purchased it. All I know is that at some point, in deciding to address this need for story, for plot, and catharsis, I turned to Aristotle. The book is remarkable for many reasons, including the pleasure to be found in reading Aristotle on tragedy, as if it has just been invented, speaking confidently about how no one knows the origins of comedy, but that probably it is from Sicily. He notes that the root of "drama" is the Greek verb *dran*, which means "to do" or "to act," and this became one of the most powerful insights for me. Memorable action is always more important to a story—action can even operate the way rhyme and meter do, as a mnemonic device. You remember a story for what people *did*.

> Tragedy is a representation of an action of a superior kind —grand, and complete in itself, presented in embellished language, in distinct forms in different parts, performed by actors rather than told by a narrator, effecting, through pity and fear, the purification of such emotions.

Here the text is footnoted:

> *purification:* the Greek word *katharsis,* which occurs only here in the *Poetics,* is not defined by Aristotle and its meaning is much controverted.

Pity and fear and grand action. And purification. This was what I was after. I had reached for the right instructions.

Reading Aristotle to learn how to structure a novel means reading at an angle, almost at cross purposes, but I understood him all the same. And rereading him now, I still thrill to his descriptions of beginning, middle, and end, or his casual mention, in the section on scale, of "an animal a thousand miles long—the impossibility of taking it all in at a single glance," and understanding that, while he was speaking of scale in the story, this was, in a sense, what a novel was: a thought so long it could not be perceived all at once. His assured way of saying that a story "built around a single person is not, as some people think, thereby unified" gave me an understanding of both, and what it meant with regard to his description of the way Homer "constructed the *Odyssey*, and the *Iliad*, too, around a single action"—of the grand kind—was for me like watching lightning. A single grand action unifies a story more than a single person, the characters memorable for the parts they play inside it. Or it did, at least, for the novel I was writing. And that is the thing that is harder to describe. Each of these lessons meant something specific to me as I constructed the novel, and were not necessarily useful to anyone else.

Also of great use to me was the very simple explanation of "something happening after certain events and something happening because of them." I think of this as a chain of consequences, made from the mix of free will and fate that only one's own moral character creates. But his description of poetry versus history struck me as precisely the difference between fiction and autobiography. Or at least, fiction and life.

From what has been said it is clear that the poet's job is not relating what actually happened, but rather the kind of thing that would happen — that is to say, what is possible in terms of probability and necessity. The difference between a historian and a poet is not a matter of using verse or prose: you might put the works of Herodotus into verse and it would be a history in verse no less than in prose. The difference is that the one relates what actually happened, and the other the kinds of events that would happen. .

For this reason poetry is more philosophical and more serious than history; poetry utters universal truths, history particular statements.

This was where my biggest problem lay. *The difference is that the one relates what actually happened, and the other the kinds of events that would happen.* Recounting the way in which these terrible things had happened to me did not lead the reader to the sense of a grand act of the kind Aristotle speaks of. A simple recounting did not convince. The plot I needed would have to work in this other way, out of a sense of what would happen to someone like me in this situation, not what did happen or had happened to me. The story of my mother's bankruptcy, for example, even if it felt like one of the great tragedies of my life, would not pass muster with Aristotle as something that would arouse the audience to pity and fear in the way that finds purification. As a story, it was only the account of good people undone by misfortune. And any poetic truth to it belonged to my mother, to share or not share as she preferred.

I chose one of my favorite operas, *Lucia di Lammermoor,* based on the novel *The Bride of Lammermoor* by Sir Walter Scott, as a model for my plot. A young man seduces and then betrays the daughter of the man who destroyed his father, as an act of revenge, but he unleashes a terrible murder beyond his control. I decided I would queer it: instead of the daughter, there would be a son. And instead of a marriage, the doomed love of a student for a teacher.

The choir director character in my draft thus far had a son, age two at the time of his arrest and trial, and this was the clear Aristotelian tragic line to draw: sixteen years later, he is the spitting image of the best friend my narrator had been unable to protect, his father mostly unknown to him for having been in prison. The narrator meets him when he takes a job at his school, falls in love with him, and is seduced, unknowingly, by the son of the man who molested him as a child, these many years later. Only after they fall in love do they discover the truth about each other.

I set about making up someone like me but not me. I brought the father back to life and restored the mother. The grandparents I had never known well because they lived in Korea I moved into the narrator's family home, to live with him.

I turned my attention to my main character's family in greater detail, through the plot's other parent: the myth of the *kitsune*, the shape-changing Japanese fox demon. When I read in the lore that red hair was considered a possible sign of fox ancestry, I recalled the single red hair my father used to pull out of his head and the benign stories he made up for me at bedtime about foxes, and went looking for a more ancient fox ancestor. I found the story of Lady Tammamo, a medieval Japanese fox demon who had come to Japan from China. According to legend, she escaped her pursuers by leaping from a rock that split from the simple force of her standing on it, just before she vanished into the air. When I looked up where the rock was — said to emit murderous gases until exorcised of her ghost — I saw she could fly in a straight line to the island off the coast of Korea my father's family came from. I could continue Lady Tammamo's story, braiding her, fantastically, into the ancestry of my autobiographical narrator.

The foxes in these *kitsune* stories were said to be able to take the shapes of both men and women, but the stories were only ever about foxes as women. I queered the myth much the way I had the opera, making a fox story about a fox taking the shape of a boy. I decided to give my cipher a life like mine but not mine, one in which he was always made to feel uncanny, and then made that feeling literal: he suspected himself to be part fox, a little alien in the way that makes you entirely alien. A complex tragedy, then, as Aristotle calls it — with two characters, my cipher and the director's son, no single narrator, reversals and discoveries, "fearsome and pitiable events," my plot born of a Japanese legend, hidden and in exile in Korea, and a Scottish novel turned into an Italian opera. The original reason for the title *Edinburgh* was no longer in the manuscript — I had discarded my plan to send the main character, Fee, to the University of Edinburgh — but I kept it because it made sense to me for new reasons that had nothing to do with my life, a symbol of this novel's eventual separate life.

I made a world I knew, *not* the world I knew, and began again there.

5

SOMETIMES THE WRITER writes one novel, then another, then another, and the first one he sells is the first one the public sees — but mostly, the debut novel is almost never the first novel the writer wrote. There's a private idea of the writer, known to the writer and whoever rejected him previously, and a public one, visible only in publication. Each book is something of a mask of the troubles that went into it and so is the writer's visible career.

Edinburgh was almost that for me. I finished a draft in 1999 and applied for the Michener-Copernicus Prize, a postgraduate award of the Iowa Writers' Workshop. That's twenty dollars I've wasted, I remember thinking as I mailed the application. I'd applied before with unfinished excerpts of the same novel; this was the first time I sent the entire thing. Frank Conroy called my agent a few months later to tell her I would be getting the prize. She then called me and left the most thrilling voice mail of my life. I remember listening to it in a phone booth on the corner of Third Avenue and East Fourteenth Street. Conroy had picked up the novel in the morning and read it all day until the end, when he decided to give it the prize. He called my agent, alerting her in advance of the official announcement, and told her he would do all he could to help sell the novel. It seemed like publication was close.

Instead, the submission process would go on for two years, and the book would be rejected twenty-four times. Editors didn't seem to know if it should be sold as a gay novel or an Asian American novel. There was no coming-out story in it, and while the main character was the son of an immigrant, immigration played no part in the story. "It's a novel," I said when the agent asked me what kind of novel it was. "I wrote a *novel.*"

The agent eventually asked me to withdraw the manuscript from submission.

The days of imagining that I could write a "shitty autobiographical first novel just like everyone else" and sell it for a great deal of money were five years behind me. The award, when I received it, came with a monthly stipend for one year that allowed me to work less and write more. It was meant to help a writer during what was typically the first year of work on a novel, since debut authors often receive small advances. The grant was more than twice the advance eventually offered by the independent press that picked it up, when, after refusing to withdraw the novel from submission, I left my first agent and found the publisher on my own. With a Korean American editor from Maine, Chuck Kim. It was a coincidence out of a novel—my novel, actually.

It's the story of my life, Chuck said when we spoke of it.

I really hope not, I said, hoping he had a happier life than this one, the Greek tragedy I had made myself.

You're my Mishima, he said, once I agreed to the contract.

I really hope not, I said, wishing to have a happier future than the Japanese writer and suicide Yukio Mishima.

I was the first living author for this house, the now-bankrupt Welcome Rain, which I called "Two Guys in a Basement on Twenty-Sixth Street." Chuck and his boss. They were smart, ambitious men who made their business publishing books, mostly in translation, mostly by dead authors. Chuck frequently had me to his house for dinner with his wife and brother, and we would speak of Korea and Maine equally. I had based my main character, Fee, a little on someone I knew in childhood, a young woman who would always try to kill herself, and fail every time, and who turned out to be a friend of Chuck's as well.

I feel as if you're on a mission with this novel, and I don't think it's in your best interest to complete it, my first agent had said when she had tried to get me to let it go. No one will want to review this, given how dark the material is, and they won't want to tour you with it, she said. One editor had rejected the novel with a note saying, "I'm not ready for this." I don't want to say the entire problem was the whiteness of publishing at the time, but it was not lost on me that the first editor to try to sign it up was Asian American also: Hanya Yanagihara, who then worked at Riverhead Books. She had ultimately agreed to submit it for the

Pushcart Prize, which allowed editors to nominate works they had tried and failed to acquire. I was preparing my manuscript for this when I met Chuck.

With Chuck behind the novel, everything changed. His enthusiasm for it was peerless. He got it in front of scouts, in front of editors at *The New Yorker*, and he hired a freelance publicist to pitch it to newspapers and magazines. Eventually the paperback rights went up for auction and eleven of the houses that had turned it down for hardcover asked to see it again. One editor even sent a note: "I feel as if we let something precious slip through our fingers." The winner, Picador, had in fact turned it down for hardcover.

But the result that mattered most came when I received a postcard from a friend of mine, the writer Noel Alumit, who also works as a bookseller. He had enthusiastically pressed the novel on a friend, who sent it to a prisoner he was corresponding with, a man serving time for pedophilia: he'd been convicted of having a relationship with a teenage boy. The card, written by the prisoner to the friend, described how he read the novel in four days and didn't speak the entire time. People thought he was ill. "This is the only thing that ever told me how what I did was wrong," he wrote.

I still didn't know I had written it to do this, but then I did.

I wish I could show you the roomful of people who've told me the novel is the story of their lives. Each of them as different as could be.

I still don't know if I'd be in that room.

THE GUARDIANS

I

IN 2004, a memory returned to me after twenty-five years. And with the memory's return, I understood that I had lived for a long time in a sort of intricate disguise.

It was not so different, on reflection, from making an autobiographical character.

This version of me was living the life of a thirty-something writer in New York City, as if in a play. I had an apartment on the nineteenth floor of a building at Sixteenth Street and Third Avenue, a one-bedroom with a balcony and views across the top of the city in three directions. The many landmarks were outlined at night by their lit windows, as if in klieg lights, and I liked to stand with a scotch and a cigarette looking north on Third Avenue and imagine that I had made it. This was only a sublet, and I would be there for only six months, but it made me feel like either Batman or Bruce Wayne, depending on whether it was day or night. I had spent so much time in New York without a view, I looked at it almost as if I were hungry and this was a feast. I was there with these thoughts from Sunday to Wednesday, and then, every Thursday night, I left on a train for Middletown, Connecticut, where I taught at my alma mater, Wesleyan University, as their visiting writer.

At Wesleyan, I rented a room in the apartment of an art professor who was never there when I was, and so it was like having an entire second apartment for the weekend, another fantasy I indulged. I often stayed over on Friday night, after my class, and Saturday too, before returning to Manhattan. The apartment was on the second floor of an old house on a corner of the campus, done up a little like a summer home, barely winterized, and painted dove gray. A darker, nubbly, Spartan gray carpet covered the floors, dressed up by kilims, and the ceilings and floors were warped and thus changed height from room to room, disorienting as I walked the apartment. I sometimes banged my head on a doorframe. My bed there was an antique with a flat, hard mattress, covered by an old quilt, and the books in every room, on every shelf, were what I thought of as the wrong books by the right writers, the books that had disappointed, and they haunted me as I began my second novel.

Each week was a movement from New York to Connecticut and back again, from light and air in Manhattan to darkness and enclosure in Middletown, and I took to calling myself a Connecticut Persephone. This was a joke, of course, as only occasionally did I feel as if I were descending into the underworld upon returning to Wesleyan. I had a crew of student writers, smart, ambitious, funny students who reminded me of myself at their age and the friends I'd had then. Many of my former teachers were now my colleagues in the English Department, along with a few younger faculty members who quickly became friends. But every so often I would turn a corner in the night and feel as if I had wandered across the years into my own past.

I was teaching stereoscopic narratives to my writing students that fall: the same story told from two or more points of view. I had used one in my first novel, but I employed the structure of *Batman* comics as my example, as I did not want to be the kind of professor who taught his own book. *Batman* stories offered basic and effective versions of this dual narrative. There is a mysterious crime, then Batman's attempt to apprehend the criminal. Typically the criminal, at one point or another, captures Batman and tells him the entire story from his own point of view, and the crime is made knowable, the criminal also. During the monologue, Batman manages to escape and bring the criminal to justice, explaining his methods, and the reader then has the complete story.

This was also how I felt about being back at Wesleyan. I was faculty now, had been a student before. I was inside my own story, looking at myself as I once was through the eyes of the professor I had become. I was also seeing what my teachers likely had seen of me when I was their student.

I thought this story of my education was the only story to see this way. I was wrong. It was just the beginning of the stories I would see this way.

❖

BACK IN NEW YORK, I had a regular visitor to my apartment who was like my own strange secret—a relationship so oddly closeted, it was as if it wasn't happening at all. He was a young writer who had set out, in his awkward way, to seduce me, after reading my first novel when he was my student. I had made him wait until he graduated before we even had a conversation about his feelings, much less mine. I wanted us to meet again, away from the circumstances of the class, and to see if the attraction was the same. I was sure it wouldn't be. That I would just be an ordinary older man, and not his teacher.

This was something I had never, ever wanted. I had always disdained it for what may seem the obvious reasons, but also, my whole dating life until then had been directed toward men my own age or older. My type was someone in his thirties or forties, even when I was in my twenties. When the professor I'd rented my apartment from at Wesleyan had warned me against sleeping with students, I found the whole thing so ridiculous, I held the phone away from my mouth so he wouldn't hear me laugh. But if he hadn't heard me, perhaps the gods had instead.

I could tell you that he was different from the other students, but it would sound like the same excuse offered by the few professors I knew who had crossed this line, the ones I had only contempt for. I was also hoping to be relieved of what I felt for him. The state of things between us was at least not a simple case of attraction. He was talented, and I had even consulted him for his thoughts on my new novel draft. I had what I knew was a crush, and feared I was in love with him, despite knowing that there was likely little to no hope in the matter. He was not entirely out of the closet at the time, and as my sense of how out he was kept changing, this was just one of the reasons I was cautious. He would invite me to join his group of friends, for example, at social events with all of them out in Williamsburg, but they were not aware of his sexuality, and I could see they were often confused as to why he had invited his thirty-something former writing teacher to hang out with them.

It is hard to be with someone in the closet, because you are never sure which version of the person you are with — the one who is hidden or the one trying to be free. Despite his being closeted, after we left his friends he would turn passionate and kiss me, often on the subway platform while we waited for the L train to take me back to the city. I kept thinking he would draw back, but he was at his most amorous in public, which confused me.

I loved him, in part, for what he might be someday, which is never a good way to love someone. It was in fact a way of rejecting him, a way of rejecting who he is now, and I think in some way we both knew this.

One night in the middle of the fall, he was at my apartment having drinks with me and some friends of mine. After the friends left, I kissed him on the balcony, and he seemed less inhibited, more passionate, and then his eyes flared, and he began gathering his things, nearly running.

What is it? I asked.

I have to go, he said. I need to leave.

But why? I said, and leaned in and kissed him goodbye. He kissed me again and drew back, his eyes still wild.

I have to go, he said. I'm afraid of me and I'm afraid of you.

We didn't speak for several days. They were some of the loneliest days. I knew what he was trying to do, though. I had put together his seemingly disparate stories, not included here, and I had seen this expression on his face from the other side—this had happened to me when I was his age.

It takes one to know one.

He was trying to face what he wanted, and it was also what scared him away. His desire for men brought back memories and sensations he didn't want, pushed down so far he was sure they were gone, until suddenly, there they were again. He eventually tried to tell me all of this. And I can't say any of what he told me, or what I guessed, because it belongs to him and not to me, and his journey in that regard is his own. I just knew then that I had become the man I ran from when I was having my own flashbacks. And so I was patient as he fought whatever this was inside him, even as I knew how my own relationships then had ended. I was in yet another stereoscopic narrative.

He could be as old as I am now when he is at last ready to tell anyone about it all. He might also never get there. Based on my own experiences with flashbacks, I developed a theory that he could only kiss me in public places, because it made him feel safe to know he could leave if he needed to. But I didn't like it, and I didn't understand why until the night we were in the bar where we'd first kissed, in Brooklyn, a place we always kissed, in fact, and he leaned in and kissed me again. I remember that people were watching. That night, it made me strangely angry to be watched. And then for the first time in over twenty years the reason why it made me angry came to me, and the memory I am speaking of returned.

Watching him have his flashbacks, I had imagined I was done with mine. I was wrong. Now I was the one who had to make excuses, all these years later, and leave.

In *Sleeping Beauty*, the handsome prince makes his way through a forest of thorns and kisses the princess as she sleeps, awakening not just her but the entire kingdom. The barren wilderness is transformed into a paradise. This is not quite what happened here. I can say one kiss put me under a spell. Another kiss woke me. And I was full of horror to see the devastation around me.

2

WE ARE NOT WHAT WE THINK WE ARE. The stories we tell of ourselves are like thin trails across something that is more like the ocean. A mask afloat on the open sea.

There were moments before the memory's return when I experienced what I now understand as its absence as not a gap but a whole other self, a whole other me. As if a copy of me had secretly replaced me. An android of me moving through the landscape, independent of the other me, exactly like me but not me. Every now and then, I could see the distance between us. Three times, in particular, this other self had appeared before me.

◈

IN 1993, the film *Sex Is . . .* , an independent documentary about gay men and their sex lives, debuted at the March on Washington. As one of the interview subjects, I was invited to attend. I went and watched in horror as I described the sexual abuse I'd experienced in the boys' choir I'd once been in, declaring it an education, even a liberation, and that it hadn't harmed me at all. The film sped along to another interviewee. I said more things later, but could see, in the dark of the theater, only my huge, lying mouth.

At the time I filmed the interview, my first relationship with a man who loved me, and whom I also loved, was falling apart because of my PTSD related to what I was describing. Worst of all was the smile I had on my face on-screen as I said this lie, a smug sort of superiority that I hated.

The film went on to win Best Gay Film at the Berlin Film Festival and had a national, and then international, theatrical release. By the time I moved to New York in 1994, I was regularly being recognized for my role in it. I remember taking part in New York City's Gay Pride celebration that year, in Greenwich Village, walking against the crowd, searching for my friends, when I noticed two teenage boys coming toward me arm in arm. One lit up in recognition of me and his arm shot out. "You're the guy from the film," he said.

I paused, terrified, but also curious. Yes, I said. I asked where they were from.

"Saskatchewan," they said, and then wished me a Happy Pride, and were on their way.

I have to fix this, I remember thinking. Wishing for a solution as big as the mistake, or as big as me.

❖

IN OCTOBER 2001, I had my phone in my hand, about to call my mother. My first novel, *Edinburgh,* was about to appear in bookstores the very next day. The story is of the legacy sexual abuse leaves in the life of a young man angry at himself about it, and his apparent powerlessness over that silence. She'd complained that she hadn't seen the novel in manuscript, and I had pacified her by assuring her I wanted her to have the bound book. This was partly true. I was proud to finally be able to hand my mother the physical thing, to say, *Here. I'm a writer.* But now the bound book was in my hand, and I was preparing to send it to her, and I stopped, pulled up short by the memory that I had never told her what had happened to me.

The scope of this gap terrified me. How had I let this happen? I was thirty-four years old. I was about to publish a novel about sexual abuse based on my own experiences, but had never told her one thing about them. Not only that, but in all the time that had passed between when the events had occurred and that moment right then, I could see I had been very angry at her. A child's anger. The child in me had wanted her to figure out what had happened. I had hoped to avoid the humiliation of having to tell her, wanting her instead to guess my thoughts. That adolescent wish that the mother knows your pain without your having to describe it. But children have to learn to say they are in pain. To name it. The naming even helps heal it.

Even at that moment, I was trying to stop myself. I was frozen in the act. I wanted to put the phone down and never tell her. I tried to imagine if there was even one way I could continue to pretend with her. But I knew she would be deeply hurt to be surprised by what was in the book. I could see how I passed myself off to others as someone who had gotten over it all on my own, the disguise I had put on of being unhurt simply a way for me to fix myself in private. I had never told her because I had hoped I could heal in secret and she would never have to know. And yet here I was, still in pain.

As I prepared to call and tell her, I did so knowing it had taken me eighteen years to tell her. Almost as long as it had taken me to tell myself.

And then I made the call.

❖

IN THE SPRING of the same year as the memory's return, I was working as a writing tutor to a graduate student in nonfiction who felt I understood her better than her teachers did. She sent me a draft of her memoir, and as I read through scenes describing how she had attempted suicide and then, in therapy afterward, raged at her therapist for not knowing she had attempted suicide, I wondered at the therapist's reaction to the suicide attempt itself. I sent her what I thought was an ordinary email: "I don't see that you've included scenes describing what it was like telling your therapist about your suicide attempt, or how she reacted. If you could describe this, it would help the reader know why you're so angry here."

I received an email back, the letters in the tiniest possible font, smaller than she normally used, such that I thought, at first, it was some strange mistake, or even a hacking.

I never told her. I've never been in therapy for it, either.

My immediate thoughts: How could she not have told anyone? Did she not know how dangerous it was to just go around untreated? She could relapse at any moment. And then I remembered: most suicides hope to die without interference. Telling someone means allowing the person you told the chance to stop you. I had discovered something like the back passageway she'd left open.

Staring at those tiny letters, I realized I was meeting the person she actually was, underneath her performance of competence. All her life since then she had been waiting to see if someone would notice, and I had. And then another cold truth came to me out of those tiny letters.

I was almost exactly like her.

All of my attempts at therapy previous to this had been about the issues that moved above certain ruptures in myself that remained undescribed. The difference was that I had never raged that a therapist had not figured this out about me. If anything, I was proud of it. I had endured, I told myself. I was so strong. But this is not strength. It is only endurance. A kind of emotional or therapeutic anorexia. I was not strong. Or if I was, it was the adrenaline of the wounded. I was really only broken, moving through the landscape as if I were not, and taking all my pride in believing I was passing as whole.

3

PRIOR TO THE MEMORY'S RETURN, if you asked me, I would tell you there were things in my life that I couldn't remember. I would allow you to think that they were like your own missing memories, gaps made by pure human fallibility and impressionistic thinking. Associations that didn't associate. And yet I recall feeling an empty confidence at those times, the hollow power of a lie. When I began *Edinburgh,* I knew there was something missing, something I wasn't letting myself know. It is just one of the reasons why I wrote it as a novel instead of a memoir. I had written it as if the memory would never come back — as if this could stand in for it. I had imagined the missing memories were gone forever. I thought of the novel as the solution for what was lost.

Instead, it was a summoning. As if I had called and it came back to me.

Even now, though, as I try to write this essay, it dissolves in my hands. There is still a part of me that insists what I'll tell you cannot be told. That insists that if the truth were known I would be destroyed. I try to write this essay and freeze, lose the path, lose my thoughts, my drafts, my edits, all of my purpose. I look up at the ticking clock in front of me and stop. My editor writes back, curious: What happened to this? And I am also mystified to find what I thought was the careful draft full of repetitions, mistakes, missing pieces.

My writing process is informed in general by my relationship to this — a process with a deep mistrust of myself.

The impulse to hide this from myself and others pushes at me. I change my sense of the structure again and again, moving events around, until the document becomes a mass of repetitions and fragments, elliptical, incomplete. A self-portrait.

Most people misunderstand the crime of sexual abuse. They think of stolen youth, a child tucked under the arm and spirited away. But it isn't like someone entering your house and stealing something from you. Instead, someone leaves something with you that grows until it replaces you. They themselves were once replaced this way, and what they leave with you they have carried for years within them, like a fire guarded all this time as it burned them alive inside, right under the skin. The burning hidden to protect themselves from being revealed as burned.

You imagine that the worst thing is that someone would know. The attention you need to heal you have been taught will end you. And it will—it will end the pain you have mistaken for yourself. The worst thing is not that someone would know. The worst thing is that you might lay waste to your whole life by hiding.

You could mistake your ability to go this far for strength. So you go on. Strength is admirable, after all, and you are ashamed of everything else about yourself. This endurance, at least—this you can admire. You were too young to know what you believe is your complicity was something taken from you, but in your silence, you have become complicit with the continued pain, the wound that risks replacing you the longer you let it stay. But among the things you cannot imagine is that anyone would understand, or be kind. This is all you understand.

When I ask myself why it was so hard for me to let this secret go, the answer is that holding on to it was the only source of my self-esteem for years. It was all I thought I had.

I'm sorry, is what I would have wanted to have my replacement say in that documentary. Sorry I was so lonely as a child. Sorry that I was a child, with a child's reasoning. Sorry I didn't understand how this man could be punished, as I had only ever seen children punished. Sorry I dreamed of a kiss and then, when

I accepted it, didn't know how it would make my mouth a grave. Myself living inside of it. Sorry that years later, for having had that kiss, I would boast of avoiding the pain that was eating me alive from the inside out, and that this would be said on film, and it would go everywhere, around the world. Sorry for at least that, and more than that. But I wouldn't know this for years.

Edinburgh is a palinode. The gods, offended by a speech, require the speaker to make another, its opposite. *Phaedrus,* quoted in *Edinburgh,* is one example of this form. But there were no gods to make me do this, just me. And after it was published, the work wasn't done.

4

THIS IS THE MEMORY I put away.

In September 1978, I am eleven, asleep in a dream in which I am at a lake with a boy who is a year older than me, a boy I know from choir. He lives one town over from me. We sometimes carpool. He's as beautiful as the elves are supposed to be in the games I play about magic and wizards. He has blond hair and incandescent blue eyes.

In the dream he swims toward me, his hair plastered dark against his head. He chuckles and it echoes lightly. He reaches up from the water and gives me a kiss, a spark in his eyes. An excitement that is just for me.

I wake up in the morning dark. The dream is so real, I expect my mouth to be wet.

I'm gay is the first thought. *And I am in love with him.*

The choir is my refuge. My secret kingdom, an escape from the children who set traps for me at school. Classmates who have spent years tricking me into humiliating setups—pretending to befriend me before turning on me, or simply attacking me—situations that end with me being demoralized and alone. I had never encountered racism before this—in Guam, I was just one of many multiracial children in a diverse group of students. The intensity of it leaves me full of despair. In photos of me as a child, you can see that the light in my eyes at age six leaves my eyes in the photos of me at age seven, just a year after the move to Maine.

My mother was called in for annual visits with my teachers, during which she was told that I inhabited a dream world of fantasy, and that I would have to live in the real world eventually. Afterward, she would come home and tell me this, and each time I would say, I don't have to live in the real world. Coolly, flatly, as if she were telling me I had to live in Boston and I could refuse. By the time I joined the choir at age eleven, it had been five years of being called a flat-faced chink, or being made fun of because I like to play with girls, who, yes, were all white, and soon joined in these traps organized by the white boys at my school. My nickname at this time is Nature Boy, because I like to go off into the woods alone, and part of the reason I like it is that I don't have to be with them, see them, think of them. But the choir is made up of boys like me, and I soon enjoy a popularity there I've never had. I have friends, finally. Now my mother warns me about too many sleepovers, or of Dungeons & Dragons games that go on too long.

The boy from the dream is a part of this, though not entirely. He doesn't like D & D as much as my other friends do. I don't see him except at rehearsals. He is one of the soloists, and his voice is as beautiful as he is, if not more so. When I'm invited to go on a section leaders' camping trip with the director, I accept eagerly, knowing he'll be going also. The car is small for the four of us

—a Pacer—and the dream boy sits in my lap, laughing, relaxed. He seems not just to touch me, but to meld, and I'm in a kind of bliss I didn't imagine.

I remember my dream of the lake and the kiss, and it seems certain to come true.

We park the car at the trail's parking lot and set off. During this hike to our campsite, the director jokes about how it is so hot we should hike nude. This seems impossible to me. He frequently talks to us about nudism, American prudery, sexual immaturity. How children should be able to vote, divorce their parents, choose whom they want to have sex with.

At the campsite, after the tent is set up, he begins to take off his clothes.

You don't have to take off your clothes, he says to me.

But the other boys do, and soon they are all swimming together naked in the swimming hole we have chosen for our campsite. And so I take off my clothes and jump in. He takes photos of us, but especially of my dream boy, who is clearly his favorite, and who poses happily.

Soon it is evening and we are all in the tent. We are all still naked. The director has told me he knew about the crush, and he wants us to kiss. That the kiss is something he wants to see. The dream boy had told him of my feelings for him, and they had used it to bring me here. The director smiles as he tells me this, as if he hopes I will be amused, and also indulge him. The dream boy is there in front of me, also smiling at me, kneeling, naked, coming closer. There seems to be no way out, as if something is being cut off from me even as it is offered, and I can't prevent it. As the kiss happens, I like it and hate it at the same time.

This is my first kiss.

After that night, the dream boy will never kiss me again. I will still want it. It is as if I didn't get it, not like I wanted, and everything is wrong afterward.

I included something like this scene in the novel. I describe looking at my face's reflection, and how this is when I began wanting to die.

I had, until that day in the bar in Brooklyn, remembered most of it except for the dream and what the dream led me to do. What I cannot, do not, let myself remember in that tent is the reason why I despaired. I put away the dream that night, and any memory of how I believed it was a dream coming true. I put away how I hated my silence, my inability to act, my shame at being humiliated this way—to have my secret known by those I thought were my friends, who then only used it against me. My despair was the despair of realizing that this was just another trap, that there was perhaps no end of traps. The boy from my dream was there to make everything the director was doing to me and the other boys seem okay. This trip is the extent of the director's interest in me this way. He never tries to be alone with me again. He only wanted to control what I wanted—access to his favorite —and when I received it, and how.

As an adult, I understand my powerlessness. I can see I was in the woods without access to a phone or a car or another adult. I now know that the director chose me in part because my family was in crisis—he knew my mother needed a place for me to be after school, and that I needed the refuge the choir offered. Until the camping trip, the choir had been like a paradise for me: other boys who were smart, who liked me, who didn't mock me, who wanted me as their friend, just for who I was. I can see that I was only a tool to the director, and this display of power over my desires was done to put me in my place. And that new place was to make everything seem okay to the other boys, much like my own dream boy had done for me. But what's new, supplied by the memory, is how I gave up then, gave up believing my life could ever be any better. I would never escape the people intent on humiliating me. There was no place for me in this world, and there was nothing I could do about it. The despair I have lived with my whole life overtook me then, and until that kiss in the bar twenty-five years later, I had kept this secret, even from myself.

I was twelve when I put this memory away. The force exerting itself in my life was the power of pure childhood imagination, unmediated by any sense of my own power to speak, to create understanding and compassion. Instead, there was in me a dream of fear, so powerful I made a doll of myself to stay in my place, and I ran away. The doll woke up, stretched, looked around, and believed it was me.

5

IMAGINE walking into your apartment and finding someone ripping up a piece of paper. You put your hand on his arm and this person turns to face you. It is you.

You read the paper, and as you do, you feel as if you are falling into it, endlessly, away from yourself and into yourself at the same time.

In the months after the memory returned, I continued with my life as best I could. But my recovered memory, for me, was like receiving a telegram one morning and finding inside the answer to twenty-five years' worth of mistakes, twenty-five years of confusion and pain, and watching as around me the day turned as black as night. There was a story I needed to understand, the one I had tried to avoid, and it was all I wanted to listen to, and everything else I had to do was in the way.

The young writer I'd been involved with eventually moved on that fall. We never really spoke of what had happened, or whatever it was we'd unsealed for each other—my attempts at such conversations did not end well. Like me at his age, he did not seem ready to speak of it. We remain friends.

There was one more story I was inside of then, yet another stereograph. The one from the spring. The one in which I was someone who had not told his therapist the story he needed to tell.

❖

THE FIRST NEW THERAPIST I FOUND had been recommended to me by a friend. As her office was near where I was living at the time in New York, and she had helped my friend to a remarkable recovery after a sexual assault, and that friend had recommended her highly, I went. This therapist listened to me for ten or fifteen minutes as I described why I had come to her, and then she said, "I'm not sure I know how to help you. The people I work with usually can't even name what happened to them, much less write a novel about it."

I was suddenly very aware that I was sitting on a couch surrounded by stuffed animals and toys, as if I were visiting a nursery. I wondered if the toys were for her other patients even as I knew they were, and I fought the impulse to pick one up. She told me I seemed fine, perhaps a little neurotic, at least not as damaged as others—not in danger. She agreed to keep seeing me, and I did see her twice more. But inside the self performing as someone who was fine was the self who was not, and the vision I'd had of my life, the one that had me wanting to scream, was a vision of how living this way, inside of this performance, had blighted my life. I felt like a tree struck by lightning a long time ago, burning secretly from the inside out, the bark still smooth to the end — the word FINE painted on it.

I had even used this image of the lightning-struck tree in the novel I'd written, and it was just one of the ways the novel allowed that hidden self to speak in public. The novel that seemed, that day, to have become yet another obstacle for me.

I thanked her and left. When I reached the dark sidewalk, I told myself I would find another therapist. But I felt something new. A wild fury of failing — *no one believes I am not fine; why does no one believe it?* — thundered in my head as I stood there. The one who knew he was still burning was trying to say so. And the one who was determined to say nothing did not allow it.

I had told my story but I had not told my story. I had written a novel and found catharsis, but I had not found healing, had not found recuperation. I had read self-help books to research the novel about sexual abuse, but I had not done the work, had not applied those books to myself as much as I had used them as a map to a character. Through it all I kept telling myself that nothing had happened to me, *nothing had happened to me, nothing had happened to me, nothing had happened to me.* I was *fine.*

But I was not fine. It would take me four years to try again. As I examine the reasons why, I first find a strange little lie that does not add up when I examine it: an angry feeling that the therapist did not believe me. But she did. She simply told me she couldn't help me. And the copy of me who believed I could be fine without ever speaking of it took over again. No one believes you, the copy told me. A last — last? — lie. For that night, at least.

I am built for this terrible pain, I told myself, and sent myself on my way.

❖

I LEFT THE APARTMENT in the sky when the sublet there ended and moved back to Brooklyn briefly, to an ill-fated rental there, a one-bedroom apartment with an unfinished wood floor my land-lord tried to pass off as hardwood—the carpet staples still in it. I did not complain, unable to tell him he was lying to me. I didn't bother to unpack, and three months later moved out to Los Angeles—another sublet, this time with a friend in Koreatown, a share in his 4,000-square-foot apartment in a building named for a silent-film star, where I drove his borrowed white Porsche and tried very hard to be who I thought I should be at parties filled with professionally beautiful people I vaguely remembered or didn't know at all.

I told myself I was chasing pleasure after so much grief. That I was writing my new novel. But I was desperate to escape the slow creep of deadness inside, the paralysis I felt in the face of this memory and all that came with it. The grief at following my dream of a boy into the woods, into what was just another trap in what felt like an unending series of traps. That I was still doing this was lost on me, though it came to me in moments, and I pushed the knowledge away each time. The paralysis that had stopped me again and again, this was what I was trying to kick away. I ran from myself by moving across the country, and even did the move twice, once out to Los Angeles and then back again, to Maine. I told myself I was making smart decisions, and sometimes I was—selling my second novel, applying to the Mac-Dowell Colony, applying for a job at Amherst College—but that feeling followed me, the feeling of needing to stop and also to scream, as if I thought I could stop what was freezing me from the inside out by scaring it out of me. And there was always a new man, another will-o'-the-wisp of desire that I followed into whatever woods I found. With each move, a raft of boxes followed me, many never unpacked, joined by new ones full of unanswered mail from the previous address.

◈

FOUR YEARS WENT BY.

When I finally found another therapist, I picked him by calling several therapists in the area and listening to their voices — I chose him for his timbre and tone. I went to him for what I thought would be triage after a breakup, something I'd done before. I had just moved to Amherst, Massachusetts, to begin a new job, and I had broken up with my boyfriend shortly after arriving, having discovered a sexually transmitted disease, despite being in what was supposed to have been a monogamous relationship. As I had caught him, the previous fall, trolling online for sex with strangers, and after discussing whether we wanted new rules — non-monogamy, specifically — or an end to our relationship — we had continued, as he'd insisted he wanted neither to be in an open relationship nor to end our relationship. This time, however, after certifying I had gotten my little hygiene problem in the way I believed I had — from him — I ended the relationship with no discussion. It was a minor illness but an unacceptable risk. This was what I thought I would be talking about with the therapist. And while it was where we began, we soon went elsewhere.

I had been talking about the patterns in my ex's relationships, but the therapist kept turning me back to mine. He told me I had

242   How to Write an Autobiographical Novel

to stop trying to understand my ex and just accept the fact of him. I needed instead to understand myself. My habit of chasing after a fantasy. Do you know this phrase, the therapist with the nice voice asked me after a number of sessions, "In repetition is forgetting"?

I don't, I said.

It's Freud, he said. It refers to the Freudian repetition cycle. We repeat something so that we can forget the pain of it. We set out to get it right instead, to fix what went wrong. But we can never fix the past, he said. We then only repeat it.

In repetition is forgetting.

He was a popular therapist in this town, and in conversation with a friend who was also seeing him, he had mentioned that one of our therapist's specialties was treating gay men with a history of sexual abuse. I had silently noted this.

We can only break the future, came the thought.

There is something I should tell you, I said.

And there, on his office sofa, I remembered my student who had never told her therapist enough, and began at last to try to tell someone everything.

◆

I AM WRITING this from my future. The one I made from the one I broke, possibly only after that day.

The therapist gave me an exercise. You can't get rid of the guardians who've kept you safe until now, he said. You have to give them new jobs. The jobs they have, they've been doing since you were a child.

I had never thought of them as protectors. The liar on the screen. The one who hid his wound from his mother in shame.

The one who kept his hurt secret from his other therapists, trying, alone, to fix himself, unable to even think of saying the words. But finally able to write them. Of course each one was doing what I'd essentially told them to do, even if I no longer felt that way or wanted it done. They all were.

And then there was the one who'd left me the fragments of that novel like a trail through the woods, from the land I was in to this one. The one planning this world that the novel would make.

I had written a novel that, after it was published, let me practice saying what I remembered out loud for years until the day I could remember all of it. Until I could be the person who could stand it. The person who wrote that novel, he was waiting for me.

HOW TO WRITE AN
AUTOBIOGRAPHICAL NOVEL

I WILL TELL ONLY THE TRUTH, you decide. It's right there, after all. Like you could hold it, perfect, in one try.

This vision of the novel you are sure you can write sits in your life like a gift from any god you might be willing to believe in. As suddenly real as any unexpected visitor.

You must write it, you decide. It would be so easy.

You watch each other, carefully, for years.

When you begin, you are like someone left in the woods with an ax and a clear memory of houses, deciding to build a house.

You decide you will teach yourself to furnish everything with that ax. You are the ax. The woods is your life.

And yet when you sit down to try, the perfection is gone.

The beautiful symmetry, the easy way of it, all of it is replaced by awkwardness, something worse than if your mind made only noise.

When you stop, dejected, you see it again, perfect again. As if it is mocking you.

Soon you learn that you see it only when you do not try.

Thinking this may be its way of stopping you, but either way, you stop trying. And then start. And then stop.

Perhaps you are unfamiliar with why you would try to undo yourself. Why you would be your own worst enemy or best friend, or that person who is sometimes both. Now you try to live with what you know.

You still see it, even if it eludes you when you reach for it. What is the way into the place where it is? you wonder.

Perhaps it is like the Venetian towns built to confuse pirates. You think you are headed toward the square with a fountain, and instead find yourself in an alley, or out along the cliff wall. Another life.

There is that noise still in the mind, drawn over the surface of the entrance like camouflage.

You find this only when you decide you must try again.

You don't know this yet, but gods, even when you don't believe in them, do not give something easily. Not even when the god is you.

You didn't make this up, people say to you when finally you write it and give it to them to read.

I did, you say, but you feel as if you have dropped your disguise.

Is this me? they ask coldly. Their disguise, also dropped.

You had hoped they also would see how perfect it was. You wonder if it *is* them, and you forgot somehow, you are stupid in some way you didn't anticipate.

The living reside uncomfortably in prose. This includes you.

You like the child who believes they are invisible because they stood in a shadow.

This person, your reader, now says, There is no plot.

You see this also. The novel revealed now as a string of anecdotes, and you cannot see what comes before or after. The events of your life like an empty field and you there, shouting, "Novel!"

The writer who cried "Novel!," yes. Yes, that was you.

Invent something that fits the shape of what you know.

To do this, use the situations but not the events of your life.

Invent a character like you, but not you.

You, in the forest of yourself with the ax, building the house, sealing yourself within its walls.

You are the ghost of the house you build and never live in, this house you make of your life.

The space you occupy more like the space between the wall and the paint.

This also the difference between you and the one you have invented to be you.

This golem of the self, this house, now something anyone could visit and understand. Unlike you. That is what you hope for now.

This golem more or less careless than you, more or less selfish, more or less remorseful.

More or less you, but not you.

Or it is remorseful in exactly the same way as you, but something else is what changes as you write it, until you understand you and it are apart.

If you are a professor, then the character is a professor. If you are tall, he is tall. Angry, then angry. But then change other things that will make the difference.

Give the character your name only if it will make this difference plain. Anything else is museum theater.

Or choose a name with the same music.

Invent the other characters also, the same way.

Or change all the names. Change everything.

Use the names of neither the willing nor the unwilling. Especially those who will change from willing to unwilling once the novel is published and they understand what they have given you.

Know that this may be anyone, even you.

You do this because you must betray this character in the way all writers betray all of their characters, done to reveal the ways they are human.

To do less than this is only PR.

You have invented this self because the ways you are human are not always visible to yourself. All of this a machine to make yourself more human.

For this reason, be prepared, always, to stop and set the novel aside until you are prepared to do what you must do.

Why is it not a memoir? people will ask.

I tell more truth in fiction, you might say. You hope this is true.

The memoir a kind of mask too, but one that insists you are only one person.

All fiction is autobiographical, people say. People who say this want to believe it more than any novel itself, much less the one you wrote.

It is time to speak of the price.

The price is you do not get it back after you write it, whatever you took from yourself for its heart.

Give this over, then, only if you can make something greater than what you had.

Anyone who unhappily saw themselves in your characters will most likely see themselves, even if they were not described. Those you do include will pass themselves by, seeing themselves in other characters.

The legal standard is that a stranger must be able to recognize the character in life from the description in the novel before the person can sue.

You cannot sue yourself.

There is another standard for yourself, and its demands and punishments will stand unrevealed until you find the book finished, out in the world, waiting in the place where you once lived.

Anyone not in your life will believe it is your life, and sometimes the people in your life will too, despite what they might remember.

This price is paid until no one is left alive.

Here are the warnings, then, dressed as thieves.

You can't stop me, you think. I must do this, you are thinking.

I will not stop you and I don't want to. You will stop you. A hundred times. A thousand.

You lost in the trap of "that happened," and you struggle because "that is how that really happened," and yet you cannot make it convincing in fiction, cannot figure out what happens *next*.

Your novel only an anecdote, your plot a series of aversions, dodges in disguises, trauma dressed as friends saying, "Yes you can no you can't yes you can."

Ready to steal as much of your life as you let them, more than what they already have taken.

One last price, hidden behind the rest.

Write fiction about your life and pay with your life, at least three times.

Here is the ax.

ON BECOMING AN
AMERICAN WRITER

I

HOW MANY TIMES have I thought the world would end?

This was the question that appeared in my head the morning after the election, the election that for now we all speak of only as "the election," as if there will never be any other. The question appeared like a black balloon determined to follow me around, bobbing in and out of my vision, a response to my first thought: *This is the end of the world.*

I was standing in my kitchen, at the stove. I was supposed to teach a class that morning. Canceling the class seemed out of the question, though I did not know how to do all of the things that would get me there. The coffee seemed impossible to make, as did breakfast. Going downstairs, getting into the car, driving the twenty minutes south to the college where I teach. Walking into the classroom. I couldn't imagine any of that.

What I did imagine: a white supremacist, evangelical Christian, theocratic, militaristic government. My Muslim friends rounded up and deported. Being hunted by right-wing militias for being gay, or for being mixed race, or both. Climate departure, the next step after climate change, when the weather turns in violent shifts, monsoons and blizzards, floods and freezing. The ocean a hot soup, empty of life. A government opposed to environmental protections, labor protections, abortion, birth control, and equal access to health care.

I was, I knew, in shock. The previous night, when the results seemed final, my partner of three years had proposed marriage, and I had accepted. We decided to marry before the laws could be changed, and I knew it would help if we ever needed to seek asylum. Before this, my now husband had expressed a deep antipathy to even the idea of marriage. My sister called afterward, distraught, having just been able to put her children to bed—they had begged her to move, to leave the country. That had all happened between 2:30 and 3:30 a.m.

My phone was in my hand. A tingling and numbness ran from the top of my left shoulder all the way down to where my phone digs into my palm, pushing on a nerve there when I scrolled with one hand, as I did, walking from room to room in disbelief and horror. This is what I was doing just before I came to a stop in the kitchen. The pain that began that day lasted almost a year.

I checked Facebook, an autonomic response. WHAT WILL YOU TEACH, my friend the poet Solmaz Sharif had posted.

What will I teach? *What do I know?* This somehow brought me out of my trance. But I was still motionless in front of my stove.

Can you make coffee? I asked myself. No. Can you buy a coffee? Yes. Go buy a coffee, I told myself.

I put on a coat. I got my coffee and a breakfast sandwich and drove south to the school. The views along Interstate 91, of the White Mountains and the Green Mountains, usually console me, but that day all I could think about on that drive was the death of the world.

❖

I ARRIVED in the college's town to find it as empty as if classes were canceled. As I walked to my office, a young woman left the library and crossed the strangely empty lawn. As she drew closer, I saw tears streaming down her face. She did not look at me.

In my office, as I collected the materials for class, I overheard another young woman crying as she described her anger to a colleague about the future in a country that had elected a sexual predator as president.

What will you teach?

It felt as if a president had been assassinated, but the president was alive. Instead, the country we thought we would be living in was dead. As if a president had assassinated a country.

I walked into my classroom. My students were all present. The room was very quiet, and tense, as if they were trying to find a way to tell me one of them had died. Many of them were crying or had just stopped crying. I hadn't been sure if any of them would be celebrating the new president before this, but now it was clear none of them were.

"I'm not going to pretend last night didn't happen," I said. "Let's just talk about whatever it is we need to talk about."

"What is the point," one of my most talented students asked after the shortest pause. "What is the point even of writing, if this can happen?"

❖

THE DAY THE UNITED STATES invaded Iraq in 2003, I was at my alma mater, Wesleyan University, preparing to teach the next day. In the art professor's apartment I was subletting, I watched the news of the invasion on his antique television, the screen the size of a paperback book. I was surrounded by art as a segment aired declaring that the museums and antiquities of the ancient Persian culture preceding Saddam Hussein would likely be destroyed by American shelling. A country's historic legacy lost, perhaps forever. To these concerns, Secretary of Defense Donald Rumsfeld was shown, responding to this. He offered, "What's a few less old pots?"

He was chipper, even affable, as he said it. He thought he was funny. Yes, who wants them? Who wants any of it? A strange chill dropped over me, the sort of shadow felt even in the night. How cheerful he was as he consigned these parts of one of the world's oldest cultures, the source of so much of our art, literature, and science, to rubble. I turned off the television and sat alone and angry in the cold apartment, a pile of manuscripts to mark next to me.

What *was* the point? The task of being a writer suddenly felt inadequate. As did I. That next morning at Wesleyan, I faced something entirely new in my teaching career: I didn't know what to say to my students. And I very much wanted to know.

2

MY GENERATION OF WRITERS—and yours, if you are reading this—lives in the shadow of Auden's famous attack on the relevance of writing to life, when he wrote that "poetry makes nothing happen." I had heard the remark repeated so often and for so long I finally went looking for its source, to try to understand what it was he really meant by it. Because I knew it was time for me to really argue with it. If not for myself, for my students.

Auden wrote this line in an elegy for Yeats. And Yeats, it should be said, was a hero of Auden's. To read the whole poem is to know he meant, if not the opposite of what this line is so often used to say, something at least more subtle: an ironic complaint. This isn't even the sharpest line Auden wrote on the subject. But somehow, the line handed anyone who cared a weapon to gut the confidence of over fifty years' worth of writers in the West. As we faced the inexorable creep of William F. Buckley's intellectual conservatism that used anti-intellectualism as its arrowhead, this attitude, that writing is powerless, is one that affects you even if you have never read that poem, much less the quote. Pundits, reviewers, and critics spit it out repeatedly, as often now as ever, hazing anyone who might imagine anything to the contrary. I don't blame Auden or Yeats, who had both hoped to inspire political change with their poetry earlier in their lives. His poem meant to express his disillusionment. I don't think Auden meant it as a call to stop trying. But America was a young enough country, American literature was young also. It was easier to believe that we were wrong than to believe what writers around the world believe: that we matter, and that it is our duty, to matter.

◈

STUDENTS OFTEN ASK ME whether I think they can be a writer. I tell them I don't know. Because it depends, first and foremost, on whether you want to be one. This question is not as simple to answer as it seems. The difficulties are many, even if you truly want to be a writer. What seems to separate those who write from those who don't is being able to stand it.

"I started with writers more talented than me," Annie Dillard had said in the class I took from her in college. "And they're not writing anymore. I am." I remember, as a student, thinking, *Why wouldn't you do the work? What could possibly stop you?*

I began teaching writers in the fall of 1996, at a continuing education program based on the Upper West Side of Manhattan. I called it the MASH unit of creative writing, because you can't turn anyone away from your classes there. The program pays instructors what it has always paid them, even now, twenty years later, and they do so because there is always an MFA graduate like me who needs a first teaching job, and every other place that offers writing classes in New York is more or less like this. But I loved my students, and what I still value of this experience is that it was there that I first discovered that good writing was, as Annie had said to us, very teachable. Talent mattered less than it was made to seem to matter. I watched in my first classes as I applied techniques I'd been taught to students who seemed at first to be unlikely writers and they turned into excellent ones. I learned a different kind of humility there in the face of their efforts, which I think still serves me as a teacher: you don't know who will make it and who will not, and students' previous work may or may not be an indicator of what they can do, good or bad.

Most of what Annie had taught me was about habits of mind and habits of work. As long as these continued, I imagined, so would the writing. I will always want my students to know that if what you write matters enough, it makes no difference where you write it, or if you have a desk, or if you have quiet, and so on. If the essay or novel or poem wants to be written, it will speak to you while the conductor is calling out the streets. The question is, will you listen? And listen regularly?

Teaching these classes I also learned what could stop a writer. So many of the students in my classes were stuck. Some were struggling with a story they both wanted to tell and had forbidden themselves from telling. Some were struggling with a family story that they believed, if told, would destroy their family, or them, or their relationship to the family. A close friend to this day will not write the novel he wants to write about his late mother, who was closeted until he came out to her, and she then came out to him. He is afraid of the reaction of a single cousin.

Why does the talented student of writing stop? It is usually the imagination, turned to creating a story in which you are a failure, and all you have done has failed, and you are made out to be the fraud you've feared you are. You can imagine the story you might tell, or you can imagine this other story—both will be extraordinarily detailed, but only one will be something you can publish. The other will freeze you in place, in a private theater of pain that seats one. These writers were—are, in many cases—people who know how to write. What they don't know is how to become unstuck. How to leave that theater they made for themselves, how to stop telling themselves the story that freezes them.

I discovered I needed to teach not just how to write, but how to keep writing. How to face up to who you think is listening. Is the person listening more important than you? Or is the story you would tell more important than you? I was teaching how to stand up and leave that room in your mind so you can go and write—and live. But the question after that, always, is, *Live with what?*

And one answer was always going to be America.

❖

WHEN I WAS A STUDENT OF WRITING in college, I was guilty of believing that I would have the sort of life of an author that proceeded along lines that kept me well within the limits of the middle class. It is the American art trap: make art but be a good member of your social class. A friend of mine even has a belief that I think is worth testing—that the primary deciding factor of whether a writer becomes a writer is their relationship to being middle class. If they are working class or upper class, or even an aristocrat, they are at least comfortable betraying that class in order to write.

Put another way: Will you be able to write and also eat, or even eat well? Will you have to work another job? Will you be able to pay for health care, a house, dental work, retirement?

These fantasies frayed and fell apart fast enough as the two places I chose to focus my career—writing and teaching—have both met with extraordinary income destruction in the last two decades. I learned quickly that if you stop writing, nothing happens, but I also learned that I had nowhere else to go. I mastered my diligence in the face of that, but I am still not free of the demon that can stop me in my tracks and make me doubt my sense of my own worth and power. And there isn't just a single demon, nor are they only personal ones at that. You are up against what people will always call the ways of the world—and the ways of this country, which does not kill artists so much as it kills the rationale for art, in part by insisting that the artist must be a successful member of the middle class, if not a celebrity, to be a successful artist. And that to do otherwise is to fail art, the country, and yourself. Should you decide that writing is your way to serve your country, or to defend it, you are almost always writing about the country it could become.

❖

I READ THE FIRST REVIEW of my first novel on the Thursday after September 11, 2001, in the empty computer center of a dormitory at the girls' school in Maryland where my sister worked.

My brother and I had left the city together. He lived seven blocks from Ground Zero, and I, with my history of asthma, found that for the first time in decades, I was unable to breathe easily even out in Brooklyn, where I lived, as long as the site continued to burn. So we left for a week to take a break from the air. We were very naïve to think the fire would be out by then. I will always remember the cloud of smoke, as long as the island of Manhattan, visible from the Verrazano Bridge.

As I read the review—a rave, the sort of review you hope for as a debut author—I had the sense of being a character in a science-fiction film, one in which the writer, who finally sees his novel published, then watches as the world ends.

We did return to New York eventually. The world did not end. Instead, all through that fall, people said things to me like, *It's too bad your book isn't about the war,* and I said nothing to that, because there was nothing to say. I taught my writing classes at the New School, where I was teaching then, and each time I passed through Union Square station, I consulted the thousands of flyers for missing persons, in case one of them was someone I knew. I thought of how my own flyer might read, with the details people who knew me would decide might be helpful if you had to find me, and you might find only an arm, or the body but no head. For one terrible moment, I resolved to acquire more distinguishing characteristics in case this happened to me, though I discarded the idea as a mania driven by fear. I boarded empty flights to the two readings my publisher could afford to send me to, and ate the extra meals the nervous flight attendants offered. I went and spoke on the radio, answering questions about my book that was not about the war, and met readers, and more reviews appeared.

There were news reports of an epidemic of writer's block in New York City, and after those appeared there were reports of writer's block in many other parts of the world too. Writers known and unknown spoke of how they couldn't think of writing anything that approached the scale of the attacks. As if this were the task.

I didn't know anyone who was lost that day. When I think of the lost, I think mostly of a man I heard speaking on the radio on the morning of the attacks. He had called the station from inside the first tower to describe what was happening. The host quickly thanked him for calling in and then said, in a bit of a panic, Why are you on the phone with me? Why aren't you on your way down?

You don't understand, the man said. The whole center of the building is gone. I can't go down. That's why I'm calling.

I don't know how to describe the feeling I had in the silence that followed, except that it was approximately the length it would take you to read this sentence aloud.

What do you mean the whole center's gone? the host asked, the panic in his voice no longer slight.

I mean, I can see down the center of the building, he said. The stairs are just . . . gone.

Then the line went dead, and the radio host was weeping, asking us all to pray for the missing caller.

Later we would know for sure the towers had fallen. In that instant, I did not know, though I felt certain. It was unbearable. I turned off the radio. I was in my apartment, about to make coffee for myself, but found I had none. The enormity of what had happened was not yet clear, but I decided if the world was going to end that day, I was going to need coffee to face it. I left to get some at the corner café where I knew a couple of my friends would be working. I could get coffee and be less alone. In the hallway, I saw people leaving the building as if it were an ordinary day. They did not know what had happened. I didn't know how to tell them. I blurted it out.

They looked at me as if I were insane. As if their disbelief could make it not true.

At the café, I found my friends had scalded themselves with spilled coffee when the first news of the attacks came on the radio, and so I helped them do what they needed to do to close the store, and then, as we prepared to leave, I noticed, outside the window, what seemed to be faint grayish snow was beginning to fall out of the sky.

Is it snowing? one of my friends asked, incredulous.

I thought of a date I'd gone on two days earlier, with a welder. I had been interested in his work. Can you burn steel? I remembered asking.

Yes, he said. And he told me the temperature at which steel burned like firewood, 2,000 degrees Fahrenheit.

It would be disputed later, all of it, all the details of that day. Whether the steel had burned, the heat of the fire, whether the planes had set off the destruction or the building had been rigged to blow. A "false flag" operation, some said. I would, and still do, doubt whether I heard the radio conversation I heard, though it is nothing I would ever make up. All I knew in that moment was that this ash was from the towers, a mix of the building and those who had died in it and the plane that had struck it, and that we could not breathe in what was falling, and yet none of us could endure waiting to leave, because who knew how long it would be before another attack?

Get some sort of wet cloth, I said. We each need one. A napkin or a bandanna.

We bound wet cloths over our faces and heads. When you get

home, I said, take off your clothes and put them in a plastic bag and throw them away. Then take a shower.

They stared at me.

This is the ash from the towers burning, I said.

And so my friends and I walked home this way, wet cloths over our noses and mouths, through the falling ash in Park Slope, miles from the site. We waved goodbye to each other, saying nothing.

After taking off my clothes and putting them in a trash bag and showering, I went to make sure my windows were sealed. I had a very specific fear: I did not want to breathe them in. It seemed disrespectful. There was talk for months afterward of recovering the bodies of the missing, yet I knew on the walk home that the ash that day held most of the remains. I thought of the families, how they might react if they knew what the ash was. Later that day I regarded the pale gray snow that had fallen over my garden with the attitude of someone visiting a grave. When I returned from a trip to Maryland a week later, rain had washed the garden clean. But I knew they were still there.

Three years later, as I prepared to leave the apartment, I found the trash bag on the floor of my closet. I had never gotten rid of the clothes. I finally threw them away.

❖

WHEN WRITERS IN NEW YORK complained they could not write after 9/11, it seemed to me they were frozen by writing for that audience, by writing for the missing. Who we all felt, somehow, were watching. Waiting to see if we were worthy of being alive when they were dead. Waiting to see the stories we would tell about the life they would no longer have among us — waiting to see if it was worth it.

3

IN THE WINTER before the war in Iraq, I lost two friends, one old, one new.

The first friend died of cancer in December 2002. She was just thirty-six. She had been misdiagnosed by her doctor. First she was told she had a rash, and then that she was imagining the severity of it. She was told to take antidepressants. After further tests, she learned she had non-Hodgkin's lymphoma. A lifelong hypochondriac who always looked to be in the bloom of health, she had finally fallen seriously ill and was not believed. And when she eventually was believed, when the truth of her disease was incontrovertible, there was not time enough to undo the damage, and she succumbed. She had once been my boss at a magazine launched in the early nineties. I had met her in San Francisco, when she was the girlfriend of my boyfriend's roommate. When I moved to New York to be closer to my boyfriend, she and I sometimes spent whole days together. She herself dreamed of writing a novel one day, and in the meantime wrote poems more or less in secret, showing them rarely. When I was an editor of an experimental literary journal called *XXX Fruit*, we asked her for poems, and published some of them. I remember looking at the typeset page and thinking of it as a picture of her secret self.

By then, she had moved on to a job at a national weekly newsmagazine, which she loved, though the responsibilities often crushed what energy she might have had to write. Or at least this was what she said. Most writers I know say they don't have enough time to write. It's usually a feint.

Her lover, a poet and novelist, spoke at the memorial service of how, during the eight months she was hospitalized, my friend would tell her stories in the dark, lights out, late into the night, about their life. The stories about them were set in the future but told in the present tense. In that imagined life, it went without saying, she had been healed of her cancer, and they had pets, a house in Woodstock, friends coming over for weekends. She had thought through every detail, down to the burial of their cats at the property's edge.

She never liked to go to sleep.

Alone with her death's approach, she had told stories in her bed. She'd finally written her novel for the woman she loved, insisting on something past what was allowed them.

What would you read to someone who was dying? Annie Dillard had asked our class. She wanted this to be the standard for our work. There, at the memorial service for my friend, I thought of another: Dying, what stories would you tell?

❖

I THINK of this friend whenever I am reminded of the abandoned projects I have in my office, going back for years. This essay was one of them. Being a writer can feel a lot like writing and giving up on writing at the same time. I wrote this paragraph in a small office I kept in my home in Rochester, New York, in 2005, full of unfinished stories, unfinished essays, unfinished novels. Twelve years later, I'm editing it on a plane back from Florence, Italy, on my way to a conference at Yale, where my friend did her undergraduate degree.

In the first decade after her death, each time I would move, I would sift through the boxes, organizing the papers, and find, again and again, the CD that was made for her memorial service, the picture on it of her as a girl, sunburned, her auburn hair short, her eyes squinting in the sun. Water wings on her arms. I keep it next to my bed now, where I sleep with my husband. The boxes are in our cabin near Woodstock, where the ghosts of my friend's future twenty years ago are among my neighbors. The boxes still tell me about myself, the writer I was and the writer I am and will be, the man who once believed in their contents and the man who still struggles to do so. Until now, when there's no more waiting.

Consider, if you will, the sin of despair.

❖

OF THE SEVEN DEADLY SINS, despair is the sin of hopelessness, of believing there is no salvation. This sin can even be considered a heresy, as, to quote *The Catholic Encyclopedia* on the topic, it "implies an assent to a proposition which is against faith, e.g. that God has no mind to supply us with what is needful for salvation." It is a sin because it is the belief that grace — God — will not provide.

I was not raised a Catholic, but rather a kind of indifferent Methodist. I had no formal education in the sins, only the informal one, which is life.

Who am I to despair? I remember a boyfriend who had what could be called a depression problem, speaking with him about his despair as he lay on my bed in the apartment with the garden, where I lived for seven years before I began my years of moving. He was a Jewish lawyer from New York, involved in progressive causes, working for a progressive law firm.

He began chastising himself in my presence. You actually have a reason to be depressed, he said to me. Terrible things have happened to you. But you're still happy. What's my excuse?

You represent the American Communist Party, I said. We laughed, but only because it was true.

He was saying he did not think I was depressed, despite my difficulties, and he was right, I did not think of myself as depressed. I thought of myself as angry. Angry in the way of something held in waiting, otherwise silent or invisible. During this time, for example, writers would say in front of me, Nothing bad ever happened to me when I was a child. They were complaining about someone like me. As if they had been cheated out of being a person with the luck of terrible things having happened to them. Terrible things I was then unable to include in a novel because no one would believe them, or because I could not let myself remember. My therapist in Iowa thirteen years ago said to me, "If you were anyone else, I'd say you were paranoid. But you actually have been betrayed by many people in your life. You still have to learn to trust, though," she said. "It's still going to hold you back."

To quote again from *The Catholic Encyclopedia* entry on despair: "The pusillanimous person has not so much relinquished trust in God as he is unduly terrified at the spectacle of his own shortcomings or incapacity."

I am sometimes unduly terrified by my shortcomings, and I do not trust God. But at my worst, for now, I remember that one thing I still control is whether or not I give in. And then I go on.

❖

THE SECOND FRIEND I lost that year was a new friend, who died suddenly at the end of February 2003. Tom was his name. He was slightly older than me at forty, and healthy for a man as devoted as he was to good drink and good food, gay and HIV-positive.

He managed a café on Seventh Avenue in Brooklyn, and for the two and a half years I knew him, I saw him almost exclusively after sunset, him making coffee, me ordering it. He had met me in the season when my first novel had appeared. He had read it and would praise it loudly to anyone standing next to me in line. Soon most of his regulars knew that I had published a novel, so I spent most of our friendship blushing. When he died, I was returning from a short second tour for the paperback.

He met me, in other words, as the dream I'd had for the previous seven years was coming true. And I felt nearly dead from the effort of bringing it to fruition.

He knew me entirely as a writer. This was not how I knew myself. It was why I blushed when he spoke of my book. He had never seen me get coffee with a tuxedo in a garment bag on my shoulder, running up the subway stairs in order to be on time to serve a formal dinner on Park Avenue. He had missed the nights when, after waiting tables at the steakhouse in midtown, I would arrive in the local gay bar in a starched white shirt, sleeves rolled, and drink pairs of bourbon and beer until closing.

He mentioned that he sometimes wrote, and that he'd just come into an inheritance. He kept his job, but left on a dream trip through Europe, where he fell in love with a young man in Spain. It had almost come to something, but then it didn't, and he returned from Spain, relaxed and tanned. Heartbreak seemed to have let him off the hook somehow. For something.

In our last full conversation he told me about the novel he'd plotted and begun writing. When I arrived back from my book tour and returned to the café, expecting to see him, I found a young South African man with a mohawk pouring coffee in his place. I began to quietly panic. I knew Tom was HIV-positive, and would be absent only if something was very wrong.

Indeed, the South African told me that Tom was in the hospital. I decided I would wait two days for the cough I had to go away, not wanting to risk infecting him. He died on the day in between.

So many of my friends had been living with AIDS, I'd forgotten it could still kill them.

Tom died on a Thursday night. A wake was planned for Sunday. I was asked to read something. I spent the next few days in a cloud of apologetic prayer that eventually pointed me to the idea of writing an elegy. I found myself in the odd position of doing what I often did, which is making a poem for a friend, but in this case, one he would never read. All the other times I'd written poems, for a birthday or a wedding, I'd written them with the idea that the poem would be heard by the person it was written for.

I was able to write it only when I imagined him reading it. When I imagined giving it to him. I gave it instead to the owner of the café and his coworkers. They set it in the window, next to a picture of Tom in his sun hat in Spain, where it stayed for a year.

The writing of elegies is something uncanny, and I use that word with the sense that I've never used it before. You can't help but imagine the poem being observed by the deceased. You are even addressing it to them, asking the dead in, not to speak but to listen. And you let nothing go from your desk that wouldn't meet their standard. It's a kind of review you perhaps couldn't previously have imagined, and then after, it is a review that can only be imagined by you.

In the days that followed, whenever I got my coffee, I saw the picture of Tom next to my poem, and I thought each time about how you could wait too long to write. I was faltering with my second novel, but this stiffened my resolve. Tom had always had a knack for telling me the one thing I needed to hear, and in this way he told me this last part, again and again, almost daily, until the poem came down.

4

WHAT IS THE POINT? I have struggled with this question my student asked that morning after the election for as long as I've been a writer and a teacher.

In a comic about that morning after the election, I would draw you a picture of me driving in my car, mountains in front of me and behind me, the black balloon of my question — *How many times have I thought the world would end?* — a thought balloon as long as the drive, and revealed on the next page to be as long as my life, a trip through all that has followed me since at least the fifth grade, when I first learned to fear death by neutron bomb, or that I would have to wear a special suit just to be outdoors as an adult because of damage to the ozone layer.

I love summer. My worst nightmare is a world where I cannot enjoy it.

In one panel is the time I learned that the empty factories of my childhood meant new factories had been built in other countries where labor was cheaper, and I understood those jobs would never return until the long argument owners were having with labor — an argument longer than my life — would end in Americans being paid almost nothing again.

In another panel, near the middle, would be the trip I took in 2007, when I went to San Francisco to attend a week-long writers' conference and took a taxi driven by a man who told me Republicans had a thirty-year plan to take back the wealth of the country for the rich, and that we were in the last decade of it. "Who told you this?" I asked, because it was what I had thought was happening. "Some professor," he said as he dropped me off at the University of San Francisco. "I forget. He said it started with Reagan. But Reagan didn't start it," he said. "The people around him did."

I thanked him, tipped him, and went inside. I knew this was a moment like any in a newspaper column I'd read all too often, the pundit quoting the wisdom of his cabdriver to his audience. If I wrote about it, people would mock the trope, or they would say I sounded crazy. This is America, where you are allowed to speak the truth as long as nothing changes.

Somewhere near the end of the balloon is my realization, the morning after the election, that this is the last year of those thirty years the driver spoke of.

❖

THERE'S ANOTHER Alexander Chee in my mind, the one who I would be if I'd only had access to regular dental care throughout my career, down to the number of teeth in my mouth. I started inventing him on a visit to Canada in 2005 when I became unnerved by how healthy everyone looked there compared to the United States, and my sense of him grows every time I leave the country. I know I'll have a shorter career for being American in this current age, and a shorter life also. And that is by my country's design. It is the intention.

I have been to convenience stores where I see people working with untreated injuries, and when I leave, I get panhandled in the parking lot by someone in a chain-store uniform who is unable to afford the gas to get home on the last day before payday—someone with two jobs, three jobs. Until recently, I struggled to get by, and yet I am in the top twenty percent of earners in my country. I am currently saving up for dental implants—money I could as easily use for a down payment on a house. But I'm not entirely sure I'll see the end of a mortgage, or that any of us will.

Scientists around the world were terrified before the election about our chances for long-term survival on this planet. The widespread death of coral in the Great Barrier Reef—called coral bleaching, as if the coral were not dead, just blond—is something these scientists had feared but they'd believed they would not live to see happen. Many of them wept. Climate change denial is the product of an ExxonMobil campaign to prolong the period of its profits as long as possible—the corporation was caught spending millions of dollars to deny its existence, instead of openly working to create energy solutions we could all survive. Exxon knew climate change was real all along, has known for thirty years or more. Conservatism's oldest con is getting a voter to yell "thief" at someone the thief chooses, the thief they voted for. And now we are in the final phase.

It's a strange time to teach someone to write stories. But I think it always is. This is just our strange time.

❖

WRITING WORKSHOPS inevitably circle around to conversations about publishing, and I usually allow it at the end of a class. This way I can teach my students the ordinariness of the profession as well as the radical possibilities in their work first. And since sometimes, maybe every time, the most radical thing to do with radical work is to treat it as ordinary, I make sure to educate students on the procedures for submitting work to magazines, journals, agents, and publishers. I try to pass along everything I know about writing and publishing, and to avoid injuring their excitement for it.

There are the stories I tell the class. The stories I don't tell are about being paid last, after even the power bill, though your book is the one under the lights. How your friends will think you're rich, and your family will think you've betrayed them, even if you didn't write about them. Reviewers will misunderstand your book and it will cost you everything and no one but you will care. Or they will misunderstand it and it will still sell thousands of copies and no one but you will care.

To write and finish my first novel had taken seven years and three jobs, plus a fourth, the actual writing of the book. Sometimes I worked on it on the F train from Brooklyn, going into the city for a shift at the steakhouse where I waited tables. Sometimes I wrote it while I waited for my section to be seated. One day I gave up on it, in pain from sitting wrong for hours at a time. I won't continue, I decided, until I have a typing table at the right height. And then I left my apartment and within an hour found one at a yard sale, as if the gods were mocking me.

Here is your table, they seemed to say. The tag read $3, but what I read in that price, the table sitting there right in my way, was *Get back to work*.

The feeling I had when the novel finally came out was not initially one of exultant enthusiasm. The feeling was *You want me to do this again?*

I wasn't just tired. I also needed money, and more would be forthcoming if I could write. But I couldn't seem to write then. I had a novel I gave up on every Friday and began again every Monday, like a bad relationship. It was something beautiful I'd fallen in love with years ago and then talked myself out of, and then let myself back into, slowly. I had started another novel as well, but I didn't feel smart enough to write that one yet. And the urgency of needing the money the writing could provide led to me shouting quietly, in my head, at anything I was actually able to get down. For failing myself.

One day in the fall of 2003, I had gone to Wesleyan a little earlier for a ritual I wasn't proud of, in which I would go to the comptroller's office and request an advance on my check. It was a futile exercise, really, a way of delaying the day of the month when I would be out of money. My publisher had gone into bankruptcy owing me what then amounted to a year's pay, and then they had sold foreign rights to my first novel, and I would never see that money because of the way bankruptcy court works. Afterward, as I headed to class, instead of going in, I stopped in my office to collect myself, because I had the urge to go in and tell my students to stop now. Don't do it, it isn't worth it, there's nothing here for you.

I knew it wasn't true. I didn't believe it. And yet I was tempted. But none of this would have reached those responsible. They didn't need to hear about the failures of a system. They needed to hear about how to deal when the system fails.

I waited alone in my office, watching the time in the lower right corner of my computer screen, until I felt I could teach from that. And then I stood and went in.

What is the point? I was asking myself that day. The problem can be not just who is listening, but who is not listening. Who will never listen. The point of writing in the face of the problem was the point of samizdat, readers and writers meeting secretly all across the Soviet Union to share forbidden books, either written there or smuggled into the country. The point is in the widow of Osip Mandelstam memorizing her husband's poetry while in the camps with him in the Soviet Union, determined that his poems make it to readers. The point of it is in the possibility of being read by someone who *could* read it. Who could be changed, out past your imagination's limits. Hannah Arendt has a definition of freedom as being the freedom to imagine that which you cannot yet imagine. The freedom to imagine that as yet unimaginable work in front of others, moving them to still more action you can't imagine, that is the point of writing, to me. You may think it is humility to imagine your work doesn't matter. It isn't. Much the way you don't know what a writer will go on to write, you don't know what a reader, having read you, will do.

❖

ONLY IN AMERICA do we ask our writers to believe they don't matter as a condition of writing. It is time to end this. Much of my time as a student was spent doubting the importance of my work, doubting the power it had to reach anyone or to do anything of significance. I was already tired of hearing about how the pen was mightier than the sword by the time I was studying writing. Swords, it seemed to me, won all the time. By the time I found that Auden quote—"poetry makes nothing happen"—I was more than ready to believe what I thought he was saying. But books were still to me as they had been when I found them: the only magic. My mother's most common childhood memory of me is of standing next to me trying to be heard over the voice on the page. I didn't really commit to writing until I understood that it meant making that happen for someone else. And in order to do that, I had to commit the chaos inside of me to an intricate order, an articulate complexity.

To write is to sell a ticket to escape, not from the truth, but into it. My job is to make something happen in a space barely larger than the span of your hand, behind your eyes, distilled out of all that I have carried, from friends, teachers, people met on planes, people I have only seen in my mind, all my mother and father ever did, every favorite book, until it meets and distills from you, the reader, something out of the everything it finds in you. All of this meets along the edge of a sentence like this one, as if the sentence is a fence, with you on one side and me on the other. When the writing works best, I feel like I could poke one of these words out of place and find the writer's eye there, looking through to me.

If you don't know what I mean, what I mean is this: when I speak of walking through a snowstorm, you remember a night from your childhood full of snow, or from last winter, say, driving home at night, surprised by a storm. When I speak of my dead friends and poetry, you may remember your own dead friends, or if none of your friends are dead, you may imagine how it might feel to have them die. You may think of your poems, or poems you've seen or heard. You may remember you don't like poetry.

Something new is made from my memories and yours as you read this. It is not my memory, not yours, and it is born and walks the bridges and roads of your mind, as long as it can. After it has left mine.

All my life I've been told this isn't important, that it doesn't matter, that it could never matter. And yet I think it does. I think it is the real reason the people who would take everything from us say this. I think it's the same reason that when fascists come to power, writers are among the first to go to jail. And that is the point of writing.

❖

I BEGAN THIS ESSAY as an email I wrote to my students during that first weekend of the war in Iraq. I had felt a sudden, intense protectiveness of them. I didn't want my students to go into the draft, rumored then to be a possibility, and I was even more afraid of people like the secretary of defense. Destroying art is practice for destroying people.

I wanted to lead my students to another world, one where people value writing and art more than war, and yet I knew then and I know now that the only thing that matters is to make that world here. There is no other world. This is the only world we are in. This revisable country, so difficult to change, so easily changed.

I wrote to them that weekend and told them that art endures past governments, countries, and emperors, and their would-be replacements. That art—even, or perhaps especially, art that is dedicated somehow to tenderness, dedicated as a lover who would offer something to her beloved in the last nights they'll share before she leaves this life forever—is not weak. It is strength. I asked them to disregard the cultural war against the arts that has lasted most of their lives, the movement to discredit the arts and culture in American public life as being decorative interruptions of more serious affairs, unworthy of funding, or even of teachers. I told them that I can't recall the emperors of China as well as I can Mencius, who counseled them, and whose stories of them, shared in his poetry of these rulers and their problems, describe them for me almost entirely. And the paradox of how a novel, should it survive, protects what a missile can't.

The email I sent was not the only act, though; it was just a beginning. It was when I turned my back on the idea that teaching writing means only teaching how to make sentences or stories. I needed to teach writing students to hold on—to themselves, to what matters to them, to the present, the past, the future. And to the country. And to do so with what they write. We won't know when the world will end. If it ever does, we will be better served when it does by having done this work we can do.

I have new lessons in not stopping, after "the election." If you are reading this, and you're a writer, and you, like me, are gripped with despair, when you think you might stop: Speak to your dead. Write for your dead. Tell them a story. What are you doing with this life? Let them hold you accountable. Let them make you bolder or more modest or louder or more loving, whatever it is, but ask them in, listen, and then write. And when war comes—and make no mistake, it is already here—be sure you write for the living too. The ones you love, and the ones who are coming for your life. What will you give them when they get there? I tell myself I can't imagine a story that can set them free, these people who hate me, but I am writing precisely because one did that for me. So I always remember that, and I know to write even for them.

I am, it should be said, someone who did lose his faith. I may in fact be pusillanimous, even as a condition of my faith in myself, and at times I despair. I do not write as much as I should. I do not always think that when I die I will have the chance to see my dead again. But for now, I live and work and I feel them watching me.

And so I leave this here now, for them. And for you.

ACKNOWLEDGMENTS

I WILL BEGIN by thanking my husband, Dustin Schell, who regularly makes the value of my life and my work visible to me in ways large and small, and whose love is the center of my world.

Thank you to my agent, Jin Auh, for her friendship and fearless advocacy all these years, and to her associate, Jessica Friedman, and the entire team at the Wylie Agency, who protect me and my work so well. Thank you to my editor, Naomi Gibbs, for her thoughtful and demanding editorial acumen, and to everyone at Houghton Mifflin Harcourt for their hard work on my books. After fighting so hard for it, being in print is everything to me.

My thanks to my teachers in the writing of essays, Annie Dillard and Clarke Blaise. My thanks to the editors of the published essays here: Edmund White; Elizabeth Benedict; Rosecrans Baldwin and the entire *Morning News* family; Hillary Brenhouse, Dan Sheehan, and Michael Archer at *Guernica*; Chad Harbach and *n+1*; Jesse Pearson, at *Apology*; Aaron Gilbreath, Mike Dang, Michelle Legro, and Sari Botton, at *Longreads*; Mark Armstrong, at Automattic; Yuka Igarishi and Mensah Demary, at *Catapult*; Isaac Fitzgerald, Saeed Jones, Karolina Waclaviak, and Jarry Lee, at *BuzzFeed*. Your collective efforts have helped make me the essayist I am, and I'm very grateful.

Friends who helped especially: Garnette Cadogan, John Freeman, Melanie Fallon, Jami Attenberg, Keiko Lane, Sandi Hammonds, Maud Newton, Gerard Koskovich, and Joe Osmundson —thank you for keeping faith with me and this work. And my thanks to my writing group, The Resistance: Mira Jacob, Kaitlyn Greenidge, Luis Jaramillo, Brittany Allen, Julia Phillips, Tennessee Jones, and Bill Cheng.

❖

THIS COLLECTION began in part thanks to an invitation from Lis Harris to read in the Columbia University Nonfiction Program's series in the fall of 2014. I collected my published essays to send to her students, and I am so grateful to her for that prod. Some of the anecdotes central to my history here may have been described by me on other occasions, in interviews or in other essays, and so I reserve the right to effectively repeat those anecdotes, or plagiarize myself. The names and identifying details of some of the living people described here have been changed to protect their identities.

The following essays originally appeared in other publications. All have been edited and revised for this collection. In particular, "The Curse," initially published as "Playing Mexican," in the New School's literary magazine *Lit,* and "After Peter," first published in *Loss Within Loss,* edited by Edmund White (University of Wisconsin Press, 2001), are greatly revised from their original versions. "The Querent" was previously published at the *Morning News.* "The Writing Life" first appeared in the anthology *Mentors, Muses, and Monsters,* edited by Elizabeth Benedict, and was reprinted at the *Morning News.* "My Parade" first appeared in the *n+1* anthology *MFA vs NYC,* and was reprinted by *BuzzFeed Books;* "Girl" was first published in *Guernica* and was reprinted in *The Best American Essays 2016*, edited by Jonathan Franzen. "Mr. and Mrs. B" was first published in *Apology* and was reprinted online at *Longreads*. "Impostor" was first published at *Catapult*. "How to Write an Autobiographical Novel" first appeared at *BuzzFeed*. "The Autobiography of My Novel" was first published in the *Sewanee Review*.